TOXIC TOWN CLEANUP

A SMALL TOWN'S FATE

CHANGES COURSE

AS VOLUNTEERS FIGHT BACK

~a memoir~

Ten more years of the

PINE RIVER SUPERFUND CITIZEN TASK FORCE

St. Louis, Michigan

2014-2023

Cover photo credit: David Jones

Book cover design: Lynzee Harrison Photography

Contents

Introduction

Glossary of Terms

INTRODUCTION

The likely summation of the fate of St. Louis, Michigan was this: Known for its healing waters, to becoming known for its poisoned waters and land. A small group of people decided to combine their efforts to alter the course of history. That group, the Pine River Superfund Citizen Task Force, along with elected city officials, aid from state and federal legislators, and with money and expertise supplied by the Environmental Protection Agency, is effectively rebuilding the good reputation of St. Louis and bringing healing to the waters and land to make them safe again for both people and wildlife.

The first volume of my memoir, *Tombstone Town*, detailed the beginnings of the Task Force and recounted the efforts to gain a comprehensive cleanup of the toxic legacy of St. Louis, namely, the Velsicol Superfund Former Plant Site, the impoundment area of the Pine River, downstream in the river, and several disposal sites, including the Burn Pit Superfund site, the Gratiot County Landfill, and the Breckenridge Radioactive site.

The story continues in this volume, recounting both accomplished tasks, new tasks that have come to light as the extent of the contamination continues to be discovered, and some tasks that, once they begin, can never be allowed to end.

The town is now a vibrant community, with tons of pollution having been cleaned up, at a cost to taxpayers of over $250 million so far, with another $125 million expected to be spent soon. Once the plant site is remediated, the operation and maintenance of its permanent systems will cost $2 million per year.

Would this time and money have been spent without the volunteer labor of the Task Force? Other states also have highly polluted Velsicol sites, and little or no citizen action, and very little cleanup. Not only do we think our efforts have made a difference, but we also think other groups could learn from us, benefiting from our struggles to get the best cleanup possible for St. Louis, which was years ago labeled by a major news outlet as Toxic Town, USA.

Chapter 1
(2014 – Part 1)
Falling Trees

At the close of one of our monthly meetings, Lynn Roslund came up to me to say he was concerned about the way EPA and the city were handling the trees on his property. Excavation of yards in the 12-block neighborhood nearest the chemical plant site had begun, and part of the process was to remove the trees, along with contaminated soil in their root balls, and replace them with new trees.

We knew some residents would hate having their mature trees taken down, and we hated it, too. But this was our town's opportunity to rid itself of the leftover pollution from the chemical company, and its reputation as Toxic Town, U.S.A. I expected Lynn would tell me his concerns about tree *removal,* but instead he told me the opposite -- someone had come by his house and told him he could *keep* all the trees in his yard. Lynn really didn't like the Chinese elms in the area between the sidewalk and the street, and was able to convince the person to put them on the list of trees to be uprooted. Lynn thought the person who had come to speak with him was either from EPA or the City of St. Louis.

I had to ask him once more: "Do you mean they are going around the neighborhood and telling people their trees *don't* have to be taken down?" Lynn thought it likely that others were being told the same thing.

When the various groups conversing after the meeting had dispersed, I took Lynn over to Jim Hall, who was now chairperson of our CAG, and asked him to repeat his story. Jim and I just looked at each other. What in the world was going on now?

Had the city officials changed their minds? I knew they had met with EPA earlier in the year and at that time had told them they wanted all the trees on city property removed. The city owned the grassy areas between the sidewalks and the streets, which EPA Project Manager Tom Alcamo had told us were to be called "parkways." But maybe they had changed their minds.

I offered to call Tom Alcamo at his office in Chicago and find out EPA's policy on taking out trees in the contaminated yards, and follow up with City Manager Bob McConkie, and Jim agreed.

On the phone, when I told Tom I wanted to talk about the trees in the parkways, he was instantly defensive and began to talk about people's emotional attachment to trees, and how Dow Chemical in Midland was doing a cleanup, and *they* weren't cutting down trees. I asked if it was dioxin being cleaned up in Midland (I knew it was, but was hoping to get him into a conversational mode). And was it from airborne deposition? So it only required shallow digging, right?

Then I brought the conversation back to the trees in the parkways. He said the lawns in the parkway were Bob's bailiwick, and Bob did not want all the trees cut down. That he and Bob would meet soon about the design plan for the neighborhood, and only 37 trees needed to be removed. The rest would be hand-dug around the roots. One of our CAG members had done a rough count of the trees in the neighborhood, and there were almost 500.

I said to Tom, "Let's take one big tree, and let's say your sampling showed that contaminated soil is only in the first six inches. You will hand dig around the roots, right?"

"Right."

"Let's take another big tree that has contamination at a foot. Will you hand dig?"

"Yes."

"Eighteen to twenty-four inches?"

2

"We'll try to dig as much as possible, but if we leave some contaminated soil, it's not a human health risk."

"What about the robins who pull worms out from there?"

That set him off, and he accused the CAG of only seeing things from the point of view of contamination, and how we didn't care about the trees or how the neighborhood looked.

He was right, the CAG did see the community through the lens of contamination, wanting it all cleaned up. That was our task. But wait…wasn't that also the mandate of EPA? And hadn't the Record of Decision (ROD) set out the parameters of how the contamination would be cleaned up? The reason we had not known about EPA's "adjustments" to the ROD plan of digging up all the contaminated soil was that we had not been shown their work plan. The Technical Committee had asked to see it several times from the signing of the ROD in 2012 onward, and Tom had assured us we would have a look at it once it was written, but that never happened.

Since the parkways were Bob's "bailiwick," I called City Manager Bob McConkie to ask him why they had changed their policy, and to let him know that the CAG viewed tree and root removal as essential to getting the best cleanup possible in the neighborhood. I didn't have to explain the CAG's viewpoint, however, because Bob said the city's policy had not changed -- they wanted all the trees in the parkways removed, and as many as possible from people's yards. The CAG and the city were on the same page.

And it was not city workers telling residents their trees did not have to be cut down, but workers with CH2m, EPA's contractor. Why in the world was EPA not working in tandem with the community to gain the best cleanup possible for the neighborhood?

About this time, Scott Cornelius had begun to attend our CAG meetings, paying his dues, and becoming a full-fledged member. Scott had served as the MDEQ Project Manager for the Velsicol Superfund site from 2000-2012. He had left MDEQ to take a position with a private environmental company, but soon found it wasn't the right fit for him. Now he had started his own environmental consulting business, and also had been hired as an instructor at Alma College, working there alongside our former CAG member, Murray Borrello.

When I told Scott about the tree issue, he shook his head and said this was only the beginning, and that EPA would have a tendency to want to deviate from the ROD's stipulations in other ways, too.

Either Bob McConkie, city manager, or Mayor Jim Kelly had been attending our CAG meetings regularly, as had Council Member George Kubin (former mayor). After one of the meetings, I noticed those men, and also Utilities Director Kurt Giles, grouped around Scott. Soon after that, we learned that the city had hired Scott as their environmental consultant to assist them during this phase of working with EPA in implementing the cleanup plans.

This turn of events pleased us very much. Even though some CAG members had been driven crazy by Scott's extensive soil sampling during his years with us, we now could see how hard he had worked to convince EPA to bring the best cleanup possible to our community…at least on paper. That he would continue in that endeavor while working with the city, we had no doubt.

By the time Tom and Bob sat down for their discussion of the design plan for the neighborhood, Scott was on board as the city's environmental consultant. Resulting from that meeting were detailed comments from the city to EPA for improving the design plan, and letters to Tom and the political appointee at Region 5, Susan Hedman, from Mayor Jim Kelly.

The letters made it clear that the city was concerned about ROD compliance. The ROD clearly stated that the remedy for the contaminated neighborhood was excavation and offsite disposal of soils with levels measuring above agreed upon standards (5 ppm DDT; 1.2 ppm PBB; 4.4 ppm TRIS), and did not make exceptions for soil bound in root balls, or located under shrubbery, driveways, sidewalks, or decks. Furthermore, this was not a technical infeasibility issue.

The city had also asked EPA to provide an estimate of the volume of contaminated soil that would be left in place by following their design plan, but Tom Alcamo refused their request. Instead, Scott did the math, using EPA's numbers, and showed that the proposed design plan left about 49% of the contaminated soils in place. That was unthinkable. And we felt betrayed once again by EPA.

Certainly if it had been Velsicol wanting to cut corners, we would have expected it. But from our Environmental Protection Agency, we expected better. Even though later in the dispute EPA staff would accuse us of having created an adversarial relationship with them, it was clear to us that, once again, it was EPA that had violated trust with the community by behaving like a PRP (potentially responsible party).

Far from being adversarial, our CAG had assisted EPA and Tom Alcamo several times in recent months.

For instance, at the beginning of the year we had written a letter commending Tom for his successful requests for funds to begin the neighborhood excavations, and to accomplish design work for the plant site. The letter went to Tom's bosses, and to our federal legislators.

Also, when it was time for excavation to begin in the neighborhood, cooperation from Consumers Energy was needed to disconnect gas lines and reconnect afterwards. Calls to Consumers from Tom and from Bob McConkie went unanswered. Then the CAG offered to send a letter to the president and CEO of Consumers, and as a result, cooperation was forthcoming, as well as an apologetic phone call from a local Consumers representative.

Finally, as our group talked about the delays for the cleanups that were due to a lack of funding, we wrote to our federal legislators requesting they establish a trust fund for the St. Louis Velsicol site, with millions set aside in it that could be drawn upon by Tom or his successor as needed. Our request went unanswered, but the point is, we were doing our best to get money to Tom so that he could accomplish a thorough cleanup of our town.

During the tree removal dispute, I had written an email to the members of our Executive Committee conveying my concerns about the soil removal plan for the neighborhood, which left trees, gardens and landscaped areas undisturbed. Tom had told me in a previous phone call about this aspect of the plan, so I was surprised to receive another call from him saying my statement about gardens and landscaping was false. He also accused me of having seen the private homeowner information before writing my email, but I hadn't, and I told him that it was he who had told me about the gardens and landscaping the last time we had talked on the phone.

He went on to say that he and Dan Rockafellow (MDEQ project manager) and Theo von Wallmenich (CH2m project manager) had been blindsided by the city's letters, because Bob McConkie had signed off on access to the parkway areas, and Mayor Jim Kelly had never expressed concern about how the neighborhood would be remedied. Tom didn't say it, but I felt sure he was thinking these changes in attitude were due to the city having hired Scott, and I'm sure he was correct in this thinking. Unlike Tom, I was thankful Scott was advising the city officials.

When I got off the phone, I started to wonder how in the world Tom had known what I'd written in my email to the Executive Committee? Other than our officers and board members, Jim Heinzman, our Technical Advisor, was the only other person the email had gone to. This was my first inkling that someone on the Executive Committee had an agenda of his own.

Our group also wrote a formal letter to Tom, saying specifically what we expected in terms of cleanup in the neighborhood regarding the trees, gardens and landscaped areas, shrubs and perennials, house foundations, sidewalks, driveways, patios and decks, streets, fill material, and confirmation sampling. For example, we argued that roofs were a deposit area for airborne contaminants from the chemical plant, and were washed by rain, which meant drip lines should be excavated, with hand digging close to the foundations. Simply avoiding that area of the yard could leave plenty of DDT in the soil for robins to pull worms from.

Several CAG members attended the next city council meeting where we knew EPA Project Manager Tom Alcamo and MDEQ Project Manager, Dan Rockafellow, would be making a presentation on the residential remediation project.

During the meeting, Tom pointed out that the city manager had given access to EPA for the parkway areas. Council member George Kubin said access had been given, but not approval of the plan. Dan said that homeowner's property rights were involved, and the agencies were not going to share names and addresses with the city. George said they didn't need to see personal addresses, but the city did need to know what was going to be done in each area of the neighborhood before it could approve the remediation plan. He also asked when the city could expect a response to the comments they had submitted on the design plan. Tom made it clear that EPA had no intention of responding to the comments.

This attitude of Tom's certainly did not fit with EPA's current guidelines for interaction with communities. We had looked on line at the EPA Strategic Plan for 2014-2018, and Tom's refusal to write comments and to provide information to the community was exactly opposite of the guidelines laid out in the Strategic Plan written by EPA Headquarters.

Council member Melissa Allen wanted to know what EPA's procedure would be if robins continued to die in the neighborhood after the excavation if only 49% of the contaminated soil was removed. Dan Rockafellow assured her that we would see a lot fewer dead robins, and if they continued to be found, the State of Michigan would find out what was killing them. Our own wildlife toxicologist, Matt Zwiernik, had addressed this issue repeatedly in the Technical Committee meetings. No longer finding dead birds did not equate to having a successful cleanup. For one thing, with trees gone from the neighborhood, fewer birds would nest there. For another, birds no longer dying of acute DDT poisoning did not indicate a healthy bird population. Chronic DDT poisoning from lower levels of the pesticide were still a real possibility. Egg and nest studies were needed, and so far both EPA and MDEQ had refused to see the need for those studies. In their eyes, if the birds stopped dropping dead, that would indicate a clean neighborhood

Mayor Jim Kelly summed up the community's viewpoint on the half-hearted cleanup plan by saying: "We want it done right. We've suffered for 50 to 60 years, and we are tired of being labeled as a toxic town. I want it to go away in my lifetime."

In the midst of this tree removal issue, a scientific report came out about how the tree bark in St. Louis, Michigan was emitting toxins the trees had stored when the chemical plant was in operation. Did this mean we still had air pollution, too?

Tom Alcamo was very unhappy with the article, and told us Region 5 planned to write a letter of rebuttal, saying there were flaws in the scientist's measuring techniques.

Our CAG (focused, as we were, on contamination) saw the article as another reason to remove all the trees from the neighborhood.

Matt Zwiernik, however, cautioned us to think about the entire eco-system of the neighborhood, and that with the removal of all the trees, the eco-system would be disrupted. Yes, it would be, for a time, but not forever. In my view, getting the DDT-contaminated soil replaced with clean soil was a good thing for the ecosystem that *would* last forever (God willing).

Meanwhile, EPA had been giving away wood from the pile of trees they had already uprooted from residents' yards to be burned as firewood. I phoned Tom Alcamo and suggested this might not be a good idea, and he agreed that even though his scientists said it was safe to do so, it caused a "perception issue," and he closed down the giveaway.

About this time, I read two news articles about political shenanigans going on with our Gratiot County Board of Commissioners. A board seat was open due to the commissioner from my district having moved away. It was embarrassing to read how the Republicans and Democrats were squabbling over it, and worse. Then I saw that retired judge James Mackie was willing to fill the seat until the next election, and I thought that would solve the problem. He changed his mind, however, and if the seat wasn't filled by a certain date, the county would have to spend $30,000 on a special election.

I decided to submit my resume, making it clear that I was an independent voter, and did not plan to run for election in November. They accepted me and swore me in, and I enjoyed my six months on the County Board of Commissioners.

At that time, the State of Michigan was in the process of turning all maintenance responsibility for the Gratiot County Landfill Superfund Site over to the county. In addition to household waste, the landfill had been illegally used by various local industries as a waste site, including Velsicol Chemical Corporation. When the PBB manufacturing ended in the 1970s, tons of leftover PBB from the factory were dumped on or near the landfill. Also, chickens and cattle that had been slaughtered after eating PBB-contaminated feed had been buried at the site.

County Administrator, Jeff Huff, told me there were a number of concerns about maintaining the integrity of the site that he wanted addressed prior to the county taking responsibility for its upkeep, such as places where the clay cap had settled, leaving dips for rainwater to pool and perhaps enter the landfill; methane burning flares that were no longer working; and a broken stretch of fence.

He and I took a field trip to the site and rode around the 40-acre cap in a John Deere Gator. A county employee had already begun to truck dirt and clay to depressions in the landfill cap and fill them, but there were a lot of them, and some were wide and deep.

Since the MDEQ had supposedly reshaped the cap in recent years, I found it surprising to see it in such rough condition.

But the upkeep of the cap was the least of my worries. County employees could handle the task of maintaining it with no difficulty. What worried me was MDEQ expecting the county to repair the methane vents and to collect water samples for chemical testing in the lab. And the other worry was that the county had to pay for all of these maintenance projects. It's true, Gratiot County owned the landfill, and had held the deed to it for all the years that the State had overseen the site and kept it in repair. MDEQ had used the interest from the $500,000 Landfill Trust Fund to pay for upkeep of the site, but after the 2008 financial collapse, the interest generated from the trust fund had been much less than what was needed.

As for the county's financial state, it was good for now. The revenue generated from the construction and operation of dozens of wind turbine power generators (windmills) throughout the county would keep the coffers filled for at least seven years. To maintain the landfill, $50,000 had been budgeted per year in the county's budget, and the county commissioners had hired Michigan Consulting and Environmental out of Mt. Pleasant to handle the sampling and lab tests needed for the site. The company also planned to do a survey of the capped landfill to produce topography maps to allow the county to know best where to build the cap up higher with dirt and clay.

Later in the year, MDEQ inspected the landfill, and the project manager, Matt Williams, shared an email from one of his workers that stated maintenance of the site had "gone downhill since it was turned over to the county." This made no sense to the Board of Commissioners, since repairs that had been left undone by the state were subsequently completed by county workers, such as the break in the fence and unfilled depressions in the cap. Jeff Huff wrote to Matt and said the MDEQ worker "should have seen the landfill the day the DEQ gave it back to us and then compare to what it is today." He let Matt know that the email had stirred up some hard feelings among the county commissioners. Matt sent an email saying he was sorry if he had offended anyone.

We turned to the Mt. Pleasant environmental company again when MDEQ offered to sell the county 21 acres adjacent to the Landfill site. Jeff had asked me what I thought about the proposed purchase. Since it was onto that parcel of ground that the landfill had leaked 10 years previously, it made sense to me to have the county own the land rather than a private person, in case it leaked again. The county certainly didn't need a lawsuit from a private owner, should that happen. We hired the environmental company to do an assessment of the parcel, not wanting to purchase it if it had environmental problems we didn't know about. We paid more for their assessment ($1,800) than we did for the 21 acres ($1,000), but it was well worth it for the reasons mentioned above.

In addition to the tons of PBB contained in the landfill, traces of PBB coursed through the veins and lodged in organs of the Michigan citizens who had been alive during the 1970s PBB Disaster, causing damage to health in ways that were not fully known.

In the early years during the PBB Disaster, it was noted that exposure to the fire retardant caused skin rashes, hair loss, memory loss and joint problems. In the decades following the 1973 accident, scientists found that PBB exposure could affect the endocrine, immune and reproductive systems, and adversely impact liver function. In our area near the chemical plant, thyroid problems, breast cancer, miscarriages, and male genitourinary conditions were common.

Researchers from Emory University in Atlanta, in partnership with our CAG, the Mid-Michigan District Health Department, and the PBB Citizens Advisory Group had organized community informational meetings, combined with blood draws, for hundreds of people around the State of Michigan, including almost 500 in the St.

11

Louis area, and they had signed up hundreds of men and women of reproductive age for a study.

Then they ran out of grant money.

Dr. Michele Marcus rallied the partners to formulate a new grant proposal, in hopes of having a grant from NIEHS to continue the research on the effects of PBB in humans. Regular conference calls began, during which we planned the scope of our request, and we hoped money would be in hand as early as July, 2015.

During the 2013/2014 blood draws in our community, we had discovered a problem with the database of the original PBB Registry begun in the 1970s. The records of many people were no longer included. For instance, I was helping an elderly former chemical worker at one of the meetings sort out the papers he had brought with him that showed his results from testing back in the 1970s. He had complete records of two studies in which he'd participated. When we took the original documents to the person who had access to the computer database, she found no record of him at all, not even his name. His deceased wife had also worked at the chemical plant, and her name was missing as well.

This happened repeatedly, and it let us know that somehow a failure had occurred over the decades in transferring records from paper, to microfiche, to computer database.

A real deterrent to the public health quest of our research had to do with privacy laws. The State of Michigan had begun the PBB Registry of several thousand people in 1978, with the assumption that the health outcomes of PBB exposure should be regularly observed and analyzed by following a group of people with known exposures. As the years went by, the State fell away from doing follow-up examinations of the participants. When the entire PBB Registry research project was turned over to Dr. Michele Marcus at Emory University, the modern-day privacy laws prevented the State from giving the study results to Emory. Instead the health records were turned over to a semi-private company, the Michigan Public

Health Institute (MPHI), who contracted with MDHHS, the state health department.

In order for the records to make their way to Emory, the PBB Registry participant had to fill out a form to authorize release of the records. This meant individuals needed to be contacted and educated about the process. Most people didn't know that Emory had assumed the duties previously performed by the State of Michigan.

Complicating the process even more, MPHI was not allowed to release the names of the participants to Emory, making it next to impossible for the PBB researchers to inform people in the Registry about the need to transfer their records. How could they, when they didn't even know who they were!

That's where the PBB Citizens Advisory Board and the Pine River Superfund Citizen Task Force were able to help. Farm families on the Advisory Board knew other farm families who had been in the original study, and contacted them. Our CAG member, Gary Smith, teamed up with former chemical employee, Jim Buchanan, to find current addresses for living former chemical workers, or their survivors. Many people were notified by these efforts, but thousands more still needed to be found.

Marcus Cheatham, Health Officer for our local health department, agreed that public health was being impeded by this difficult process. In a letter to the CEO of MPHI, he requested that the records be transferred to the local health department, citing a state law giving authority to local health departments to have access to privatized information regarding public health. In terms of public health, Dr. Cheatham pointed out that the participants could then be informed of ongoing programs or studies that might benefit them. Also, the health department would be aware of any past tests performed on the participants, which could be important during other health events. And when new information about the effects of exposure to PBB was released, the health department would be able to contact the individuals in the Registry.

We followed up his letter with an appointment with Dr. Renee Canady at the MPHI company offices. Marcus Cheatham and I drove down to Okemos, Michigan, and Michele Marcus participated by phone. In addition to the other points of our visit, we asked for access to the original paper or microfiche records so that the people whose names had been lost could be restored to the PBB Registry.

Despite our good visit, and Dr. Canady's interest, nothing came of our efforts.

This was Jim Hall's first year as chairperson of the CAG. I had written a guide to the various duties of the office of chairperson for him, and he greatly appreciated it. I also let him know I would help out when needed, remembering how Ed Lorenz had helped me back in 2002 during my first year as chairperson. Jim called on me occasionally, but for the most part, he did whatever needed to be done.

This attitude contrasted sharply with our relatively new Technical Committee chairperson. I had also written out guidelines for Steve Boyd, and he told me right away that he didn't think he should have to be the one to get the key to the meeting room, or to arrange the tables and chairs. To help him out, Gary Smith and I got there early and did those things for him. Steve also didn't see the need to make phone calls ahead of the meeting, to write an agenda, or to follow up with people after the meetings by phone or email. And at the meetings themselves, he sat silent, not calling the meeting to order or adjourning it, and not keeping the participants on track when the conversation veered elsewhere.

His lack of leadership skills concerned me, and also concerned our paid Technical Advisor, Jim Heinzman. Both of us tried to gently steer Steve and to help him out.

The one thing that seemed important to Steve was the title "Technical Committee Chair." As a university professor, we knew he had pressure to prove himself in various ways, so we didn't take offense at his delight in his title.

I was the one who had asked Steve to join our CAG and chair the Technical Committee because of his background. He had grown up in St. Louis, had worked one summer at the chemical plant, where he was exposed to fumes that made him sick. He had gone on to study soil chemistry, and had the title of University Distinguished Professor at Michigan State University. Also, he sat on a committee that oversaw a $15 million NIEHS grant for a Superfund Research Program at MSU.

When he first joined the CAG, he seemed to be on the same page with us. He told us that he had attended a citizens' meeting for the Dow Chemical dioxin cleanup downstream in Midland, and how the organizational structure discouraged community involvement. He praised our CAG for its passion and its persistence in endeavoring to get the best cleanup possible for our community. He also said that he thought because we were an orphaned site (without a PRP), unlike the Dow site, that EPA had a lower standard for cleanup in our community, which lined up with what some of the rest of us thought we were observing.

Soon after Jim Heinzman's and my interventions with Steve, he began to type out a list of things to talk about at the meetings, and email it out ahead of time. Things were looking up.

Jim Heinzman had also been trying to help to find ways to ensure EPA and its contractors followed through on what they said they would do while attending the Technical Committee meetings. I suggested that our minutes, which I wrote, include an Action Items list of the name of the person and what he/she had committed to do.

We soon found the list alone was not enough. I then suggested to Steve that, as chairperson, he should follow up after the meetings with phone calls to encourage the people to complete the tasks they had said they would do. Steve resisted, saying that he didn't think anything on the lists were so urgent that any harm would come if its accomplishment was delayed a month or two. For most

15

things, that was likely true. But what about the tasks that were a year old? And how were we to keep track of the things not done as time passed?

For example, we had expressed our concern about a railroad spur that had formerly led into the chemical plant. Rail cars full of chemicals had often been parked on the spur for days. Some of the land where the rail spur had been located was now low-income housing. Almost a year before, we had asked EPA to sample the area for DDT and PBB contamination, just as they had sampled the yards in the neighborhood adjacent to the plant site. Tom said he would look into it. It was when I was reading back through emails and copies of our minutes to write about the events of 2013 that I saw that the railroad spur concern had not yet received a response from EPA. If we continued to wait for a response without reminding Tom about that task, EPA could very well complete their work in the neighborhood and then be reluctant to come back to sample the railroad spur.

Jim Heinzman had talked about using a spreadsheet to track the progress of a response from EPA for various requests. That was still an option, but we had decided to try the Action Items list in the meeting minutes as a place to start. Steve praised my detailed minutes, but was concerned that if we held people accountable, we would alienate them.

Maybe that's why Tom Alcamo, Dan Rockafellow and the EPA contractors started to behave badly toward us. They must have been feeling alienated because we were trying to hold them accountable to what they said they would do, regarding the contaminated soil removal in the neighborhood. I am being sarcastic.

As mentioned, the signed Record of Decision stated that neighborhood soils measuring above the agreed upon standards would be excavated and disposed offsite. It seemed to us that EPA thought the ROD meant only the easily obtainable soils. When we disputed their interpretation of the ROD at the Technical Committee meetings, Tom became both angry and defensive and sometimes would clam up and not talk at all. I decided to try phoning him outside of the meeting atmosphere to see if I could get a clearer understanding of EPA's intentions.

On the phone, Tom said that EPA did not intend to dig the dripline of roofs close to the house foundations. They did not intend to dig up "sentimental" trees and perennials. They did not intend to dig under streets or sidewalks.

I shared this information via email with the Executive Committee members. Steve replied only to me by saying that I had shared partial and incorrect information with the CAG, alarming people "in response to factually incorrect information." I had no idea what he was referring to, since I had shared the very information given to me by Tom. I called Steve and went over the facts with him, and he then seemed to understand.

Had the CAG become alarmed, as Steve had said? Most assuredly. For years we had dedicated ourselves to getting the best cleanup possible for our community, and if EPA did half the job now, would we, or our offspring, ever get them back again to complete it? Plus, if a signed public document directed EPA staff to do something, were they not they bound to do it? Yet Steve seemed to be worrying that we might alienate EPA if we insisted they measure up to the Record of Decision.

A little later Steve wrote a personal email to me saying he had observed an adversarial relationship being played out between the CAG and Tom. He wrote, "A constant barrage of negative feedback has to be disheartening," and he accused me of being cynical, disrespectful and attacking Tom's professional integrity. I thought about what he had written. Had I ever expressed cynicism? Perhaps, but not towards Tom. Disrespect? Never. Had I attacked his professional integrity? Certainly not. Did I, however, want him to follow through in his professional capacity to adhere to the ROD stipulations? You betcha!

17

There wasn't much time to cogitate on Steve's new attitude of finding fault with the CAG, or at least the Technical Committee, and with me, personally. The tree removal issue was paramount.

Our CAG chairperson, Jim Hall, and our treasurer, Gary Smith, both downtown St. Louis residents, spoke with several city officials, including Mayor Jim Kelly, City Manager Bob McConkie, Utilities Director Kurt Giles and several members of the St. Louis City Council reminding them of the importance of getting as much contaminated soil as possible removed from the neighborhood. The city officials also had their environmental consultant, Scott Cornelius, telling them the same thing.

I wrote a press release which the Gratiot County Herald published about the tough decisions facing homeowners, and mentioning EPA's intention to issue a letter to homeowners whose yards had been excavated that would state the property was protective of human health and the environment. On the flip side, I also pointed out that local realtors would inform homeowners that had excluded areas of their property from excavation, that the whole property must be disclosed to a potential buyer as being contaminated. This information came from my phone conversations with a local realtor, and also a realtor in a larger city. I quoted Jim Hall in the article, who said, "I hope people will look on this as an opportunity to get rid of the pollution once and for all."

With this combined pressure, Tom Alcamo partially capitulated. He wrote to Mayor Kelly, stating that all the trees on the city-owned land would be removed. He also put in change orders to excavate city-owned alleys. He was very angry about this, as was his CH2m contractor, Theo von Wallmenich. They were not shy about expressing their anger to those of us on the Technical Committee. Tom wrote to Mayor Kelly that both "EPA and MDEQ feel you have gotten bad advice with even outside experts thinking it is a bad idea to remove all the trees."

Would it change the eco-system of the neighborhood for a number of years? It definitely would. But the replacement trees would grow in time, providing nesting habitat, and the worms in the soil beneath the trees would be DDT-free, or at least we hoped they would be, if EPA followed through and did the job they had agreed to do as laid out in the Record of Decision.

Chapter 2
(2014 – Part 2)
Dying Birds

As the excavation in the neighborhood moved forward, Mayor Jim Kelly continued to hear from residents, wondering why *their* yards were not being excavated, when all the yards around them *were*, or why they were told that their yards would *not* be excavated since only the top six inches were contaminated. They were confused, some being told one thing, some another, and some of them getting angry about it. It made us wonder what kind of information the people in the neighborhood were receiving from EPA and their contractors.

Gary Smith and Jim Hall decided to talk to residents and ask a few simple survey questions to give us feedback from the people whose yards were in the 9-block clean-up area (later expanded to 12 blocks). When Gary started to report on the survey results at a Technical Committee meeting, both Tom and Theo verbally jumped all over him, shouting that it wasn't Gary's place to be talking to the residents. Gary calmly differed with them, and asked if they would like to hear about the issues, both good and bad, that were raised by the people in the houses. Neither Tom nor Theo responded, but Phil Ramsey spoke up and said, "Let's hear it!"

Understandably, some in the neighborhood did not want EPA to remove the trees on their private property. Other people had drainage issues. Some were concerned about broken sidewalks. Many were confused about the tree removal issue since almost every household had been told something different. When the neighbors talked among themselves, they didn't understand why one yard was excavated and the next yard wasn't, even though their sampling results had been the same. One resident said all the yards around her yard had been dug to at least 18 inches deep, and yet she was told her yard wasn't contaminated. How could her yard, in the middle of surrounding contaminated yards, be contamination free? She wanted her soil re-sampled, but EPA was not willing to do it again.

Since the goal of our CAG was to have as much contaminated soil removed as possible, we maintained that residents who had willfully left contamination in place by not allowing their gardens to be excavated, should not receive the letter from EPA saying their yards were protective of the environment. Tom consulted with his attorney at Region 5 who declared that everyone in the neighborhood would receive the letter, even if minimal excavation had taken place.

We then requested that deed notices be issued and attached to deeds on file with the Gratiot County Register of Deeds. We were not asking for deed restrictions, but only a notice so that the next buyer would be informed about areas of private properties that had not been excavated, such as under trees, sheds, decks and sidewalks. The EPA Region 5 attorney, Gary Steinbauer, responded that institutional controls, such as the deed notice, were only used when contamination remaining in place presented an unacceptable risk to human health or the environment.

To us, unacceptable risk to human health or the environment meant that undisturbed soil beneath a tree that had measured above the clean-up standard of 5 ppm was *not* protective. In our view, a future homeowner should have the right to know when he was having the stump ground from a dead tree in his yard that DDT might be flying around in the sawdust and soil dust.

In EPA's view, since the entire neighborhood would have less contaminated soil, taken as a whole, that meant the neighborhood was now safe for both human health and the

21

environment. They looked at the entire 9-block area as a unit, while we looked at single properties. In EPA's view, once the neighborhood was cleaned up, even if 49% of the remaining soil was contaminated, the entire project area was 51% less contaminated, and their goals had been met to reduce contamination, making the whole neighborhood safe for both humans and wildlife.

As Gary Smith said, maybe the robins would understand this reasoning, and only dine in areas where the contaminated soil had been replaced. And maybe the worms would understand that they could only run clean soil through their systems, and not crawl into contaminated areas to feed. We all saw this as bureaucratic blarney.

The city continued to request further excavation in the neighborhood, specifically under Bankson and Watson streets, as well as the entire unpaved portion of Center Street. They also asked for sampling under all the streets, including M-46, since yard sampling had shown contamination levels on both sides of each street. In addition, they wanted a Memorandum of Understanding with EPA for future maintenance and utilities work in the areas that EPA was not excavating, or even sampling. By leaving contaminants in place, EPA was leaving the city liable for future disposal expenses of contaminated soil, whenever they had reason to move soil.

EPA's response was that their risk assessing utility worker exposure model showed that only in one area under Bankson did the levels exceed what might be injurious to a future worker exposed to excavated soil. Since the other areas showed concentrations of DDT and PBB below their utility worker cleanup numbers, they did not even plan to sample under the other roadways.

All of the exertions by both the city and the CAG to get the cleanup we had been promised in the ROD grated against Steve Boyd, our Technical Committee chairperson. He apparently identified with the frustrated and angry attitudes of Tom Alcamo. In emails to the Executive Committee he pleaded the case for EPA -- that they were strapped for funds, and that we should be grateful for the cleanup we were getting in the neighborhood and not ask for more. Also, he said other communities were not getting any money for their cleanups, because EPA was spending it in the neighborhood of St. Louis.

In one of Gary Smith's responses, he told Steve that his concern was not with everywhere else in the country, but here in our town. "Getting the cleanup done correctly here in St. Louis and the Pine River watershed was my original goal and still is." He added that whenever he heard the statement "we ain't got any money, I see something that won't be done to our satisfaction."

After reading their email exchange, it seemed to me that maybe Steve needed to be informed of some of our history in working with EPA. After all, he was quite new to the dance steps of working with the agency.

I wrote and told him about a decision we had made years ago to not let EPA use guilt tactics to make us accept a lesser cleanup. In addition, a case could be made that our community had suffered decades of injustice from the U.S. government, with EPA and MDEQ having allowed Velsicol to leave the state without paying for cleanup of the river and the town; by how EPA had refused to listen to our concerns about the plant site leaking during the early days of our CAG; and by how EPA had waited a year before telling city officials the lab results that showed the drinking water wells were contaminated with pCBSA. I said that it was time for environmental justice to prevail in our community to right the injustices that had come to us both from the polluter, Velsicol, and, sadly, the Environmental Protection Agency.

In response, Steve wrote a long diatribe against me, accusing me of vitriol, bitterness and resentment, saying, sarcastically, that my email had recounted "a litany of past transgressions and injustices foisted upon you and the community." Well, they were the facts however he might choose to color them.

Chairperson Jim Hall and Treasurer Gary Smith met with me to discuss our mutual concerns about Steve. In addition to Steve's

23

personal attacks, we talked about his lack of leadership skills, our concern that he didn't understand our mission, our questioning of his allegiance to the community of St. Louis, and our worries about his divisiveness. It appeared to us as a possibility that Tom Alcamo, and our new Community Involvement Coordinator, Diane Russell, recognized Steve as the weak link in our CAG and were perhaps using him in a divide and conquer tactic, much as our first CIC, Stuart Hill, had done with the CAG and the City years before. All three of us saw the problem, but didn't, at present, know how to proceed.

As for our new MDEQ project manager, at first he seemed to be working out just fine. Dan Rockafellow had been assigned to our site after Scott Cornelius left MDEQ for the private sector. We knew it would be an adjustment, after spending twelve years with Scott, but all of us were hoping for the best.

Even though Dan's past experience was in working with the Surface Water division, we were pleased to see his willingness to educate himself about Superfund, and about our sites, in particular. When we learned that MDEQ had published a draft of the Ecological Risk Assessment for OU-3, the downstream portion of the Pine River, I asked Dan for an opportunity to see it in its draft form, with the understanding that it would only be read by the Technical Committee, and not shared further. He complied, and we took this as sign of his desire to work with us.

As the year progressed, however, and the tensions rose over the neighborhood trees and tree bark, along with questions about the downstream cleanup, Dan increasingly aligned himself with EPA, rather than advocating for the State of Michigan and the St. Louis community, including our CAG. In fact, he told me that the CAG didn't really represent the community.

The Ecological Risk Assessment document also went to EPA, and, apparently, they had gone ahead and hired a contractor to do additional sampling downstream to fill in data gaps. Our Technical Advisor, Jim Heinzman, said EPA's hiring of CH2m to

24

sample was premature – that they should not have moved forward without first engaging the community in a discussion about the outcomes they wished to see from a remedy downstream.

This view was echoed by a newer CAG member, Matt Zwiernik, a wildlife toxicologist from Michigan State University. He said our EPA people were skirting CERCLA law by leaving the community out in its discussions about downstream. And when he read the Eco Risk report, he found it flawed by omitting measurement endpoints, by using analytical procedures that were inadequate to quantify PBBs in the river, by using scientifically indefensible TRVs (toxicity reference values) for DDT and PBB, and many more shortcomings.

I took Matt's notes about the scientific flaws in the document and wrote a memo to present to EPA and MDEQ at our Technical Committee meeting. When they heard the memo, Tom and Dan were unmoved. In their view, the science in the report was adequate for cleanup purposes, end of discussion.

After many tense discussions at our Technical Committee meetings, with EPA and its contractors resisting any of the science that Matt put forth, a sudden turn of events occurred. Surprisingly, we learned that Tom Alcamo wanted to set up a meeting at Michigan State University to talk about these issues, and possibly hire Matt to do a study downstream.

Even though this was good news, it was tinged with questions of propriety. The fact was it was our CAG, led by Matt, who had spoken out against the inadequate Eco Risk Assessment for downstream. Yet Tom and Dan did not want to include the CAG in its discussions with Matt about scientific work that needed to be done in that region of the river. Even though our CAG was the community advisory group for all of the Velsicol sites, including downstream, EPA also did not want to include Jim Heinzman, our CAG Technical Advisor, in the discussions. Despite the fact that Jim had written many memos on these very scientific issues, which I incorporated into letters that were now part of the Administrative

Record at EPA, neither the CAG nor its technical advisor would be allowed at the meeting, Tom Alcamo told our chairperson, Jim Hall.

Then we learned that Steve Boyd *would* be included. As might be imagined, the rest of us had mixed feelings about that. When Steve himself said in an email that his presence at the meeting wasn't really necessary, since he couldn't add anything to the discussion, it seemed to me logical that Heinzman should be there instead, since he had done much thinking and writing about the downstream issues and could contribute a lot to the discussion.

I called Tom Alcamo and asked that Jim Heinzman be included with the other scientists at the meeting as a representative of the CAG. Tom told me that Steve could serve as a representative of the CAG. I pointed out what Steve had said in his email, that his presence wasn't really necessary, and I also said that Heinzman was our officially hired person to represent the CAG in science discussions, and hired with grant money from EPA. Despite my arguments, Tom refused my request. It was one more indication of something going on behind the scenes that didn't bode well for our CAG.

During this time, we also wrote a letter to Tom outlining, in a formal manner, the outcomes desired by the community for the remedy downstream, which included a measurable decline in the DDT levels of fish, birds and mammals that lived downstream. We did this, because the process under CERCLA law requires EPA to solicit from the community members the outcomes they desire. Even though CERCLA law was being ignored by EPA staff by failing to ask for our input, we still wanted to place our viewpoint into the Administrative Record for OU-3 of the Velsicol Superfund Site.

About that time, MDEQ released data on fish they had collected in 2010, and for once we had good news. The DDT levels in the fish had dropped significantly, with the reduction attributed by EPA to the extensive sediment cleanup undertaken behind the St. Louis dam from 1998-2006. As soon as we had the data, I shared it with the local news media to let the wider community know that things were looking up.

Meanwhile, birds were still dying of acute DDT poisoning, both in town and downstream. The stories about it in our papers and on our radio stations were picked up by larger publications, with some of them using the phrase "dead birds falling from the sky" in their titles. This greatly irritated our project managers. We didn't mind it quite as much, because we hoped the publicity would help convince EPA Headquarters in Washington, D. C. to send money to our town for a comprehensive cleanup.

When Environmental Health News led off a story by saying "Health experts are questioning the Environmental Protection Agency and Michigan state officials for their decades- long delays in cleanup of a Superfund site that is killing songbirds in yards…" Tom Alcamo took it personally. The article quoted Dr. David Carpenter, director of the School of Public Health in Albany, New York who was an expert in Superfund cleanups.

A quotation from Tom Alcamo in the article stated that EPA was using a cleanup standard of 5 ppm (parts per million), but in the neighborhood was using "an excavation level of 4.1 ppm DDT to ensure that we are 95 percent confident that we are meeting the 5 ppm number." In our Technical Committee meetings, Matt Zwiernik repeatedly asked how EPA had reached the 5 ppm standard as being ecologically protective of robins, especially when the U.S. Department of Interior calculation showed a lower number of 2.5 ppm DDT as the protective standard. Eventually Tom Alcamo referred Matt to several journal articles on the question, but there were problems with using those, since the articles referred to freshly applied DDT, and not aged, such as was in St. Louis soils, along with the breakdown products of DDD and DDE (and we knew DDE was even more persistent in animals and people than DDT). Another article referred to was about robins in an Illinois orchard. Apparently, EPA had assumed the caloric intake of worms of the St.

27

Louis robins that were building nests, laying eggs, and rearing young to be the same as the robins eating in an apple orchard when nesting season had ended. Even for a non-scientist such as me, that didn't equate.

Meanwhile, the robins continued to die in St. Louis, with one of them in the 2014 collection having over 850 ppm DDT in its brain. And the main source of the contamination had not been cleaned up. Our CAG was in its 17th year of existence, and we still had not seen a shovel go in the ground at the 52-acre buried chemical factory property.

We updated our legislators with the shocking news about the high levels of DDT still being found in robin brains, and we asked Senator Debbie Stabenow, Senator Carl Levin, and Congressman Dave Camp to write to Mathy Stanislaus, EPA Assistant Administrator in charge of Superfund funding, asking him to ensure no more delays of the cleanups in St. Louis from lack of funding. The response they received from Stanislaus stated that no money would be forthcoming from EPA Headquarters that year.

Instead our EPA project manager drew upon the Trust Fund set up after the Fruit of the Loom settlement to afford the start of excavation in the residential neighborhood.

By February 2014, the Fruit Trust Fund money was almost gone, and additional sampling in the neighborhood had not yet found a perimeter where the DDT levels fell off. By this time, 114 yards had been sampled. Tom appealed to Headquarters, and a few million dollars were squeezed out to enable work to continue. In response, we sent a letter to Mathy Stanislaus and James Woolford at EPA Headquarters in Washington, D. C., thanking them for the funding, and we publicly commended Tom for his initiative in finding ways to bring money to our town for cleanups.

About this time, a new EPA Community Involvement Coordinator began to attend our meetings. We hadn't had a CIC attend a meeting for a few years, and to tell the truth, we hadn't felt the lack. Yet, with every new person assigned to us, we hoped for the best. Each of us greeted Diane Russell in a friendly manner, wondering if she would emulate the best CICs that we had met at the conference in Seattle long ago, or the ones who had fallen short.

Also about this time, I received a phone call from Dan Rockafellow, saying that the Director of MDEQ, Dan Wyant, would like to visit our site. He said the director made a visit to each congressional district in the state once a year, and this time, he would like to spend an hour and a half at the Velsicol Site and the high school athletic fields.

I spread the word among our CAG members, and I was especially glad that Margaret Hoyt could attend, because she had worked at the chemical factory packaging PBB back in the 1970s.

It turned out that EPA and CH2m wanted to take the director out onto the plant site, and members of the public and press were not allowed to go out there. Also, the city officials wanted to have a meeting in city hall with the director to tell him personally their thoughts on the 49 percent of contaminated soil that EPA was leaving in place. Because of these other demands on his time, it meant that meant our CAG members only had a few minutes to speak with the director when he first arrived at the gates to the former plant site on North Street.

Margaret had an opportunity to tell Dan Wyant part of her story, and the Morning Sun newspaper printed a nice photo of them in conversation, along with our State Senator John Moolenaar who would later be elected to the U.S. House of Representatives, replacing Dave Camp.

Then I had the chance to speak to Director Wyant. I expressed the concern of the CAG with how EPA seemed to be cutting corners on the work they were doing in St. Louis. I gave him the example of how the neighborhood cleanup had become a fight, with the community doing all it could to convince EPA to fulfill the requirements of the ROD. I told him we really needed the State of

Michigan to be our advocate in getting the best cleanup possible in St. Louis. My words were quoted in the Midland Daily News.

The first chance she got, our new Community Involvement Coordinator challenged me on my statement.

It had become our practice during the past few years to meet for dinner at River Rock restaurant in St. Louis after the Technical Committee meeting and before the evening CAG Membership meeting. At the first supper Diane attended, she and I chatted about her little children and other pleasant topics, but after the rest of the group had left to go to the evening meeting, she brought up the quote from the Midland paper, differing with me on EPA's behavior. I listened to her, and could see that she really wanted to believe the best about EPA. I recognized in her words my own early best hopes that EPA would ride into our community on white horses and swiftly and surely clean up the mess, smiling the whole time. Needless to say, my idealistic view had changed over the years. Even though I firmly explained to her the relationship as I saw it now between community, MDEQ and EPA, I still sympathized with her position, remembering my own hopeful view from 17 years before.

I had sympathy for her position, but she had no sympathy for mine, and from that point on, Diane seemed determined to change how our CAG did things. The next month, I overheard her telling Phil Ramsey that he needed to keep his thoughts to himself until the end of the Technical Committee meetings. Phil, who was now in his 80s and quite deaf, tended to regularly relate how the community had been trying to get things cleaned up for 40 or 50 years, referring back to the late 1970s when he sat on the Gratiot County Board of Commissioners and was trying to get the PBB-filled county dump cleaned up, as well as the chemical factory. Diane told him that his statements were not technical information, and he should wait until the end of the technical discussions to voice his views.

It bothered me to hear her talk to Phil in this way, and later I told him he could say whatever he wanted to say any time he wanted to say it. I wondered what kind of training Diane had received to think it was all right to scold an elder and tell him to keep quiet?

Not only from Diane, but also from Tom and Dan we were picking up on their seeming disdain of the history of our site. We could understand that their focus was on their present-day efforts, but they couldn't seem to understand that we brought up the history because we'd been though an EPA remedy once before that had failed, and we worried that this one could go the same way if they cut corners and didn't heed the lessons of the past.

In order to emphasize the history, Jim Hall added a Looking Back segment to each of our monthly CAG meetings. He brought in U.S. Fish and Wildlife Service articles from the 1940s that warned about the widespread usage of DDT, and he brought advertisements that promoted the use of DDT. One showed a dog, an apple, a housewife, a cow, a cucumber and a rooster singing "DDT is good for me-e-e! ♪♪. Another advertised Disney character wallpaper for children's bedrooms that was impregnated with DDT. A little boy is looking at the paper and saying, "Oooh, look, Donald Duck!" A little girl is saying, "Golly, there's Pluto, too!" And a mother is putting a baby into its crib with the "protective" wallpaper behind her.

One of the most moving Looking Back items shared was a transcript of a 1943 interrogation of a young chemical worker from the factory in St. Louis. In a matter-of-fact way, 23-year-old Francis Oomen related that while inspecting drums, filling cylinders and testing cylinder valves, the inhaled fumes would make him vomit. After a day when he had breathed in ethyl-chloride, ethyl-bromide, buthylbromide, bromoform, allyl-bromide and sulphuric acid while unloading railroad tankers, he was unable to walk straight, unable to see well, and began to have dizzy spells and blackouts, and then "keeled over." He had told Mr. [Frank] Curtis, but had continued working. When he went to see Dr. Waggoner, and later Dr. Barstow, he was prescribed fresh air, mineral baths, and was

31

diagnosed with chronic poisoning. The descriptions in the account were very sobering.

Meanwhile, out on the buried plant site where Frank Oomen and many other St. Louis people had earned their livelihood, work was underway to determine what was beneath the clay cap. Geophysical scans showed wide-scale areas of metal debris underground, as was expected, because all the buildings, towers, pipes, and railroad tracks had been demolished and buried on site, along with the buildings and their foundations. In the summer of 2014, CH2m workers dug long test pits to determine the nature of the debris. They wore Level B Tyvek protective gear with air supply, and, in addition to volatile detection badges worn by them, the volatiles in the air were measured in real time using gas chromatography. Some of the volatiles were NAPL, DBCP and benzene.

During the work of test pit investigation and 150 rotosonic borings, a large amount of NAPL was found toward the south end of the plant site. Tom Alcamo said he was surprised to find so much there.

In addition to chemicals on the site, we were concerned about radioactivity. Gary Smith examined maps from the Remedial Investigation and noted that radioactivity had been found in about twelve locations on the plant site. Theo von Wallmenich from CH2m said the Nuclear Regulatory Commission had looked at the data, and had determined the levels were not high enough for concern. The radioactive substances in the plant site soil were thorium and uranium. Apparently, during the 1980's burial of the site, flat metal sheets (not lead) had been placed over the areas where radioactivity was found.

Our Technical Committee also raised concerns about NAPL leaking from the west side of the plant site into the Pine River. During the Remedial Investigation, dye tests had shown movement on that side of the site toward the river. Theo von Wallmenich of

CH2m said that our concerns were shared by EPA, and that is why the remedy planned for the plant site included further investigation and the possible installation of a NAPL collection trench on the west side of the plant site. We said maybe an Emergency Response Action was in order, ahead of the slow process of the remedial action.

In contrast to what his contractor said, Tom Alcamo stated there was no visible evidence of leaking on that side of the site, and that a response action was not warranted, since it was not an imminent threat to humans or the environment. He referred to the fish data that showed DDT levels declining in fish tissue. At least one of our scientist CAG members expressed caution about taking the new fish data as proof positive that the west side of the site was not leaking. In our discussions among ourselves, we wondered if the lack of sediment in the river bottom around the plant site meant that the DDT-laden NAPL leaking from the site found no sediment particles to latch on to, and instead flowed quickly downstream. We knew that DDT "likes" to attach to soil or sediment particles and stay put.

Across the river, at the separate Burn Pit Superfund Site, our concerns as a CAG centered on the competency of the EPA project manager assigned to the site.

With each new agency person assigned to us, there was always a time of adjusting, and with Jena Sleboda Braun, the adjustment period kept extending further because of her lack of attendance at our meetings and her very short email responses to our questions. Finally, the Executive Committee suggested I write a letter to her, requesting her presence at our meetings. In the letter, we sympathized with the fact that she had small children at home, and acknowledged her reluctance to travel in the middle of the week to attend our monthly Wednesday meetings. Nevertheless, we had high expectations for our project managers, wanting them to become part of the human effort we were waging to get the sites in our community cleaned up. Her presence at meetings would aid that effort, because we never knew when a question, comment, or discussion might be raised, and having the project manager there to respond was essential.

Since she had indicated in an email that it would be extremely difficult for her to meet our attendance expectations, we suggested that maybe it would be best for a different project manager to be assigned to the Burn Pit Site during this critical period of determining the remediation plans for that site.

Jena did not respond, but instead her boss sent us a terse letter saying that Jena would "attend all CAG meetings in which pertinent information on the Velsicol Burn Pit site needs to be disseminated."

This response highlighted a longstanding viewpoint issue between EPA and our CAG. In the view of EPA staff, informing us of their decisions was all they owed us. In our view, involving us in the decision-making process was what EPA was supposed to do. CERCLA law and all official EPA documents concerning community involvement matched our viewpoint, but the EPA employees who worked with us had not received, or had rejected, the message from EPA Headquarters about how they were to behave with community members.

In her first informational meeting in 2013, Jena had told us that the Burn Pit was enrolled in a fast-track program that would enable testing, designing a plan, and actual remediation to take place more swiftly than usual Superfund site projects. By 2014, when plans seemed to be moving at the same bureaucratic crawl, we asked about the fast-track program and found that it was no longer functioning.

Many science-based questions were asked at this meeting, and Jena's vague and ill-formed answers left many in our group wondering if she lacked enough information herself to be able to competently answer the questions. And her responses to community questions veered away from direct answers, as well. For instance, when asked how two of the main chemicals of concern on the site were dangerous to humans, she said, "oh, they're everywhere," implying that we had nothing to worry about. I'm sure that benzene and 1,2-dichlorethane are found at many chemically contaminated sites, but that doesn't mean they are safe! Benzene is a carcinogen and 1,2-dichlorethane, most often used to make vinyl chloride, is a probable carcinogen.

About nine months after her first visit to our CAG, Jena returned to inform us that she had completed the Remedial Investigation for the site, using data gathered by MDEQ in 2004-05, and in 2007, with some data gaps filled by EPA in 2012. The 2012 sampling had concentrated on the aquifers underneath the site, and it was found that the deep aquifer connected with the one under the plant site. That water, therefore, would become part of the future pump and treat process planned for the plant site. The shallow aquifer also would not be addressed right away. Plans were to use thermal treatment in the soil, and the hope was that the treatments would take care of the contamination in the shallow aquifer. EPA had also tested to see if the groundwater at the Burn Pit was traveling to the river, by placing a few wells between the Burn Pit and the river, and they determined that it wasn't. Our Technical Advisor, Jim Heinzman, a hydrogeologist, questioned if this method was adequate to determine the pathways of the groundwater to the river, but Jena didn't seem to understand his concern.

Another nine months passed before Jena's next visit to disseminate information. In the meantime, both the CAG and MDEQ had submitted comments to EPA on the Burn Pit RI document. Weston Solutions (MDEQ's contractor) also submitted comments, pointing out many inconsistencies and errors in the document that needed correction. They also asked some hard questions. In EPA's response to MDEQ's comments, Jena stated that she planned to address these questions when writing the Proposed Plan.

During this time, Ed Lorenz took EPA to task for their website description of the Burn Pit because it glossed over facts about the history of the site. It ignored the failed 1982 cleanup that the agencies had allowed Velsicol to perform by accepting their reports without verifying the true state of affairs for themselves. He re-wrote the description according to the known facts, but so far, EPA hasn't substituted the factual history for its whitewashed version on their website.

When it was time for the large, community-wide public meeting on the Burn Pit Proposed Plan, our new CIC, Diane Russell, organized the event. When I saw the agenda, I knew there would be a problem. A break was scheduled between the PowerPoint presentation and the time for questions. I knew most of the community members would leave during the break and go home. Sure enough, when the very long PowerPoint ended, most of the community members went home and missed hearing the questions and concerns others raised. In my opinion, it was simply another tactic by EPA to discourage community participation. As CAG member Carol Layman said later, CIC's were nothing more than Community Interference Coordinators.

The people who had remained asked their questions, and got the same miss-the-target answers from Jena that had troubled us from the beginning. In fact, when asked which way the groundwater flowed at the site, she stumbled about, and gave a wrong answer. After that, her supervisor, Donald Bruce, who was also in attendance, helped her with the answers, even standing up to deliver them on his own.

We followed up the public meeting with letters to our federal legislators making it clear that the proposed plan for the Burn Pit had not received community acceptance. And our excellent legislators wrote to upper management EPA letting them know that they backed the community in desiring a better proposed plan.

In contrast to Jena's mode of delivery, the written EPA responses to Burn Pit comments submitted by the CAG and others were detailed and actually answered many of our long-standing questions. Further, the document stated that improvements would be made to the Proposed Plan before it became a Record of Decision. Obviously someone else had written the responses, and that was all to the good.

At the very end of the year, a visible improvement occurred, one that every citizen and visitor to St. Louis could applaud. Finally, after eight years of doing nothing but looking ugly, the sheet-pile wall leftover from the sediment removal operation was finally removed from the middle of the river. Tom had received money from Region 5 to make it happen, and we were all pleased with the result.

Chapter 3
(2015 -- Part 1)
Rising waters

It was not a new worry. Since first learning of the plan to shut down the city wells, we had raised concerns and questions frequently about what would happen to the water table.

As far as we knew, our situation was unusual, if not unique. At what other town in the nation had all the municipal drinking water wells been permanently shut down at the same time? Surely, when the city pumps stopped pumping, the water level underground would rise. And from local history, we knew artesian wells were the norm in years past, with the Magnetic Mineral Springs well water leaping six feet out of the ground when it was first drilled in the 1870s.

When the plan to take St. Louis off its present well source and bring new water in was first proposed in 2005-2006, we thought the plant site extraction wells would be in operation, off-setting the shut-down of the city wells. The idea was that both the groundwater contamination beneath the Velsicol plant site, and the contaminated groundwater beneath the Burn Pit, would be held in place hydraulically by the proposed pump-and-treat system for the plant site. Later, when we saw that the two well projects would not coincide, that was when we began asking questions about what EPA planned to do should the water levels rise precipitously, and would the contaminants move within the aquifer and perhaps into surface water, re-contaminating the river? Our concerns did not receive answers, however. We were simply told EPA was not worried about it. That didn't assuage our worries.

As we worked to write our comments on the Proposed Plan for the Burn Pit Superfund Site, we addressed the rising water issue. We pointed out that the protectiveness assumption of the Record of Decision for the former plant site would be altered, along with the protectiveness assumption of the Burn Pit Proposed Plan, since both remediation plans had relied on the current, functioning city pumps.

In our comments, we requested that the city's pumping field remain intact until the pump-and-treat system was in operation on the former plant site acreage.

We requested that the EPA Burn Pit Project Manager, Jena Sleboda Braun, meet with us to discuss our concerns regarding the impending shut-down of the city pumps, which the city expected to quit using later in the year, when they began to receive water from wells in the neighboring town of Alma. The two towns had established the Gratiot Area Water Authority to distribute water to both centers of population.

Because Jena rarely attended our meetings, we asked Jim Heinzman, our Technical Advisor, to write a formal letter requesting her presence to begin an immediate discussion about the shut-down of the city's pumps, prior to the installation of the pump-and-treat system that was supposed to "contain" the contaminated water under both the plant site and the Burn Pit site. In our view, the shutdown of the city well pumping constituted a potential threat to the people and environment of St. Louis.

Jena's response was brief and unsatisfactory, stating that the cessation of well pumping was not new information (and, of course, her boss had told us she would only attend our meetings if she had new information to impart to us). The only reason the information was *not* new is because *we in the CAG* had been raising the issue repeatedly over the past several years. We had asked the question many times during Technical Committee meetings, and I had asked it before a large audience at a Gratiot Area Water Authority meeting in Arcada Township at least two years before, and Tom Alcamo had said then that EPA wasn't prepared to talk about it, but things would be worked out. Okay... and how would they be worked out? That question was never answered. I had spoken to Tom about it in a recent phone call, and he said the 2010 groundwater model that CH2m had constructed showed there would be no problem. The model, however, was based on the well field as it was now, with the city pumps operating.

Jena replied to our letter by saying she would discuss our concerns once she had published EPA's responses to our Burn Pit Proposed Plan comments. Gary Smith said to wait until then would mean that the ROD would be signed, and after that EPA, by law, did not have to address our concerns until the entire remediation was completed. He said, "We'll all likely be dead or afflicted with dementia by then." Ed Lorenz said, "We are approaching the time when we have to demand that Jena either dialogue with us or quit the project."

After discussion with the Executive Committee, I drafted a very direct letter enumerating each point, and advising Jena that the *timing* of the well shutdown was new information that activated a CERCLA requirement that the issue be discussed with the Community Advisory Group now. Her boss was copied on the letter.

We also contacted our federal representatives (Senator Debbie Stabenow, Senator Gary Peters, and Congressman John Moolenaar) to let them know that the Proposed Plan for the Burn Pit had *not* achieved community acceptance, and the rising water was one reason why. They wrote to the EPA Region 5 political appointee, Susan Hedman, and her terse reply, void of both information and human concern, did not endear her to them or to us. (By December, she would lose her job due to her mishandling of the Flint water crisis.)

At one of our monthly CAG meetings, Technical Advisor, Jim Heinzman, walked us through a draft of the Burn Pit comments that had been written so far. He was interrupted by Dan Rockafellow, our MDEQ Project Manager. Dan was the only person present from the agencies that evening. He suddenly said, "Where are these comments coming from?" He spoke loudly and rapidly, beginning sentences and not finishing them, and it was difficult to ascertain what had upset him. From his half-sentence references to the owners of the Hidden Oaks golf course, which was situated next to the Burn Pit, and to people who lived on Prospect Street near the Burn Pit, he seemed to be trying to say that our comments were not valid, and that CAG members were not the authentic community. At one point, I said, "Dan, please finish your sentence so we know what you are talking about!" The only idea that he completed was to say, several times, "Where are these comments coming from?"

Jim Heinzman said, "Frankly, you don't need to know where they come from. The comments are to be viewed on their merits, not where they come from."

Phil Ramsey said, "I talk to people all over the county all the time. They tell me what they think about all this. That's where they come from!"

Neither of their responses appeased Dan.

In a way, his outburst was helpful to us, because several of us had felt something negative fomenting beneath the surface when in meetings with both EPA and MDEQ. This incident let us know we weren't imagining things.

Another outcome of that meeting didn't register with me until I woke up in the night. In a couple of Dan's fitful stops and starts, he referred to a comment that had been in an earlier draft of our document, and then had been removed when the University of Michigan Law School professor, Nina Mendelson, recommended we take it out.

Since the draft document containing that comment had only circulated among members of the Executive Committee, and not the general membership, and certainly not to the agencies, how had Dan known about it? It could only mean that someone on the Executive Committee, or the Technical Advisor, had shared it with him. The next day I asked Jim Heinzman directly if he had circulated the earlier document to MDEQ and EPA, and he had not. By then, I suspected who had shared it with the agencies, but I couldn't prove it.Our comments on the Burn Pit proposed remedy covered a lot more territory than simply the shutdown of the city water wells. The

CAG wrote 23 pages of comments about the interim action at the Burn Pit site, stating in part:

- it failed to offer protection for the Pine River and all surface water
- demographics showed St. Louis fell under EPA's "environmental justice" definition
- EPA had offered unrealistic cost estimates for the best alternative, which was excavation and removal because it was most protective and permanent for the community's people and wildlife
- the plan failed to propose real time monitoring of the movement of NAPL and other contaminants during implementation of the remedy
- the ash piles, leftover from when the chemical plant burned wastes, should not be buried at the site
- the plan lacked both performance criteria and confirmation sampling

The remediation plan was inadequate at best, and we said in our accompanying letter that for EPA to achieve the ninth criteria on the CERCLA list of Nine Criteria – namely, community acceptance – the plan would need to be re-written.

The comment regarding unrealistic costs had to do with high estimates given for the remedial alternative that our CAG thought would be the best remedy. Even by EPA's risk calculations, excavation of the Burn Pit Site was the most permanent and most protective. Because we had experienced excavation and its costs when the riverbed was dug out, we could see that EPA had overpriced the excavation remedy for the Burn Pit, most likely to aid in convincing us that it wasn't doable. During the 1998-2006 remediation of the riverbed around the plant site, it had cost EPA $129.33 per cubic yard to dig up and dispose of the contaminated sediment. Jena elevated her estimates 10 times higher for the Burn Pit, saying it would cost $1,354.65 per cubic yard to excavate and dispose of the contaminated soil. Our objections to this unfair overpricing received no response.

As for the EPA responses we did receive, it seemed clear they were written by someone who had taken most of our comments seriously, and we were pleased to see that several of our suggested improvements were to be added into the remediation.

- EPA agreed to include our complete comments in the Record of Decision, instead of redacting and summarizing them as they had done for the plant site ROD
- EPA assured us of technical coordination between the remedies at the plant site and burn pit site
- EPA agreed to remove the ash piles and dispose of them instead of burying them on site
- EPA agreed to use real time monitoring as the work was underway at the site
- EPA agreed to add additional text to the ROD about confirmation sampling

Apparently, since both the CAG and the City of St. Louis had strenuously declared EPA's Burn Pit Plan inadequate, and because our federal legislators had supported our stance, EPA was seeking ways to achieve number nine on the CERCLA list of the Nine Criteria – community acceptance.

In another attempt to achieve community acceptance, there came a sudden emphasis on DBCP among the contaminants at the Burn Pit Site. For years we had been told that 1,2-DCA and benzene were the contaminants of concern driving the cleanup at the site. Yes, we knew other contaminants were in the mix, including DBCP, but now its presence was being hammered home to us as if it had just been discovered. In fact, a newspaper reporter understood it in just that way and his headline read *Another Toxic Chemical Revealed at Burn Pit Site*. It seemed to us that Jena and others were using the toxicity of DBCP to convince us that only thermal destruction was safe to use at the site, and not excavation.

When we questioned the new emphasis on DBCP, we were told it had always been an emphasis. I went back through our minutes since the time Jena had become project manager for the site (2012), and I sent her an email from six sets of meeting minutes over the course of two years that said that 1,2-DCA and benzene would drive the cleanup. If DBCP had been emphasized, it would have made its way into our minutes, since from our CAG's beginning, the various secretaries had written detailed minutes of all aspects of our endeavors.

When I pointed this out to Jena, she responded that after EPA had received our comments on the Burn Pit, "it was clear that there was not an understanding of the very real, very high risk that the residents of St. Louis and other communities along the disposal route would be exposed to if the hot spot excavation alternative moved forward." Her response validated our suppositions that DBCP was being used to convince the community to accept the alternative that was less protective and less permanent than excavation.

That was our last conversation with Jena. She never did meet with us to discuss our concerns about the possible impact the shutdown of the city wells might have on the contaminated groundwater under the Burn Pit. Within a few months, we received a brief email from her stating that she would no longer be involved, and the project manager for the Burn Pit would now be Tom Alcamo.

If it seems as if tensions were high at this time between the CAG and EPA, that is a correct assumption. There were plenty of issues that we disagreed on, such as the question of rising groundwater, the fear tactic of using DBCP to manipulate us into community acceptance, and the ongoing difficulty in getting data in a timely fashion for the Technical Committee. Despite these surface disagreements, several of us commented in private that it seemed as if there was also something negative going on beneath the surface.

Tensions were also high between the city of St. Louis and EPA. The City Council insisted that EPA sample under some paved streets where it was suspected fill dirt from the chemical plant had been used to elevate the roadways. Also, as mentioned, the city asked

44

EPA to sample and dig up one unpaved street and several alleys, and Tom was unhappy to have to put the change orders in to complete those tasks.

The CAG's Technical Committee had asked repeatedly to see the sampling plan for the ANP (adjacent and neighborhood properties), and Tom assured us over and over that he would share it with us when it was ready, as was his usual practice, but he didn't do it.

Our chairperson, Jim Hall, had begun to research EPA and CERCLA documents to find out how EPA project managers and community involvement coordinators were supposed to interact with the community. I started to do the same thing. Nothing we saw said that EPA personnel were supposed to withhold information from a community. In contrast, they were to readily share information, and to involve the community in decision-making. That's all we had ever asked for as an EPA-sanctioned Community Advisory Group.

One day as I drove around the ANP, I saw that this year's excavation of yards had begun without the sampling plan having been shared with us. I emailed Tom to remind him of his assurance to us that he would share it, and to please expedite that process. Again, he responded that the plan was not ready to release to the public, and once it was ready, EPA would share it with the CAG and the public.

In turn, I shared some quotations from the EPA Administrator Gina McCarthy as written in EPA's 2014-2018 Strategic Plan. In part, she said EPA will "ensure communities have an opportunity to participate in environmental decisions that affect them," and that EPA staff needed to "deliver information that communities can use to participate effectively." She outlined specifically that communities should be part of the decision-making process "on land cleanup" along with other things.

Tom responded that our CAG had enjoyed much more engagement with both EPA and MDEQ than any other site that he was aware of. If true, that didn't bode well for the rest of the CAGs in the country.

Later in the year, I gained some insight into the problem. The PBB researchers at Emory University had invited me to take part with them in a year-long fellowship program called Reach the Decision Makers. Every month we interacted on line with EPA employees, both past and present, learning how EPA functions. Certain speakers emphasized that a few programs within EPA had the authority to wield so much power that they functioned as their own unit, and they didn't want any new ideas to get in the way of how they were already doing things. Not surprisingly, the Superfund program was one of the programs that fell into that category.

Another source of tension made an attempt to spring up between the CAG and the City of St. Louis. Tom Alcamo told us that he couldn't meet with our Technical Committee or the CAG membership, because he needed the time to meet separately with the city and its consultant (Scott Cornelius). I wrote to Mayor Jim Kelly, expressing my concern about possible divisive tactics again being used to split the CAG and City as had happened during the early years of our co-existence. I suggested that someone from the CAG attend the city meeting with EPA, much as how city people usually attended the CAG meetings. Jim Kelly replied that the divisiveness was on the city council's mind as well. They, however, had worked hard to "open the line of communication between EPA, MDEQ and the city," and he preferred to keep this meeting separate. He suggested, though, that one or two people from the city meet with one or two from the CAG monthly to make sure we stayed on the same page, and to protect against divisiveness.

Later Scott Cornelius told us that EPA's Tom and Diane, and MDEQ's Dan had said negative things about the CAG during the meeting with the city. He felt certain Diane hoped to start another CAG with different people, just as Stuart Hill had attempted to do many years before. He said he explained to her that the people who were in the CAG were the ones who were willing to do the thankless job, and EPA would be hard-pressed to find others who would remain committed to the task.

As a result of Mayor Kelly's suggestion, Jim Hall, Gary Smith and I began to meet every month or so with the mayor and St. Louis City Manager, Kurt Giles. During those meetings, we could speak freely about our joint endeavors and our concerns about tactics used by the agencies to separate us.

One thing we had talked about doing together finally came to fruition. Since none of us were allowed onto the plant site, we wanted to mount a camera to record the work as it went forward within the boundaries of the chemical plant property. Our CAG had suggested this plan two years before as part of our comments on the plant site Proposed Plan. At first, Tom Alcamo liked the idea and even offered grant money to set up a website for that purpose. More recently, and since Diane Russell had become our Community Involvement Coordinator, the plan now met with EPA disfavor. She seemed to see the camera as intrusive, and that our CAG would be overstepping its bounds to watch what workers were doing on the plant site.

Nevertheless, we proceeded with our plan. Since the City of St. Louis generated its own electricity, they owned electric poles. We determined which pole had the best placement for our needs, and with the help of Matt Ogle, a local citizen who knew about such things, we bought a camera and mounted it, with the pictures going to our CAG website. Once work began in earnest on the plant site, the community would be able to observe the action.

Getting the work to actually *start* on the plant site was the biggest problem. Tom Alcamo did everything in his power, some of it very creative, to get money flowing for cleanup of the former chemical plant property. He had squeezed money out of the Fruit of the Loom bankruptcy settlement trust money to begin the design work for projects on the site. He was also able to persuade his bosses at Region 5 to fund aspects of the project's design. In his view, if the design plan was finalized and paid for, and if EPA Headquarters in Washington, D. C. only had to pay for the actual implementation of the cleanup, he felt they would be more likely to fund the project.

In our attempt to get the big money needed for the plant site, several CAG members wrote letters to Mathy Stanislaus, Assistant Administrator at EPA Headquarters, who was responsible for doling out money for Superfund cleanups. Both Jim Hall and Margaret Hoyt could speak from personal experience of the health consequences of living near or working at the chemical plant. We also asked our federal lawmakers to write to Stanislaus, and the three of them joined forces on a strongly worded letter, saying that the contamination presented an imminent and substantial endangerment to the health and safety of St. Louis residents, citing research on the health outcomes from exposure to DDT. Despite our concerted efforts, no money was prioritized for the Velsicol Superfund Site in 2015.

Research was growing in the areas of understanding the negative health outcomes from exposure to DDT and PBB. We felt so fortunate to be working with the team from the Rollins School of Public Health from Emory University. As they sought another NIEHS grant for more research, they formed a true partnership of four entities: the researchers, the PBB Citizen's Advisory Board (farm families), the Mid-Michigan District Health Department and the Pine River Superfund Citizen Task Force. The Leadership Team of the partnership spoke at least monthly by phone, and sometimes more often when decisions needed to be made. If the grant was funded, one study would test a substance that could help people eliminate PBB and DDT from their systems. Another study involved the new field of epigenetics, and would look at families of three generations to determine if PBB was passed to the next generation through sperm. If funded, we all felt some of the money should go to pay for blood draws and analysis for people who had formerly lived in Michigan, and now lived elsewhere in the country.

Over 500 of them had already filled out the online forms at the PBB Registry website, wishing to be part of the ongoing studies.

It just so happened that I became Facebook friends with a son of one of the founders of Michigan Chemical Corporation, later bought out by Velsicol. He described a heartbreaking story to me. Three siblings were in charge of the chemical manufacturing plant: his father, his uncle, and his aunt. Within the first 10 years of operation, his father objected strongly to some of the decisions being made about production and disposal. Arguments ensued. The father then gathered up documents and took them to a U.S. Attorney. After nothing came of the attempt to halt the bad practices legally, his father resorted to alcohol and essentially drank himself to death.

My Facebook friend was nine years old at the time his family moved away from St. Louis. He was old enough to know it was a drastic situation that had caused his father to step away from the business, and to move his family elsewhere, but he was too young to know any more details. He expressed guilt over all the health problems of people who lived in St. Louis, even though many of his Facebook friends from here reassured him that no one held him accountable.

In terms of what had happened in the past, someone from the early days of the PBB Disaster contacted me. Getting a call out of the blue was not unusual, with most of them being about what the person had helped to bury under the plant site cap, what had been dumped off site, and where slaughtered cattle had been buried. This time the caller began to talk about studies he had done with mice to show what health outcomes to expect in 20 years or more.

The caller was Dr. Thomas Corbett, a physician who had tried to warn the State of Michigan about the PBB problem in 1974 and was instrumental in bringing Dr. Irving Selikoff from the Mount Sinai School of Medicine to Michigan for the first human health study of PBB in 1976.

When Dr. Corbett called, I invited him to come and to talk to the CAG membership. He told us when the facts first began to be published in newspapers, about a year after the first contamination had taken place, and he read about cows dying from ingesting PBB in their feed, and that PBB had entered the food chain, he decided to try to learn possible health outcomes quickly by doing experiments with pregnant mice and rats in his research lab at the University of Michigan. Some of the immediate results of PBB in the rodents' food were liver enlargements and birth defects, including a condition where the skull didn't form over the brain. He believed there was a high risk that these and other problems would begin to show up in humans beginning in about 20 years.

In the summer of 1974 he met with the Michigan Department of Agriculture to present his findings. At that meeting, the officials discussed the costs of the PBB crisis, but nothing about the public health concern. Then Dr. Corbett presented his findings. Afterwards, an official cornered him to warn him not to tell anyone about his research results, and it was implied that if he didn't keep silent, grants to the University of Michigan would be cut off. Because Dr. Corbett had served his military time in the U.S. Public Health Service during the Vietnam War, his grants came from the Veterans Administration, rather than from the State of Michigan. At the time he was chief of anesthesiology at the Veterans Administration Hospital in Ann Arbor, and a faculty member at the University of Michigan's medical school. Because he knew the threat couldn't hurt the university, he went ahead and presented his results to the newspapers.

He also called Dr. Irving Selikoff, the leading researcher in environmentally caused illnesses, to encourage him to come to Michigan. Selikoff first sent one of his team members, Dr. Harry Anderson, to review Dr. Corbett's lab results. Following that, Dr. Selikoff wanted to bring his whole team, but needed an invitation from a state agency, such as the Department of Agriculture or the

Department of Public Health. Neither agency was willing to issue an invitation, believing they didn't need an outsider coming in.

Dr. Corbett then approached the governor's office about issuing an invitation, and spoke with an aide, Mark Mason. The invitation from Governor William Milliken never came, and Mason denied publicly ever having spoken with Corbett. A year and a half later, FOIA'd documents verified that he *had* talked with Corbett. This was typical of that time as officials tried to cover up the immensity of the PBB Disaster.

By then it was now an election year and Frank Fitzgerald was challenging William Milliken. Fitzgerald used the Corbett/Mason controversy in his campaign, and the fact that the governor had not invited Selikoff to Michigan.

As a result, in May 1976, an invitation was issued from Governor Milliken, and Selikoff came and conducted his blood draws. He also recommended to the State of Michigan that all sickened animals on farms be destroyed, resulting in the slaughter of a million chickens, and tens of thousands of head of livestock.

Years later EPA presented an award to Dr. Corbett for his persistent dedication in trying to prevent serious health injury to the public.

In terms of the health outcomes of PBB exposure, the International Agency for Research on Cancer (part of WHO) has determined that PBBs are a probable carcinogen for humans, but there are not enough studies to say for sure that it is definitely a carcinogen. This means more studies are needed, another reason our CAG is actively partnering with the research being conducted by the Rollins School of Public Health at Emory University.

The health of our children and grandchildren is always on our minds in everything we do. For years we had told EPA that we wanted them to sample the high school athletic field, which was built on a floodplain downstream from the chemical plant. The field had flooded many times, with at least seven feet of water covering it in the 100-year flood of 1986. Some of us remembered that some bulldozing had been done during the cleanup from that flood, but we didn't remember if the contaminated soil had been trucked away or put somewhere else. It turns out it had been pushed up behind the middle school, and since then, that high-ground area had become the practice field for football, as well as a play area for other activities.

When EPA sampled the athletic field, they found DDT levels high enough to warrant a remediation for wildlife standards, as they had found for much of the ANP neighborhood yards and for other floodplains downstream. Tom Alcamo worked hard to convince his bosses that an Emergency Response should take place, and in the summer, that occurred. It was the first time a critical removal response for ecological purposes had taken place in Region 5. A special team from the Emergency Response Branch of EPA received funding for the excavation project of the practice field, the baseball field, the discus area and the long jump area. The plan was to excavate to depths of 1 to 2 feet, with hand digging to take place in the long jump area. The project wrapped up in August with the laying of new sod. Watering of the sod was necessary, but river water was not used due to the negative impression it might have on the public.

As for the continuing concern about rising water, Jim Heinzman told us there had been a breakthrough in communication with EPA. In a conference call, he had laid out the possibilities from his hydrologist point of view to Tom Alcamo and Theo von Wallmenich, and he felt he'd finally been taken seriously.

Jim reported to us that Theo's company, CH2m, had been contracted by EPA to write a Groundwater Investigation Plan. Better late than never and late is not an exaggeration. The "before" testing would take place only weeks before the city wells shut down. Groundwater monitoring for chemical contamination would take place using the sentry wells drilled when Becky Frey had been EPA project manager, along with 34 new monitoring wells. As for

52

groundwater elevations, they would be measured in 249 other wells. In addition, four pumping wells would be put down into the lower aquifer unit to get a better understanding of the hydrogeology at depth. All data gathered would go into a computer model to help design the groundwater pump-and-treat plan for the plant site.

On October 20th, the city wells were shut down. As soon as they quit pumping, the water began to rise. First we were told it was up 10 feet, but it was not expected to go higher. By December it had risen 15 feet, but we were told it was not expected to rise higher. By February of 2016, the rate of rising had slowed, and it was up 20 feet, and not expected to go higher. By March it was up 25 feet and former drinking water wells began to spout out the top, and had to be capped. Again, we were told it was not expected to go higher.

Chapter 4
(2015 -- Part 2)
Circling Wagons

Our paid Technical Advisor, Jim Heinzman, came in for a lot of criticism from the agencies during this time. Tom Alcamo and Dan Rockafellow both said repeatedly that Jim should be doing more for us than he was. They said he should be doing the interpretation of reports and documents, and not EPA and MDEQ, now that he was being paid by a Technical Assistance Grant. Being the frugal lot that we were, and trying to not waste taxpayer money, we had contracted with Jim to wait for the go-ahead from our treasurer before putting in billable time on reports.

Gary Smith, our treasurer, had been working on a new Technical Assistance Grant (TAG) from EPA, and he calculated that if we paid Jim for much more work, the old grant monies would be used up before the new funds were acquired. And receiving a new TAG grant was not a sure thing, anyway.

When Gary spoke of this concern at a Technical Committee meeting, Tom Alcamo told him to write the new grant listing greater responsibilities and "a higher burn rate" for Jim so that more money could be paid out to him.

Steve Boyd, who served as chair of the Technical Committee, spoke to me and Gary at different times about what Jim was being paid. His implication seemed to be that he also should be paid as a committee chair. That wasn't even to be considered. We were all volunteers. The only reason the Technical Advisor was paid was to fulfill a tenet of the TAG grant, that our group pay someone to advise us on technical matters. In prior years, when Dianne Borrello had served as Technical Advisor, she rarely charged for the work she did. At that time, we were doing our best to stretch the TAG grant funds to save as much as we could for the time when design work would begin at the plant site. We knew other CAG and

TAG groups burned through $50,000 in a year, paying a full-time salary to a technical advisor. Our CAG, on the other hand, stretched that first $50,000 out over a decade, thanks to Dianne working more as a volunteer than a paid employee.

Steve was critical of Jim Heinzman in other areas, and, to my way of thinking, seemed to be trying to undermine him. For example, one month Steve had received notification from Tom Alcamo that EPA would not be attending our meetings (which seemed to be an increasing occurrence). Jim suggested there might be some merit in having the Technical Committee meet anyway to discuss the difficulty we were all perceiving in gaining information from EPA, such as sampling plans, and the trouble we were having in discussing anything with Tom without him getting angry or defensive. Jim Hall and others agreed with Jim's suggestion.

On the day of the meeting, Jim Heinzman emailed to say he had received a last minute phone call from Dan Rockafellow about whether or not a Technical Committee meeting would take place, since Tom Alcamo would not be in attendance. Jim told him our plans to have a discussion without the agencies present. Dan took umbrage and stated that he, then, would attend, and if we didn't want him there, we would have to ask him to leave.

Steve responded sharply to Jim's email recounting this incident, saying we had not made a decision to exclude anyone from the meeting, and that Jim had taken too much responsibility on himself by communicating our plans to Dan.

At that afternoon's Technical Committee meeting, Dan attended, as did Diane Russell, our new EPA Community Involvement Coordinator. Tom had sent his EPA report via email, and we discussed that and other technical issues for a while. Quite suddenly, Steve changed the direction of the meeting, voicing his observation that the relationship between the CAG and EPA and DEQ had deteriorated in the short time he had been involved with the group. He said the CAG was at fault for their lack of trust in EPA. Why didn't we trust EPA? He also took exception to the idea that the CAG needed to persuade EPA to take action on various issues. Phil Ramsey spoke up and said he could give a lot of reasons why we didn't trust EPA, but the big one was their failure to tell the City for a year that the drinking water contained the DDT by-product pCBSA. And I cited the example of how EPA was eventually persuaded that we were right about DDT hotspots in yards after hearing our local historical knowledge about the chemical plant giving free fill dirt to residents.

Diane Russell frowned while we were speaking, and interrupted me to say how she was angry with us for telling these stories, that we should forget the past and live in the present. She said we made it sound as if EPA wouldn't have done anything if the CAG hadn't kept after them. Phil Ramsey said, "You're damn right about that."

Then Steve spoke up and said the CAG should recognize that there is a time to stop asking for something – that if EPA doesn't respond, then the CAG should stop asking. He reached an arm across his body and clapped his hand on the sleeve of his other arm, and said, "I feel like I have an EPA patch on my arm."

The statement from Steve that if EPA didn't respond to us, we should quit asking was absurd. Not only did it violate CERCLA standards for community involvement, but it meant CAGs were unnecessary at Superfund cleanups. His statement echoed something his mother had said years ago when the CAG and City of St. Louis met to iron out our differences. She had said, "Why do we even need a CAG? EPA knows what to do."

And Diane's anger at hearing about our past...really? As a community involvement coordinator did she expect to come into a community and criticize its past experiences with EPA? I was put in mind of a novel I'd read in high school called *The Ugly American* about how the U.S. diplomatic corps tended to enter other countries and show insensitivity to local language, customs and the past experiences of the people. That's what Diane was doing.

As for Steve's accusatory question – why didn't the CAG trust EPA – that was easy to answer using the examples from the 1982 consent judgment, the 1998 refusal of EPA to listen when we said the plant site was leaking, the years of intentional divisive tactics to split the CAG and City, the 2005 withholding of information about the contaminated drinking water, the 2012 refusal to believe our explanation for the hotspots in residential yards, and a host of smaller incidents.

In thinking about all of that, it seemed to me the real question was this: Why doesn't EPA trust the CAG?

I tried my hardest to think of anything we had said or done to make EPA distrust us. Had we ever secretly undermined their efforts in any way? Had we ever said one thing and done another without telling them? Had we ever said we would do something and then not follow through?

Not convinced that I was thinking of every possibility, I called Jim Heinzman, who had previously worked for MDEQ, and asked him if the CAG had ever done something to cause EPA or MDEQ to distrust the group? He couldn't come up with anything. Then I called Scott Cornelius, who had worked as our MDEQ project manager for 12 years. He said nothing came to mind, but if he thought of something, he would get back to me. Later he called again, and said the CAG had always freely shared their thoughts, opinions and facts with him, and he had never distrusted the group.

Later I put the question to others on the Executive Committee. Gary said EPA didn't like the fact that we questioned their actions and their results, or that we often sought answers from other sources. He said, "Obviously, they don't like this because they have to divulge more information. Logic dictates there is a reason to hide or suppress information and a benefit in doing so."

Ed Lorenz said we should "appreciate the contradictory pressures on the agency" from elected officials, polluters, and reduced budgets. He said, "Mostly we need to always remember,

EPA and DEQ/DNR didn't make this mess; Velsicol did. EPA and DEQ simply have not done enough to remediate our community."

That took us full circle back to the beginning: The CAG believed in using our persistence to persuade EPA to higher standards, while Steve believed we needed to stop trying to persuade EPA to higher standards in this cleanup.

My conclusion was that the issue of lack of trust was not worth talking about. The only thing the CAG wanted was a complete and thorough cleanup completed by EPA. If EPA did that that, we would be satisfied. We were not seeking marriage with EPA, or any other human relationship. We needed them to behave professionally and to do the work without cutting corners. And the sooner they did it, the sooner we could dissolve our Task Force and get on with the rest of our lives.

Others in the CAG thought we should try to discuss the lack-of-trust issue and other communication issues with EPA. Jim Heinzman felt that way, as did Jim Hall. In my view, it was a waste of our valuable volunteer time, especially since the premise was why we didn't trust EPA, instead of what had we ever done to cause EPA to distrust us? It reminded me of the Stuart Hill attempt to get us to hire a conflict resolution/storytelling/song-singing mediator to waste our time.

While the two Jims tried to work with EPA in organizing a time for discussion on our relationship, Gary Smith called for a special meeting of the Executive Committee. He said it seemed to him that too much of our volunteer time was being spent on EPA being upset with the CAG, and, in the eyes of some, not doing something right. Gary had been gone for the meeting when Steve clapped his hand on his opposite arm and declared he felt he was wearing an EPA patch, but Phil and I had told him about it.

At the Executive Committee meeting, Gary related a recent conversation with Dan Rockafellow. Dan had described the CAG as kids in the backseat who are given some M&M's and they keep asking for more. Gary said, "Apparently Dan sees us as problem children who are never happy, instead of seeing us as concerned citizens who are striving to get the best cleanup possible for their community."

Steve spoke up to say the CAG and the agencies were polarized in an "us-versus-them" head-butting contest. He said it didn't seem to be a productive way to relate. Gary asked if he could suggest a better way, but Steve had no ideas to offer.

Gary then started to talk about how we got to where we were with the agencies, but Steve interrupted him and said if Gary planned to recite the list of things that have happened in the past, he had heard that list many times.

Gary pointed out that Steve, although he had been aware of CAG activity, hadn't been immersed in it for 15 years or more. Even though there had been a lot of back and forth with EPA, Gary felt that because of that, the CAG had persuaded EPA to do a better cleanup. He gave the example of EPA's plan to let all the water out of the river and dry dredge the impoundment area, and how Dick Roeper and Murray Borrello were able to persuade EPA to adopt the sheet-pile wall method that was less destructive to the ecology of the river.

Jim Hall read from an EPA document on CAGs that said CAGs are to assist EPA in making decisions, and that EPA is to seriously consider the unique viewpoints put forth by members of the community. Jim said, "We can't just say 'okay, whatever you want to do is fine with us.' Instead, we have to try to communicate our views."

Steve said, "I hear both sides of it. EPA does not view it the way you view it." He went on to say, "It is the way it is said; the manner in which it is expressed. When you recite history, it comes across to them as demeaning. Facts can be expressed in a respectful way and not in a demeaning manner."

I asked Steve what he thought about Diane Russell's comment that hearing our history made her feel angry. He replied that he didn't think she really was angry.

59

Jim said somehow the CAG needed to find a way to make EPA want to give information; that we couldn't go on year after year asking for the same information, and voicing the same concerns. After a while, it made us frustrated and maybe we then changed our tone.

Steve said the project managers feel that when they give information to us, it comes back to "bite them in the ass."

The issue was raised that our CAG had now been assigned two Community Involvement Coordinators, one to attend our meetings and the other to write newsletters and fact sheets. Steve said it was deliberate; that EPA was pulling away from the CAG/TAG because of polarization. Gary asked if they planned to start a new CAG, and Steve said he didn't know.

As mentioned, Jim Hall and Jim Heinzman had been trying to set up a meeting with Tom Alcamo to discuss the lack-of-trust relationship issue. A date had been set, and Tom was to send an email ahead of time listing his concerns. On the day of the promised email, he had called to say he didn't think the timing was right for the meeting.

At our session with Steve, I asked him if he knew why Tom had cancelled the meeting, and he said he got the impression from Tom that I had not been in favor of the meeting, and that the cancellation was due to something I had said to Tom. What?

It's true, I had told Tom my opinion of the pointlessness of discussing relationship issues when all we both wanted was for the work to get done. But I don't think learning my viewpoint was what changed his mind about the meeting. When I had asked Tom why he thought the meeting was important, and he said because I seemed angry with EPA. I said I wasn't angry, but did he mean me or the CAG in general? He said he meant me, Phil and Ed. Surprisingly, he didn't list Gary's name! Then he began talking about Steve and his excellent academic background in soil chemistry, and how fortunate we were to have him in the CAG, and that we should give him more responsibility. When I said, "Steve is part of the

60

problem," Tom grew very quiet, and then replied, "He is?" I said "Yes," and left it at that.

I think that is why Tom cancelled the miscommunication meeting.

Two days after our Executive Committee meeting, I received a 3-page email from Steve finding fault with how I wrote the minutes, which often included direct quotes from participants. Steve said quoting people was inappropriate and unacceptable, and that they were not exact quotes, they were selective, and they were taken out of context.

In my view, Steve's email was inappropriate and unacceptable, and I was fed up with him. I wrote to Jim Hall that I was thinking seriously of putting my volunteer hours into other projects instead of into the CAG, including the upstream part of the river where there was a nutrient and *E. coli* problem, the Emory University research team work, and into the Reach the Decision Makers fellowship program. I said, "Battling on two fronts is too much for me. The agencies are one thing. Steve is another. His attacks are directed at me, and they are working."

Looking back, I was worn pretty thin from other life events as well, including sitting with a friend who was dying of cancer, and traveling with a cousin to help her brother, who was in a coma.

Before I stepped down from the CAG, I decided to see if something could be done to remove Steve from the positions I had put him in -- because, yes, I was responsible for asking him to be the chair of our Technical Committee and to serve on the Executive Committee. Having been chair of the CAG at that time, I had made those appointments.

During the recent Executive Committee meeting, Steve had freely admitted that he shared internal CAG business with EPA prior to the time the CAG was ready to share the information. This was something I had suspected he was doing, and I was quite amazed that he not only admitted it, but felt it was his duty to inform EPA. Here is an example of his informing action and its consequence: the

61

Executive Committee had talked about asking our federal politicians to write a letter in support of the inadequacy of the Burn Pit Proposed Plan. We hadn't made a decision to do so yet, but Steve shared our discussion with EPA. Because Tom and Diane had the information ahead of time, EPA instructed their political people to talk with our senators and congressman to sway their thinking about the CAG so that when our letter arrived, it wouldn't be taken seriously. We learned about the actions of EPA from the aide to one of our federal lawmakers.

I asked that the Executive Committee meet without Steve to discuss whether or not he should remain on the Board of Directors.

We met, we voted, and the split vote was in favor of not dismissing Steve. The four who had voted to not dismiss preferred a non-direct approach to be played out over time.

After much thought and prayer, and to protect myself from further verbal abuse from Steve, I decided to take a break from the CAG. I told the others my decision -- that after they had dealt in their own way with the Steve issue to let me know, and I would then gladly resume my position as a CAG member and officer.

A month went by. Two months. One day Gary stopped by my house. While he was still on the porch, and before he could say anything, I asked if the Steve issue had been resolved. He said it hadn't, and I told him there was nothing for us to talk about until that issue was resolved, and I went back inside.

Without me to pick on, Steve began to find fault with Ed Lorenz. Ed had written a heart-felt letter to EPA and MDEQ personnel about the problems of official communication with citizens in general, and our citizens in particular. In part, Ed said "The problem in St. Louis is that the local experience is clearly exceptional, and some agency staff seem to think the community can be fit into the normal, oversimplified 'high modernist' ROD process."

Steve characterized Ed's written thoughts as abstract sociology, and concluded by saying, "Perhaps the thing I value most

62

about my paying job at MSU is that we are free to express and challenge ideas openly without fear of repercussions such as losing your position. It would be healthy if such open discourse were acceptable within the CAG, don't you agree?" His implication was that the CAG discouraged open discourse, which was the opposite of the experience of the rest of us. We promoted open discourse with EPA, and they discouraged it in a long list of ways.

During one of the months of my vacation from the CAG, I learned that Steve would not be attending the Technical Committee meeting, and I told Jim Hall and Jim Heinzman that I would attend and take minutes since Steve would not be there. After the meeting minutes were written and sent out, I received an email that made me laugh, remembering how Steve had criticized the minutes I wrote. The email was from Matt Zwiernik, a professor at MSU, and a former protégé of Steve Boyd. Matt wrote, "Wow! You do a great job capturing the minutes. I'm always impressed."

I made it clear to Jim Hall and Gary Smith that when Steve returned from his trip, I would again be absenting myself from the CAG/TAG.

A week or so later, Jim called to say that he'd had a talk with Steve, telling him he didn't really fit well as chair of the Technical Committee, and hoping Steve would take the hint and offer to resign. Steve argued with Jim, and accused me of being the problem. When Jim told him that the entire Executive Committee wanted him to step down from his position, he demanded the right to face his accusers. So Jim began organizing a time and place for the Executive Committee to meet with Steve.

A few days later, Gary called to say and he and Jim planned to meet with Steve to tell him again that he didn't fit well, and Gary said he planned to say it over and over until Steve got the picture.

In another few days, Jim sent out an email informing the Executive Committee that Steve had resigned as TAG chair, but wished to stay active with the Technical Committee because of his expertise in that area. And Jim said that Steve would remain on the

Executive Committee because the CAG had elected him to that position.

I returned as secretary to both the TAG and CAG meetings, and immediately the harassment began. Steve's first issue was about the minutes being sent out BCC (blind carbon copy). Steve wanted the names of the complete distribution group. I didn't write in reply, but I sent him a fact sheet from a website that explained online privacy for nonprofits. Steve replied argumentatively, and said I was overusing BCC. I replied that he was making a mountain out of a molehill, and that I always sent the minutes and other mass mailings from the CAG BCC, and "that's just how it is. It's nothing new."

Next I received an email from Theo von Wallmenich about the way I wrote the minutes. He used phrases that had been used previously by Steve in his 3-page email of several months prior, and even said, "I believe this was pointed out to you in the past by Dr. Stephen Boyd."

I wasn't surprised to learn Theo was unhappy with that month's minutes. He had said something out loud, and in a public meeting, that EPA and MDEQ had only said in more private settings. Theo had told the CAG we should be using our paid technical advisor (Jim Heinzman) to answer questions that we were directing toward EPA personnel, because we had a grant from EPA for that purpose. Later, Tom Alcamo told me Theo's comment was taken out of context. Since I was present and Tom wasn't, his words didn't hold any water.

Nevertheless, it was time to do two things: 1) Explain why our group recorded detailed minutes, including occasional quotes from individuals, and 2) Discuss with EPA why they felt we were under-served by Jim Heinzman.

We initiated a third thing as well. I began to electronically record the meetings. Steve Boyd had said using a recorder would have a "chilling effect" on discussion, and Dan Rockafellow questioned its legality. Again, I put far too much of my volunteer time into research on the topic.

At the next technical committee meeting, I gave the participants a handout about minutes from information I'd gathered. Number one was that the minutes were for dues-paying members and for the public, and that the agencies did not have a say in how the minutes were recorded. Other items detailed how minutes from non-profit corporations differed from for-profit corporations, and how the electronic recording of minutes is both legal and usual in this day and age.

The response was silence. I hoped it would be silence henceforth on the subject of the minutes.

The next month I tape-recorded, transcribed the tape, and gave the complete document of eight pages to each member of the Technical Committee, and there were no complaints about misquotations, or things taken out of context.

Jim Hall called another Executive Committee meeting. Steve Boyd was notified, but did not attend. The main purpose of the meeting was to have Jim Heinzman explain the role of a Technical Advisor, and it was interesting to learn how the position differed at sites that had a responsible party rather than at orphaned sites, like ours. He attributed part of EPA's confusion over his role to this set of circumstances.

At the meeting, Jim Hall officially appointed Jim Heinzman Chair of the Technical Committee.

Carol Layman was not happy that Steve Boyd was still sitting on the Executive Committee, because of the "loose lips" problem we'd had with him. She made a motion to let him know that his performance as a board member was not acceptable, and that she moved that we "separate him" from the Executive Committee. The vote was split and defeated. The others believed it would be best to let him serve out his term, which would end in a few months.

Ed Lorenz made a motion to notify EPA, MDEQ, and their contractors that Steve Boyd was no longer chair of the Technical Committee, and did not represent the CAG in that capacity. That motion was also defeated. Instead, Jim Heinzman would speak personally with the agency personnel to let them know that he was now the person in charge of technical matters, and not Steve.

When it was time to nominate people for our biennial elections, Steve nominated himself. Later, when the votes were counted, he received only one vote. That removed the problem.

The "relationship" problem with EPA escalated when Tom told his contractors to no longer attend our Technical Committee meetings. Since Tom relied on his hired help for the technical answers to our questions, the meetings deteriorated to nothing more than Tom giving a general report on what he hoped would happen in the future.

About this time, Dan Rockafellow, the MDEQ project manager, announced he was taking another job. In his email to Jim Hall, he said some very kind things. He wrote, "I am amazed by the challenges that St. Louis has faced over the years and yet there continues to be a vibrant community in the center of Michigan. I have also been blessed to be able to work with some amazing people over those 3 years. I wish you and the citizens of St. Louis the best today and into the future."

As for the CAG's relationship issues with the EPA, Diane Russell said her goal was to revise the Community Involvement Plan document that Mike Joyce had prepared in 2012 when he was our Community Involvement Coordinator. Interviews with individuals and groups would be conducted. To do that, the EPA's national Conflict Resolution and Prevention Center had been contacted in Washington, D.C. and a contractor was hired who had worked with groups on numerous Superfund sites in New York, Massachusetts and Connecticut.

Like most conflict resolution attempts on the part of EPA, this one created doubt and questions about the motives of the agency. The positive thinkers in the CAG thought it would be a good chance to tell an outside person how difficult it was to work with EPA; however, when they found out that it was an EPA contractor who would be conducting the interviews, their hopefulness faded. The conspiracy theorists saw it as another divisive attempt on the part of EPA to start a different CAG. The pragmatists saw it as another colossal waste of our volunteer time. In their view, the interviews would take place, the revised plan would be written, it would be put on a shelf, and EPA would continue to behave the same as always.

And none of us liked the idea of EPA spending their scarce dollars on frivolous undertakings such as this when they could be spending it to clean up our sites!

In the midst of this, Gary Smith and I drove to Midland to attend a meeting of the Dow Chemical Corporation group, called a TAP. Diane Russell was the Community Involvement Coordinator for that group, too. TAP stands for Technical Assistance Plan in the EPA lexicon, and TAPs are funded by potentially responsible parties (PRPs) through provisions in a negotiated settlement agreement. EPA TAG grants are available for TAPs, and EPA maintains "a strong oversight role," according to the EPA website.

Dow Chemical and EPA had reached their negotiated settlement in 2007, and were now in the process of remediating dioxin contamination along the Tittabawassee River. From what we heard at the meeting, the remediation methods consisted primarily of institutional controls and land purchases. Dow was buying property along the river from landowners, and then posting signs saying no animal grazing was allowed in those areas. It is unlikely that deer, rabbits, birds and other wildlife could read the signs.

The meeting itself was run in a rigid manner by a paid facilitator. Only one woman among the 15 or 20 people grouped around a large square of tables in the room dared to speak without prior approval from the facilitator. The public was seated in a small section of chairs located in a corner of the room, and they were not involved in the program taking place among the agency people and the selected representatives from the business community. Later we learned this meeting format was what Diane Russell hoped to bring to our CAG meetings. More on this topic later.

As we neared the end of 2015, Gary Smith rallied us to one last effort to get money out of our no-longer-responsible-party, Velsicol, to finish the cleanup at the Smith Farm site that had been partially remediated by MDEQ in prior years. The Velsicol Pollution Insurance policy that covered the Smith Farm site would expire in December.

We sent our documents to Professor Nina Mendelson at University of Michigan Law School, including the stop-gap Intent to Sue papers that the Traverse City law firm of Olson, Bzdok and Howard had filed on our behalf in 2010. Nina had many questions, and we were kept very busy in November and December finding and sending information to her.

Even though we had sought help in the past from Sher, Leff, the attorneys who had handled the City of St. Louis case against Velsicol, Ed Lorenz contacted them again, and one of their attorneys, Esther Klisura, asked for documents, some topics of which we were not sure about. Gary went to the county Register of Deeds and found a list of prior property owners, and Tom Alcamo aided us by having EPA files on Smith Farm (also known as the Alma Iron and Metals site) copied and sent to us.

I had notified Don Long, Supervisor of Bethany Township, which now held the deed to the site. Esther from Sher, Leff felt that the deed holder had the best case, and that the CAG should drop out. We agreed.

With the lawyer's help, Bethany Township filed a complaint for damages and other relief in Circuit Court. Don needed to sign the complaint, but before he did that, he brought it to my house and he and I and Ed Lorenz read the seven pages over to make sure everything was understandable.

Our little surge of hope was short-lived. In a couple of months, the lawyer notified Don that they would not be taking on the case. When 2016 arrived, our foreseeable options for the Smith Farm site would expire.

In November we lost another long-time CAG member, Norris Bay. Theo von Wallmenich wrote a tribute to him that was shared with the CAG. Norrie had aided Theo in the early days by providing him with documents, maps, and engineered drawings of the plant site. From those historical treasures, Theo, MDEQ, and EPA were able to determine the locations of each of the primary chemical production facilities, feedstock chemical storage, rail transportation, pipelines, sewers, flumes and discharge points into the river. In his tribute, Theo wrote that the 1944 engineered drawing, with its revisions, "did more to shape the current remediation plan than any other single historical document, helping us to understand where source areas were and how contamination may have moved off the site." If Norrie had just let the past go, as Diane Russell had suggested that current CAG members should do, all of these documents would have gone in the trash years ago. It was a good concrete reminder that the CAG's respect for the past and our determination to keep it as part of our current discussion was the right thing to do.

Throughout the year, Jim Hall had been thinking about the importance of the past to the present efforts, and he decided the CAG should initiate its own Hall of Fame to recognize those people who had contributed time and talent to the cause of cleanup in our community. He took nominations from the entire membership, but asked only the Executive Committee to vote. We chose four of our deceased CAG members: Arnie Bransdorfer, Fred Brown, Gene Kenaga and Joe Scholtz. At our Christmas potluck in December, short talks were given about each of the inductees, and many family members of the four attended. Now, a large plaque hangs in the new St. Louis City Hall building with these four names listed, and room for many more.

Chapter 5
(2016)
Waiting Games

I'm not sure I breathed at all while watching our video on a large movie screen. There was the old green bottle from the St. Louis Magnetic Mineral Springs and the title *From Mineral Springs to Toxic Town* up on the screen for everyone in the darkened movie theater to see. I was prepared to overlook how amateurish our video would seem in comparison to the others at the film festival, but it looked good! And the sound was full-bodied through the large speakers.

I wished others from our CAG could have been there for that big-screen experience. When I had learned that the NIEHS health conference in North Carolina planned to hold a film festival one evening, everyone agreed we should enter. I filled out the forms, and was thrilled to report to the CAG when our video was accepted. I was there in attendance along with the PBB researchers from Emory University, who were giving a presentation at one of the sessions.

When the 11 minutes of video ended, and when I was breathing again, a rushing sense came over me to think how long our CAG had been struggling to get chemical contamination cleaned up in St. Louis. Instead of the cleanup being finalized in 2010, the year we had made the video, we were now in year eighteen and still waiting for funding to *start* the cleanup of the Velsicol plant site.

Not only were we waiting for the EPA Prioritization Panel to designate money for the plant site and Burn Pit site, but we were in waiting mode for a number of other things: results showing the DDT levels in our blood; the assignment of a new MDEQ project manager to our CAG; a release of the PBB Registry records from the State of Michigan; and, always, the sharing of information by EPA with our technical committee *prior* to final decisions being made.

In addition, our treasurer, Gary Smith, had applied in March 2015 for another EPA Technical Assistance Grant, and now, a year later, we were still waiting for the funding. When Gary made the initial application, both our project manager and community involvement coordinator had promised to give him feedback. When the comments finally came months later, they ranged from confusing to petty.

Even though Tom Alcamo had told Gary to list greater responsibilities for our Technical Advisor and "a higher burn rate" for his wages in the application, now he questioned why Gary had written a work plan that gave "administrative work" to the advisor. That was confusing.

A comment also asked the "specific purpose" of the video camera the CAG and city had mounted on a pole at the end of Center Street, and it was followed by a question saying, "Are you aware the TA/your group is not an "Oversight Agency…?" (capital letters). We tended to use the word "oversee" in describing the function of the CAG – for instance, that we were overseeing the cleanup of Superfund sites in our town – and apparently it rubbed someone at EPA in the wrong way. And, further, we believed their concern sprang from a worry that we intended to use the video camera to watch the work at the plant site, once it began. And they were right, because, in our view, showing the community at large what was happening was merely a part of our educational outreach.

Speaking of educational outreach, one of the comments stated, "… the CAG members must share what they learn with the rest of the community." That was a petty dig. Not only did our CAG hold monthly meetings, give newspaper, television, and radio interviews, share news articles and videos electronically with our membership, speak at organizations, college classes, and schools, but also, two of us had written books for the wider public. Ed Lorenz had written a thorough study of the corporate underbelly of Velsicol, entitled *Civic Empowerment in an Age of Corporate Greed*. And I had recently published a memoir of the first 16 years of our CAG entitled *Tombstone Town*. The belittling smacked of more than ignorance.

As Gary moved forward with the TAG application, he learned that everything now had to be done online, and he found the program difficult to navigate. Tom assisted him via phone and email, and finally, the new application was submitted.

Then we learned that we had to fill out another form designating a civil rights coordinator. One of our members was a certified signer for the St. Louis School system, and she offered to be the civil rights coordinator.

Then we learned that grant training certificates some of us had previously received had expired. Later we learned that maybe we didn't need new certificates, but that we should send EPA the old ones. I hunted through files for my certificate, but couldn't find it. It wasn't the kind of thing to frame and put on the wall!

I asked for the link to the training so that I could re-take it and get a new certificate. The link came, I went through the pages and clicked on the answers, and then there was no submit button! Jim Hall, who was also doing the training, finally figured out how to get it to submit, but by that time I was told that I didn't need the training after all since I was no longer the chairperson.

Gary questioned the competence of the people involved in this process, and that angered Tom. The emails flew back and forth during this time.

During half of 2016, we didn't have an MDEQ project manager. After Dan Rockafellow had moved on to a new job in MDEQ, a state geologist named Matt Baltusis had attended some of our meetings as a temporary project manager. His name was familiar, because he had worked with our former project manager,

Scott Cornelius, in the remedial investigation of the Velsicol Plant Site. More recently, he had accompanied Dan Wyant when the MDEQ director had met some of us and toured the plant site.

Matt was friendly and helpful, finding links for online information that we needed, and giving us a list of things he thought we should discuss with EPA regarding the plant site cleanup.

I asked Matt if he thought he might be assigned to us as a permanent project manager, and he was certain he would *not* be chosen because his role at MDEQ was as a geologist.

We worried that an inexperienced person would be assigned to us who had no knowledge of our 18 years of work to get the sites cleaned up, and maybe no experience in Superfund projects at all.

St. Louis City Manager Kurt Giles and Mayor Jim Kelly had the same concerns, and we decided to write a joint letter to Governor Rick Snyder laying out our reasoning for the State to assign to our sites a person with experience in CERCLA law and Superfund remediation. Copies went to several people at MDEQ as well.

Right away, I received a call from David Kline, Section Chief for the Superfund program at MDEQ. He asked to come and speak with the CAG membership at our upcoming meeting, and when he came, he assured us that he would provide us with an experienced project manager. Later the current MDEQ director followed up with a letter voicing the same assurance. A few months later we received notification that Matt Baltusis had been assigned to our sites, which pleased us. So far he had been an advocate for both the CAG and the State of Michigan.

It was during this time period that the city of Flint, Michigan had come into the news, with the discovery of high lead content in its drinking water. During the crisis, Dan Wyant resigned as director of MDEQ, as did the Region 5 EPA administrator, Susan Hedman.

Many op-ed pieces and newspaper articles compared the Flint water crisis with the 1970s PBB disaster, which still held the dubious title as the largest food contamination event in U.S. history.

There were many similarities, and one major difference – scientists had proven the danger of lead ingestion, while the dangers of PBB had been unknown when the chemical entered the food chain. Because lead was a known danger, both the state and federal governments moved fast to aid the 99,000 residents of Flint affected, unlike the slow and reluctant response back when the 9 million residents of the State of Michigan unknowingly ingested the fire retardant PBB in their meat, milk, eggs, cheese and butter for a more than year before the problem was made public…and not by the State, but by the press.

The Flint crisis also reminded us of the pCBSA drinking water crisis in St. Louis. Even though EPA had found the DDT byproduct in our drinking water in 2005, they had waited a year before alerting the city council, the public and MDEQ. Once again, however, little was known about pCBSA's health outcomes for humans, in contrast with the known outcomes of lead contamination. Here in St. Louis, it took a lawsuit by the City, and persistent persuasion by the CAG, until, thankfully, uncontaminated water began to flow to residents in the town and the prisons, starting at the end of 2015. It looked like the Flint people would not have to wait 10 years for their contaminated drinking water to be made clean. Even so, early on in the Flint Water Crisis, the CAG sent $500 of our own money (not TAG grant money) to a charity in Flint that was distributing water to residents in need. Our hearts went out to them.

Later in the year, several CAG members attended a conference on environmental justice in Detroit which centered on the Flint water crisis. It was interesting to hear the talks from the Flint people who had made known the problem. As can be imagined, we recognized a lot of our past in their stories and explanations.

Also of interest to us were the conclusions reached by the Flint Water Advisory Task Force that described the "substance and tone" of governmental and bureaucratic communications with the residents of Flint as "aggressive dismissal, belittlement, and attempts to discredit…the individuals involved." Our CAG members had certainly experienced those attitudes in our long years of working with agencies.

And more so recently, ever since the new Community Involvement Coordinator had come on board. Our way of responding in meetings and even our behaviors were questioned by her. She had us under a microscope. Ed Lorenz was teaching from a book at Alma College that discussed the Administrative Procedures Act that lays out how agencies of the federal government are to inform the public when issuing new rules of procedure. Ed rallied the rest of us by emailing, "The important thing for us in the case of EPA is that the rules tell officials at EPA, such as Tom and Diane, how to behave. Those rules do not tell us how to behave in dealing with the agency." He went on to say that we should continue to state our opinions, to call and write to our legislators in Congress, and to go over the heads of officials when needed. He did not want us to change our behaviors or become intimidated by the tactics the CIC was now using.

Two of the legislative aides who often attended our meetings were becoming concerned about how EPA ignored our requests for information on the groundwater situation and on the landscaping problems in the neighborhood. They wanted to know if this was a new development. It certainly wasn't new. Gary and I went back through our notes from 2014 to the present and wrote two pages of questions and concerns we had asked during that time, and for which we had been promised responses, which never came. Many of the listed concerns had been raised multiple times.

The legislative aides also wondered about the abrupt and defensive attitudes of the EPA personnel when we asked questions.

For instance, during a CAG meeting I wanted to find out for sure if legal difficulties had been resolved with the contractor EPA had used in 2014 for the residential yard remediation. Recorded, it goes like this:

Me: I have a question for you. I know you had problems with the contractor you used in...

Tom: No we didn't. We didn't have problems.

Me: I haven't asked my question yet. It is my understanding that the contractor...

Tom: We didn't have any problems with the contractor that did the landscape work.

Me: Tom! I have a question. Would you like to hear it? [No response.] This is a yes or no question. Are the problems you had with the contractor in 2014 resolved?

Tom: We didn't...

Me: Yes or no.

Tom: Yes.

Good grief. Part of it was Tom's personality, and for the most part, we had learned to deal with his defensiveness. But part of it was a reluctance to share information with the CAG, even though all the CERCLA and CAG guidelines stressed the duty of EPA personnel to not only share information, but to involve the citizens in the decision-making process.

As for the withholding of information about the cleanup in the residential yards, Tom said privacy laws precluded him from sharing those with us. We then encouraged more residents from the neighborhood to attend our meetings and share their issues out loud with the group. Several came to one meeting to voice their displeasure in how things had been handled, and Tom spoke up, saying he didn't think CAG meetings were "the proper venue" for the neighbors to voice their complaints. Several CAG members spoke out, saying our meetings were exactly the right venue. And the legislative aides raised their eyebrows at Tom's attempts to quiet the resident's complaints.

Previously, when Gary Smith and Jim Hall had conducted an informal survey of some of the neighborhood residents to gain information, it had caused Tom, Theo and other EPA personnel to erupt in anger, as if Gary and Jim had done something illegal. Now the two of them, along with Teri Kniffen, decided to do a more extensive survey, and to collect the data into charts and graphs.

Jim decided we should present the results to our legislators, both state and federal, as well as to EPA. He organized a tour of the residential neighborhood where excavation of contaminated soil had taken place, and the restorative landscaping was less than hoped for. Aides for all three of our federal legislators attended, as did State Senator Judy Emmons and State Representative Rick Outman.

We met at St. Louis City Hall at eight in the morning, where Jim handed out packets of the survey results. He also laid down a rule. As we toured the neighborhood, Jim stressed that this was a time for EPA to listen to the residents, and not talk. Later, when an EPA person began explaining something to a resident, Jim spoke up and cut off the words, reminding us of the listen-only rule.

Among the complaints we heard were drainage problems, the initial work plan not being followed, the plants and trees not being replaced like for like, and the chief problem was about the quality of topsoil that had been used. It was called topsoil, but hardpan would have been a better term. Or baked brick. Jim is a big guy, and he stood on a shovel in yards to demonstrate that it could not penetrate the topsoil underneath. The newspapers ran a photo of him standing on a shovel, with our state representative, Rick Outman, looking on. Before his involvement in politics, Outman had been a contractor who had spent many years working with heavy equipment, and he knew soil.

We followed up with a letter to Tom Alcamo, who had not attended the tour. We described what had been seen and heard, and we stressed that the property owners were not the responsible party for the contamination problems. They should not have to bear the costs of the inadequate restoration of their yards following the removal of Velsicol's contaminants. Attached were quotations from the EPA Work Plan (that we had received when the project was almost completed), and in our letter we pointed out that a number of statements in the plan had not been fulfilled.

Later we learned that the legislators had followed up with phone calls to EPA personnel. As a result, EPA hired workers to come in with equipment to take plugs out of the remediated yards to allow moisture in and room for grass roots to grow. It was hoped this aeration would help the newly laid sod take root in the better soil that lay below the hardpan. Also, the City of St. Louis offered customers in the neighborhood a credit on their water bills to help pay for the additional water usage on the newly sodded yards.

On paper, the neighborhood was part of the plant site cleanup, as was the huge infrastructure project to bring uncontaminated drinking water to St. Louis from Arcada Township. Whenever we voiced our concerns that EPA Headquarters in Washington, D. C. was not sending money for plant site cleanup, Tom would remind us that EPA had sent millions for the new water system. And he was right. Years ago when the decision was made to include a new water system in the Velsicol cleanup plan, we knew the plant site would take a back seat, and we had agreed with that decision. Clean drinking water was the top priority. We just didn't know it would take so much money and so many years to build the wells, pipes, water tower, treatment plant and everything needed for the new water system to function.

Those of us who lived near the newly dug municipal wells in Arcada Township, 7 or 8 miles from St. Louis, worried about our private wells when the huge city wells would begin to pump. Sure enough, the first summer that one of the new wells was in operation, three private wells failed, and others had difficulties. Within another year or two, two more large wells would be in production, and we worried what would happen then. Engineers assured us that only one of the municipal wells would pump at any given time, and a clause in an agreement with the township board said water would be provided to us if the fault didn't lie with our own well and pump. Somehow we didn't take great comfort from that clause, and we asked for our static water levels to be tested, as well as our water quality, prior to the installation of the two new wells, so we would have a baseline to argue from, if necessary.

As for the plant site itself, design work continued. A contract was awarded, dependent on funding from Headquarters, to a company to perform the ISTT (*in situ* thermal treatment) remediation in Area 1 of the site. The plan was to insert metal rods deep into the ground, run high voltage electricity through them to heat the ground and liquefy, or turn into gas, the NAPL, DBCP and other volatile and semi-volatile chemicals buried there. A sophisticated treatment system would capture the toxic gases and liquids, sort them, and filters used to collect the contaminants would be disposed of in a hazardous waste landfill. The object was to protect workers and people living in the area from toxic fumes that might otherwise be released into the air through excavation. The plan called for the soil down to the till layer to be heated to 100 degrees Centigrade for about 6 months, with each area receiving a minimum of 90 days heating, even if the computer showed nothing being destroyed. The only drawback to this method that our Technical Committee could see was that the high levels of metals and DDT in the soil would not be destroyed. We had asked repeatedly for information on this topic, but our requests had been ignored. When we sent an email to the NAPL expert who worked directly with Tom, asking for information, Tom wrote back that his expert didn't have time to spend answering our questions.

The City of St. Louis made its own electricity, and would contribute some of the 6 to7 million kilowatt/hours needed for the thermal destruction project. We hoped this would benefit the city financially.

Only certain areas of the plant site would be treated thermally. Other areas would receive chemical oxidation treatments, or be excavated.

None of this could get underway without funding. Our federal Congressman, John Moolenaar, supported a bill in the House that would have provided more than $27 million more for Superfund projects around the country, but the bill failed to pass.

Meanwhile, the downstream study of the Pine River was underway. The 33 miles of river downstream from the St. Louis dam was labeled OU-3 (operable unit 3) of the Velsicol Superfund remediation. The point of the study was to calculate risk to wildlife from contaminants of concern in the sediments and soils.

EPA had hired our former CAG member and consultant, wildlife toxicologist Dr. Matt Zwiernik, who had conducted the dead bird studies in the residential neighborhood. His study downstream would address the concentration of contaminants and the disrupted mechanisms due to exposure in birds and mammals, such as thyroid problems and poor breeding success.

All of the property owners from the dam in St. Louis to North County Line Road had given Matt access to their land. Matt and his Michigan State University graduate students had installed 110 bird boxes for songbirds, and would directly measure nesting success, clutch size, nest attentiveness and fledgling success, which would relate to assessment endpoints. For some birds, individual animals would serve as surrogates for a group. For instance, the great-horned owl would serve for the raptors. Nesting platforms for the owls were installed.

In addition to birds, small mammals would be studied, from shrews to mink.

Matt planned to analyze tissue samples using a new ToxCast procedure, which incorporated a series of molecular and biological assays. It would be the first time the ToxCast procedure would be used in an ecological risk assessment. Most contaminated sites have only one or two contaminants of concern, but with a site containing many COCs, the ToxCast would speed up the lab process and also give information on the interaction of the COCs on wildlife.

Tom had carved out money for the study from the Region 5 budget for a year's worth of work. Matt said two years minimum would be needed, and knowing how good Tom was at finding money, we were all quite sure Matt would get his two years.

As for the fish downstream, Joe Bohr, an aquatic biologist with MDEQ, gave the CAG a presentation on the 2015 fish collection analysis of data as compared with earlier years. Previous data had shown significant declines in DDT in tissue samples since the sediment removal project in the impoundment area (1998-2006), and the new data now showed slight elevations in DDT from 2010 to 2015. Joe did not have an explanation for the rise, but said perhaps the fish collected in 2015 were older ones that had accumulated more DDT in their fat. Gary Smith pointed out, however, that the fish caught in 2015 were smaller, which tended to indicate younger specimens. Our Technical Advisor, Jim Heinzman said that when the city well field was shut down, the artesian system recovered, and the new hydraulic head could now be driving dissolved contaminants upward and into the river. Our former MDEQ project manager, and now a CAG member, Scott Cornelius, said he had advised Tom and EPA to not jump to a conclusion that 2010 data showing a decline in DDT was directly a result of the sediment cleanup in the impoundment area. He said the 2015 data was possibly a corroboration of his advice.

Speaking of DDT, the community at large still was waiting for the blood draw results that would show how much DDT or its congeners still coursed through our systems. Of the three tubes of blood drawn from each person three years prior, we were supposed to learn our PBB levels, DDT levels, HBB levels and a few other chemicals. The only results we had so far were for PBB.

CAG members often asked about the results. Gary Smith emailed the researchers at Emory asking about the delay, and told them how it was eroding confidence in the researchers. "As the new deadline dates for delivery of the results come and go, those who are participants, and those who are watching and waiting to be participants, start to doubt. The same thing is happening all over again, we're told one thing and it never happens. Just watch, this will go nowhere, just like it was with Velsicol and the State kinda sums up the thoughts."

Since the 1970s, the community had been volunteering for studies, giving blood, urine and even fat samples in the past, and often never seeing the results, and never hearing any more from the researchers. So far, the researchers from Emory had behaved differently, but the delay in the DDT results was undermining their good reputation.

In conference calls with the researchers, we learned that the lab at Emory had suffered a catastrophe of some sort, and the DDT assays had to begin all over again. After many months, we learned that apparently the lab director was putting better-paying projects ahead of the DDT results for our community. Our Executive Committee decided it was time for us to write to the lab director ourselves.

The response received described how each analysis had to be done separately, how the instrument had downtime and then needed to be checked before re-use. Also, funding was a problem, since the lab had received only half the funding originally agreed upon, and had to find funding in other places.

None of this appeased the people who were waiting for their results. The lab director said she would have results to the Emory researchers by December, but once again, the deadline was missed.

The funding for the blood sample results was coming out of the former NIEHS grant that the researchers had received. With the new grant recently awarded to them, they planned to conduct a clinical trial of a substance that helped the body eliminate organophosphates, such as PBB and DDT and, an epigenetic study on three generations of PBB-exposed families to determine if sperm might transmit to offspring a tendency to experience PBB health problems.

The CAG, local health department and farm families had asked that part of the grant money pay for community meetings and blood draws, such as had occurred in 2013 and 2014 in the St. Louis area. We had been directing people who were interested in being part of the studies to fill out the forms on the PBB Registry website to get their names on the waiting list for future blood draws. By now the people waiting numbered over 1,000.

Disappointingly, we learned that because NIEHS had cut all grant amounts by 20%, the blood draws would not be funded out of this grant.

Our CAG thought that fundraising efforts should take place to try to supplement the grant money to help pay the costs of analyses of blood drawn from people now on the waiting list. At 1000 people that amounted to $300,000. That was a lot of money.

The Leadership Team decided to form a Fundraising Committee, and also a Recruitment Committee to find the right candidates for the clinical trial and the epigenetic study. Despite efforts, no money was attained in this way.

Meanwhile another grant opportunity arose to improve the infrastructure for research cohorts, such as the PBB Registry. With input from Jane-Ann and Marcus, both of whom had the technical and informatics background to be helpful, the researchers pulled together an application for the infrastructure grant, too.

It was sorely needed. The original cohort records gathered by the state health department had not all been transferred to their quasi-contractor, Michigan Public Health Institute (MPHI); some were handed over on paper and microfiche and not entered into the data base, and when people moved, their addresses had not been updated, but instead participant records were labeled "Lost to Follow-up." For those records actually in the MPHI data base, *all* had the wrong birthdates for participants. We knew about much of this from seeing the original study documents community members had shown us that did not match up, or sometimes didn't even show up, in the MPHI database.

Sometimes we were told there were 4000-plus original participants in the state's PBB study, sometimes 5000-plus, and recently 6,800. The data was a mess. Not only did the broken parts need fixing, but it needed to be made accessible to the participants and their family members, and to researchers.

Frustrated with the bureaucratic slowness, one of our CAG members decided to start her own anecdotal health survey. Joanne Scalf, sister of our chairperson, Jim Hall, started a private group on Facebook asking past and present St. Louis residents to describe the health status of themselves and family members and the location of their residence in St. Louis. Joanne wanted to make a map of the health problems showing where people presently resided, or had resided in the past, in relation to the chemical plant. This idea caught the attention of a faculty member at the Central Michigan University School of Medicine, and he decided to work with Joanne on the project.

Finally, in terms of health projects for 2016, Ed Lorenz and his students mounted a large public health conference called Intergenerational Risk from Environmental Contamination. It began with a dinner held at St. Louis City Hall with Carolyn Raffensberger speaking about the precautionary principle. That evening van loads of participants were brought to the gates of the plant site where Jim Hall and I talked about the contamination, the failed first remedy, and the plans for the second remedy. The next day the conference featured David Carpenter, a public health physician who had done much research around Superfund sites; Jonathan Chevier whose research focused on human health and exposure to flame retardants and pesticides; and Michele Marcus, whose research focused on the multi-generational health effects from exposure to PBB. Small group discussions took place in the afternoon, with college students recording the comments and questions asked. Plans were made to write a consensus document. The evening speaker was Matthew Tejada, the director of the Office of Environmental Justice at EPA in Washington, D.C.

Those of us who had taken part in the Reach the Decision Makers Fellowship had conversed with Matthew Tejada in D.C.

while interviewing many EPA people for the course completion. Matt arrived early for the intergenerational conference, and I gave him a windshield tour of the various sites in and around St. Louis. I had to miss his talk at the conference because I was the keynote speaker for the Chippewa Watershed Conservancy banquet that evening, giving a presentation on my recently published book.

Ed was pleased with the conference, but unhappy that Region 5 EPA people had not attended. The conference, in Ed's view, was designed to help EPA do better cleanups by listening to the experts who had shown scientifically that human health was not being protected by the risk assessment standards EPA was using. With "protection of human health and the environment" as EPA's mandate, it seemed to Ed that the regional staff would have welcomed the opportunity to attend the conference.

Nearing the end of 2016, our Technical Advisor, Jim Heinzman, decided to resign because of a health issue his wife was facing. We hoped he would continue to attend our meetings when he could, because his knowledge of hydrogeology was invaluable to us.

Because the Technical Assistance Grant we received from EPA required that we have a paid technical advisor, we placed an ad in several publications and waited the 30 required days for the ad to run, and then waited for EPA Region 5 to approve our contract language.

More waiting games.

A nice tribute to our CAG appeared in the City of St. Louis newsletter. Mayor Jim Kelly wrote: "On Earth Day I attended a meeting with the Chippewa Tribe and while Jane was giving a talk, one of the women leaned over and asked me how much the CAG members got paid. I told her it was all volunteers and she almost fell out of her chair. She couldn't believe that so many people would do so much for no pay. Our community owes a huge debt to the Citizens Advisory Group."

Following that talk to the Saginaw Chippewa Indian Tribe, their newspaper did a feature story on Jim Kelly and me, with photos of us standing by the tombstone, now nicely situated outside the old depot which houses the St. Louis Area Historical Society.

Chapter 6
(2017)
Funding Quests

In the early months of the year, the lack of funding for cleanup of the Velsicol plant site was a constant concern, and it became more urgent when our EPA project manager, Tom Alcamo, said he would be working only at other sites if funding didn't soon come through. We wrote again to EPA Headquarters in Washington, D.C. pleading for enough money to get the remediation of the buried Velsicol Chemical factory underway. At the end of 2016, we had received discouraging news from Mathy Stanislaus, then Assistant Administrator of EPA, saying ours was one of twelve projects in the nation that could not be initiated due to a lack of funds, and it was uncertain that things would be different in 2017.

After the election of President Donald Trump, nationwide media that covered environmental issues plunged into a negative state of mind. I received an email from Mark Brush at Michigan Public Radio alerting me to the Trump plan to stop all contracts and grants given out by EPA. After doing some research, and contacting our EPA project manager, I wrote to our CAG members and to Mark Brush letting them know what I had learned. Essentially, the halt on grants and contracts would not apply to our site, since the money we were waiting for was not a grant, and since the process to receive the money was already underway.   Further encouragement came from listening to the confirmation hearings for the new EPA Administrator, Scott Pruitt. He said twice to senators that Superfund sites were at the top of his list for cleanup.

Next President Trump proposed cutting EPA's budget by 30%. Tom was very concerned about this, but in my limited experience with having seen EPA Headquarters, having talked with several in the administration, and having listened to how EPA dollars were being spent on research at the science conferences I attended, it seemed to me that EPA could be streamlined and more dollars spent on actual cleanups in communities. And I believed that Superfund would be all right, because of what I'd heard in the confirmation hearings. As it was, very little was cut from the overall EPA budget, and none from Superfund.

In the midst of all this, Mustafa Ali, who had helped found the environmental justice office at EPA, stepped down. I had met Ali in D.C., and later we spoke again at the environmental justice conference in Detroit. He was a good spokesman for the cause, encouraging EPA to consider the people factor when planning remedies in communities. I was sad to see him go.

More bad news came from Kali Fox, aide to Senator Debbie Stabenow, saying that Trump proposed a 43% cut to Superfund. She asked if I could put into writing what this would mean to my community. The letter I wrote and sent to our U.S. senators and congressman began by saying: "If we could do the work ourselves, we would. Men and women from our community would use their excavators and trucks to clean up the 52-acre site of the defunct and buried Velsicol Chemical Corporation. We have persistence, determination and know-how. Three things keep us from doing it ourselves: 1) Federal and state laws won't allow citizens to clean up a Superfund site 2) The cost is way beyond our means 3) The dangers to human health from the buried waste are dire." After giving our low-income statistics, and other detail, I ended the letter by saying: "What will happen in St. Louis if the Superfund budget is cut and money is not allocated to the sites in our town? The birds will continue to die. The fish will continue to be poisonous to eat. Babies will continue to miscarry or be born with urinary and genital abnormalities. Parents and teachers will continue to see high rates of autism and ADHD problems in our school children. And St. Louis will continue to be known as Toxic Town."

All three of our federal legislators thanked us for the letter, and Bruce McAttee, aide to Senator Gary Peters, said it was one of the best letters he had ever read.

And as it turned out, very little was cut from the overall EPA budget, and, thankfully, none from Superfund.

In May, we wrote to EPA Administrator Scott Pruitt, remarking on his statement that cleaning up the more than 1,300 Superfund sites in the country was a priority for him, and inviting him to consider funding our site as an excellent public relations example. I wrote: "Our highly contaminated site, one of the worst in the nation, is ready to go. Over the years, our project manager has diligently sought money from other sources to complete the design work on the [site]. All we need now to get underway is several million dollars to be designated to our site by the EPA Prioritization Panel. If you can get those dollars to us, work can begin at once, and you would have an example to point to." At first we received a generic response, and then we received a letter from James Woolford, director of EPA's Office of Superfund Remediatin and Technology Innovation, thanking us for the invitation to visit the site. Scott Pruitt didn't accept our invitation for a visit, but we like to think he might have smiled at our proposal. And later, The Washington Post quoted from my letter about our site being a possible public relations example.

During our June monthly membership meeting, Tom received word on his phone that $9.7 million had been allocated to our site, enough to complete the first phase of underground heat destruction of volatile contaminants. When he made the announcement, the room burst into applause! Finally! As Chair Jim Hall said, "We are now moving from Toxic Town to Turnaround Town!"

Yes, $9.7 million was a drop in the bucket, considering that $382 million was needed to complete the cleanup, but it was a start! Our deceased friend Joe Scholtz had said often, if we can just get them to put shovels in the ground, they will have to finish the job! And now, at least in a sense, shovels would at last be put in the ground.

In July, we wrote a thank you letter to Scott Pruitt, and once again invited him to visit us.

As mentioned, Mustafa Ali had departed his post at EPA, and we wondered if Matthew Tejeda was still there. Matthew was the Director of the Office of Environmental Justice at EPA Headquarters in Washington, D.C., and had given a talk at the Intergenerational Risk from Environmental Exposure conference that we had conducted in 2016. He replied to our email that he was still there, and planned to stay.

The issue of environmental justice was on our minds because of the recent EJ screening tool that EPA had developed. The tool included many screening parameters to determine if a community had environmental justice issues or not, and population was one detail calculated into the formula. Despite the small population of St. Louis (4,500 not counting the prisoners in the three State prisons), our town had made the list of EPA's top 25 EJ communities in the Michigan, along with Detroit, Grand Rapids, Saginaw and Southfield. To us, that meant the other measurements must have been high for us to make the list with such a small population.

Recently I had agreed to accept an appointment to Governor Rick Snyder's Environmental Justice Work Group at the state capitol in Lansing. Again, the community representatives were all from the big cities, except for a tribal representative from further north, and me, representing rural Michigan. Our charge was to make recommendations to the governor in the areas of guidance, training, curriculum and policy.

We held listening sessions in three parts of the state: Detroit, Grand Rapids and on tribal lands near Traverse City. I offered to make a presentation to the group on EJ issues in rural Michigan, and they agreed. I focused on three areas: industrial, with the Velsicol cleanup in St. Louis as the example; agricultural, with the bacteria and over-nutrification problems in the Pine River above Alma; and bureaucratic, with our ongoing battle with the state health department over the PBB records.

After many months of long discussions, the EJ group finalized a report and got it on the governor's desk in February, 2018. I enjoyed working with the cream of the crop of environmental justice proponents from around the state, and hoped that, in the long run, our recommendations would benefit the people and environment of Michigan, including those in rural Michigan.

When an industry pollutes land, air and water of a community, the health of the people suffer. Increasingly, volunteer time of several Task Force members was spent working with the researchers from Emory University. Sadly, much of that time went to a bureaucratic battle with the state health department over the PBB records of study participants.

We first became aware of the problem in December, 2013 during the blood draws in our area of the state to determine levels of PBB, DDT and other chemical contaminants in our bodies. When elderly chemical workers arrived for the blood draw, some of them had their original documents in hand from the beginnings of the PBB Long-term Study begun by the State of Michigan in 1978. When employees from Michigan Public Health Institute (MPHI), a contractor for the State of Michigan, looked at their computer screens to verify the data, they found no listings for these people who clearly had been in the study, as shown by the old, yellowed documents they'd brought with them.

As recounted in an earlier chapter, I accompanied Marcus Cheatham, Health Officer for our Mid-Michigan District Health Department, to the MPHI headquarters in Okemos in early 2014, and Dr. Michele Marcus, who headed up the PBB Research at Emory University, joined by telephone as we talked with the director of MPHI, Renee Canady. Despite our positive take on the meeting, nothing happened to resolve the issue. Over the next two years, neither Emory's letters nor letters from our state legislators made a difference. When we learned in May of 2016 that MPHI had not completed its annual renewal of paperwork to maintain its IRB approval since 2014, it meant no consent forms submitted from study participants since the expiration date were valid.

As our PBB Leadership Team heard that deplorable news, I spoke up and said this was a community issue, as well as an institutional issue, and the community needed to respond. I encouraged the Emory researchers to keep working through their university channels to resolve the problem, and meanwhile, our Task Force would write a letter from the standpoint of how this unresolved issue further demeaned the exposed community. We did so, and the reply from the Director of the Michigan Department of Health and Human Services, showed a complete lack of understanding of the circumstances, and he seemed blind to viewing the issue in terms of public health.

Then we learned that a thumb drive containing data from the original records had been left on a desk at MDHHS and later disappeared. Ed Lorenz said it was time for the CAG to take on the role of bad cops, and start cracking some heads.

In the letter Ed wrote, he pointed to the "problem of record keeping by MDHHS and MPHI," saying it required "major immediate attention and intervention by state leaders." He wrote, "After the 1970s PBB Disaster, the people of St. Louis became guinea pigs for both chemical exposures and also public environmental and health agency indifference. Unwittingly, we were pioneers in demonstrating policy failures that most recently the residents of Flint are coping with. Instead of devoting efforts to aid an exposed population, public servants have wasted taxpayer dollars in doing their best to hide the problem."

The letter ended with an offer to meet in person with Director Nick Lyon. When Lyon didn't invite us to his office, but sent an uncomprehending reply that expressed irritation with us, we decided to set up an appointment ourselves. We considered contacting the state attorney general and ask to meet with him, with Nick Lyon present, but Jim Hall thought we should first try to work through our state representative, Jim Lower.

Representative Lower agreed to meet with us, and Jim Hall, Marcus Cheatham and I explained the problem as clearly as we could. Jim Lower said he thought going to the attorney general was not the best path, but to first meet with Nick Lyon and then go directly to the governor. He felt that his association with the governor could help resolve the issue sooner.

As we waited to hear back from Representative Lower about the meeting he had offered to set up, we saw on the news that Nick Lyon had been indicted and later charged for misconduct in his mishandling of the water crisis in Flint, and he was also charged with involuntary manslaughter involving one of the people who had died from the outbreak of Legionnaire's disease, also linked to the bad water in Flint. We assumed these events had slowed the setting of a date for a meeting.

When Jim Lower finally called me, he said that Nick Lyon and others did not want any community people to attend a meeting. He was willing to speak with Jim alone. Jim explained to him that the details of the issue were not something he had fully in his grasp, and he needed people from the community there to explain. It was agreed that one person could attend, and Jim asked me to be the one.

As I prepared for the meeting, I felt a weight of responsibility on my shoulders that I would have gladly shared with others from our CAG. I said this to them and several of them wrote pertinent facts and their thoughts for me ahead of time. I listed questions for them of things that were not clear in my mind, and their responses helped me to be better prepared. The issue of the PBB records was complicated by the passage of time and the number of entities involved: the state health department, MPHI, Emory University, and the individual participants in the original 1970s study. Over that stretch of time and number of organizations, some records were in data bases, some on microfiche, some on paper, and each of the organizations had some of the 6,000- plus records, and apparently no one had all of them.

CAG member Norm Keon, a former state health department employee, warned me to expect a lawyer in attendance, and he was right. When Jim Lower and I walked into the conference room at the Anderson Building in Lansing, there were five people already seated, and not one of them was Nick Lyon. The only man at the table, other than Jim Lower, was Kory Groetsch who I recognized from his work with our Task Force years ago when we designed and put up DO NOT EAT THE FISH signs along the Pine River.

I asked who was standing in for Nick Lyon, and Sue Moran said she was next in line in the authority structure. Another woman murmured that Nick had other things on his mind right now. It turns out that she was the lawyer, named Karla Ruest. Afterwards, Jim Lower's aide, Danielle Sirianni, told me that the state health department had become so afraid of lawsuits since the Flint water crisis that they now always brought legal representation.

Karla asked me in a suspicious way to explain about myself and my interest in the proceedings. I told her that I was there representing my community, and Kory questioned what that meant. I said, in terms of PBB, it meant the entire state of Michigan. Karla didn't know anything about the PBB records issue, which was my launching point to explain the ins and outs as best I could.

After an hour of talking, Sue Moran said she planned to speak with MPHI about the records problem. She also looked forward to a proposed webinar that the Emory researchers planned to show her. Jim Lower said he would like everyone to return for a follow-up meeting in two months. I left the meeting feeling encouraged, although having learned that both Nick Lyon and Sue Moran sat on the board of MPHI, as well as working for MDHHS, left me wondering about conflicts of interest since they represented both a "company" and its contractor.

Later I listened in on the webinar, which presented in slides Emory's sophisticated way to make the data from the original PBB records both accessible and usable to the participants and researchers. There was little feedback from the MDHHS participants, and no enthusiasm. On that conference call, Sue Moran agreed to write a letter of support for the grant Emory University was seeking from NIEHS to develop the new infrastructure.

The second meeting with MDHHS at Representative Jim Lower's office was coming up, and I asked Jim if CAG member Marcus Cheatham could attend with me, since he understood the proposed infrastructure better than I did. Jim replied in the affirmative, and added that we would let the MDHHS people know Marcus was attending when we entered the meeting room.

Attending this meeting from MDHHS were Sue Moran, Sarah Lyon-Callo, Kory Groetsch and a different legal liaison with Nick Lyon's office, Jeff Spitzley. Jim Lower led off and asked Sue Moran to summarize the progress made since our last meeting.

She said MDHHS was working to determine the disposition of 600 records, and MPHI was doing the same with over 5,000 records. I asked if the chemical workers were included in this number, since they had been dropped from the study early on, and Kory said they were. Sarah said something to indicate that perhaps they would not be sharing all of the records with Emory, and I said that didn't make sense. If every record was looked at to determine if the person was deceased, or had refused to continue, or whatever, then that entire number of records should go to Emory with the proper notations. Jim Lower supported that idea, and from what was subsequently said, I believed that we had won our point.

Sue said the State planned to renew its contract with MPHI, which would expire at the end of the year. I explained how "MPHI" has become a bad word in our community, and how we were fed up with MPHI for assuring us since 2014 that things were moving only to find out repeatedly they were not and that they hadn't even renewed the IRB, making all the consent forms from participants since the expiration date invalid.

I also spoke about the expense of the consent form notification process that ate up grant money that the community would rather see spent on research, on educating people who have been exposed, and on educating their health care providers. Kory nodded in agreement, but Sarah Lyon-Callo said the process is necessary and legal, and for about the fourth time during that meeting said that people needed a chance to refuse. I said, "I've noticed how you have referred quite often in this conversation to people refusing, and I agree that people have that right, but that hasn't been our experience. Our experience has been eagerness on the part of people to know more and to re-consent or sign up for the PBB Registry." I pointed out that the waiting list for blood draws had grown to over 1,000 people as, by word of mouth, exposed people have asked to take part in the PBB studies. This was in addition to the 6,000-plus original participants, and the newer sign-ups of 2,000 or so people.

Even though Sarah and I had differed on this point, I had the feeling that we had the beginnings of a respectful relationship. I decided to call her to talk specifically about the letter we hoped MDHHS would write in support of the cohort infrastructure grant. During the webinar she had said the proposed language provided by Emory for the letter was "too committal," and in our phone conversation, she echoed that thought. She asked that Emory draft a different letter for MDHHS to consider. She also said she was concerned about the amount of time between now and the deadline for the grant. Previously, division chiefs could write and send letters of support, and now even the bureau chief had to have letters of support vetted by the communications office, which slowed the letter writing process. (I suspected this, again, had to do with the lawsuits emanating from the Flint water crisis.)

Afterwards, I contacted Representative Jim Lower to ask if his office could encourage MDHHS to provide a letter of support on time, and that's what they did, and the letter arrived for inclusion in the grant submission. Later in the year, when the state health department had not yet renewed the contract with MPHI, and we worried that Emory's work would have to cease if there was a lapse of time between contracts, Lower's office again stepped up and made phone calls to MDHHS to encourage them to finalize the contract before the expiration date, and they did.

As for the PBB studies themselves, researcher Melanie Jacobson completed one on thyroid disease. Of the participants of recent blood draws who were *not* on thyroid medication, 93% had PBB in their systems more than 30 years after the PBB Disaster. Thyroid disease was common for members of the PBB registry, with 25% of the exposed women afflicted, as opposed to about 12% nationwide. In our own experience, several of our male CAG members had suffered thyroid cancer, including Chair Jim Hall, and, most recently, Treasurer Gary Smith. Despite the fact that thyroid disease was bad news, it was gratifying to have science prove an observation of our local community of the prevalence of a disease due to the chemical contaminants we had been exposed to in the recent past. And the impetus for this study came from local knowledge within the community shared with the researchers.

Recruitment was underway for two other studies mentioned earlier – the clinical trial and the three-generation sudy. Again, both studies arose from the researchers listening to the questions raised by the community. How can we get rid of the PBB in our bodies? And does my dad's exposure affect me and my children?

Dr. Michele Marcus and I spoke on this very topic at a gathering of the International Society of Exposure Science in North

Carolina that fall. Joining with two other communities and their researchers, we emphasized the importance of scientists listening to the people, learning their concerns, and benefiting from the local knowledge they offered to researchers.

Our community was still awaiting DDT results from our drawn blood. We had been told about a lab disaster at least a year before that necessitated starting over the analysis, and other reasons for the ongoing delay had been passed along to us. Finally, the PBB Leadership Team was shown the results, and they struck us as unbelievable. Supposedly, people in the St. Louis area had far *less* DDE in their systems than the national average. Not possible. We asked that a different lab analyze the samples, and when the results came back from a second lab, the results showed higher levels than the national average, which made sense to us. That wasn't the end of it, though, and the whole issue continued into the next year.

In terms of clean drinking water, a vital component of good health, St. Louis had achieved that goal at the end of 2015 when the combined Alma/St. Louis system, called the Gratiot Area Water Authority, began to distribute water to both communities. To assure a supply equal to the capacity of the former St. Louis wells that had been shut down due to contamination in the groundwater from the chemical plant, two new wells were scheduled to go on line late in 2017. As mentioned, the need for new drinking water sprang from the groundwater contamination beneath the chemical plant site. From the time EPA first sampled in 2005 until 2015, the DDT by-product pCBSA had appeared in *all* of the St. Louis drinking water wells, as well as in monitoring wells placed around the plant site and in other locations in town. How long the chemical had been polluting the drinking water was unknown, but since it moved swiftly through water, it likely had been entering the water supply continuously since DDT was first manufactured in St. Louis.

EPA Groundwater sampling continued even after the new drinking water began to flow from Alma and Arcada Township.

Shallow monitoring wells located near the residential properties that had lately been excavated for DDT-contaminated soil showed many contaminants in the groundwater: 1,1,1-trichloroethane, various SVOCs, DDT and associated isomers, HBB, PBB and the pCBSA. We worried these contaminants might be migrating further away, polluting even more groundwater. EPA's analysis, however, determined that the contaminants were in virtually the same area as when the remedial investigation had concluded its study in 2006. Once the planned pump and treat system was installed and operating at the plant site, it was predicted that the levels of chemical contamination would gradually fall over 100 years or more of pumping, and that no more contaminants would migrate because the pumping action would "contain" the polluted water beneath the site. Our long-term worry as a CAG was how to let future generations know how vital it was to keep the pumps in action. Institutional memory is very short, and we hated to contemplate how the poisons could move in the future if the pumps were allowed to shut down.

As for the water levels that had risen significantly when the city's old wells were no longer pumping, they had reached stasis.

A second year of funding also came for Dr. Matt Zwiernik to continue studying the floodplains downstream. He presented his findings from the first year at a CAG membership meeting, and a number of indications of heavy DDT contamination in the floodplains worried us. In the first few, there were no mosquitoes to plague the researchers, and very little other insect life at all. There were no small, worm eating mammals found, such as shrews, which again indicated DDT-laden worms. There were some birds, including a few nesting robins, but their courtship and nesting behavior was not typical, and indicated possible chronic DDT poisoning.

EPA would use this data, and the second year's data, in writing the necessary CERCLA documents for cleanup of the floodplains.

In addition, while researching TAG guidelines on line, I learned that each Superfund site is eligible to apply for a TAG grant. I suggested to Gary Smith that we apply for one for the Burn Pit site, since it had been separated out from the main Velsicol Site. He did the paperwork, and after many months, we were approved for a second Technical Assistance Grant. Later we would question whether it was worth having any TAG grants due to the expanding paperwork required for us volunteers to complete, but for now it was a funding accomplishment. In fact, all of our funding efforts to that point were either accomplished or on their way to accomplishment, and the community was benefiting.

Chapter 7
(2017 – Part 2)
Exploding Fireworks

My first thought when I heard the plan was how much our deceased friend Joe Scholtz would have enjoyed it! After helping found our CAG, Joe later served as mayor of St. Louis, and he had an ironic sense of humor. The plan to use the former chemical plant site as a launching pad for our Fourth of July Fireworks would have pleased him. Finally, the 52-acres had become useful to the community, at least for one evening! Undoubtedly, he also would have joked about the volatile chemicals buried out there, many of them ignitable, and how the fireworks event could become an even bigger display.

July Fourth night I sat on the Mill Street bridge with friends and watched the fireworks go off without a hitch, and thought about how the explosions typified the heated times we were experiencing as a CAG in dealing with EPA.

In addition to the constant and inevitable tension between agency and community due to their desire to spend as little money as possible and our desire to get the best cleanup possible, no matter what the cost, we had the frustration of being left out of the decision-making process. This wasn't the intention of those who had written the guidelines for CAGS and TAGs, nor of the EPA Administrator whose plan stressed the inclusion of the community in making site decisions. Even worse, ever since the question posed to us by the EPA staff – why don't you trust us? – there had been overt and covert attempts on their part to make us appear as the bad guys to the wider community, with the goal of undermining the importance of our CAG.

Working on bettering our relationship with EPA had become a major time expenditure for our Executive Committee. I thought it was a waste of our time for the most part. A quick example: trying to prove that, yes, we were stakeholders in the eyes of CERCLA law and EPA guidelines, despite the fact that the EPA Community Involvement Coordinator said we were not; or having to prove that we did reach out to the wider community beyond our monthly CAG meetings, when our activities were laid out every quarter in the reports we sent to EPA and often published in the local newspapers, which the CIC only had to read to see how we were fulfilling our obligation to the wider community. I felt we were being harassed, and it was reminiscent of the days of Stuart Hill, only uglier and louder.

Even though I thought it was a waste of time to try to prove our worth, I proposed things we could do to help the cause. For instance, when it was claimed that EPA Project Manager Tom Alcamo didn't have enough time to attend both the Technical Committee meeting and the evening membership meeting of the CAG, I suggested the meetings be combined to help him out. We voted to try it for six months. When the six months was up, and the combined meetings had not made a difference in his lack of attendance, we went back to the way we had done it for umpteen years before that with a 3:00 Technical Committee meeting and a 7:00 Membership meeting on the same day.

After Jim Heinzman stepped down as Technical Advisor, we began a conversation with Scott Cornelius about hiring him. Scott had served as the MDEQ project manager of our site from 2000 to 2012, and now was an environmental consultant to the city through his private company. As we spoke over several months, Scott felt convinced that he could work for both the CAG and the city, and he thought the expense for some of his efforts could be shared by both.

We went through the process of advertising statewide, selecting from among four candidates, and then working on contract language with Scott. The contract had to be approved by EPA, and we knew from experience the process could be slow. Even though the TAG guidelines say that EPA does not choose the advisor, we worried that our EPA people would object if we chose Scott, because of his insistence that they follow the Record of Decision for our sites instead of deviating by doing less work for less money spent. We decided to send the contract for approval without revealing the name of the person we wished to hire.

Meanwhile, we looked over Scott's expense-sharing idea, and decided to meet with the city manager and mayor to discuss it. I couldn't see how the city would want to share in the costs of Scott traveling to our CAG/TAG meetings, and I was right about that. Also, the city had much less work for Scott to do now that the residential properties had been dealt with. And, because of the burdens placed on small communities by both State and Federal governments, the city didn't expect to use Scott's services very often. We decided it was best if we didn't try to share expenses, unless something specific arose down the road.

We also discussed the potential for a conflict of interest, and concluded that one would not exist, because as any private contractor is free to do, Scott could have more than one client.

While we waited for Region 5 EPA's approval of the contract, the Executive Committee identified issues that we wanted Scott to address with EPA should he be hired as Technical Advisor. In addition to technical concerns, such as confirmation sampling in the residential area, learning the extraction depth of the proposed pump and treat system, EPA's risk assessment process, removing the hill of debris buried at the plant site, the rise of DDT in fish, and sampling of the former railroad property, board members brought up the perceived relationship problems with EPA. Even though I agreed with the frustration at having these difficulties, I voiced my opinion that it wasn't something *we* could fix. Most of the others disagreed with me, and Scott said solving the relationship problem was key to ending the information sharing problem, with data that came too little and too late to aid us in taking part in the decision-making process. He believed that if we appealed to Tom and Diane's boss, the Region 5 director, the relationship problem could be concluded in our favor.

Region 5 approved the contract for Scott, but as soon as they learned the name of our new Technical Advisor, we had trouble. Once again, neither EPA nor MDEQ were in attendance at our CAG membership meeting, so Jim Hall wrote a letter to Tom and Matt Baltusis afterwards saying, "It was a real shame that neither of you were at the PRSCTF community meeting for this big announcement, so I thought I would make the extra effort to let you know," and went on to announce that we had hired Scott who had "an exceptional understanding of the site." A legal response arrived, informing us of having violated the conflict-of-interest federal regulation that bars hiring as a technical advisor "a person or entity doing work for the Federal or State government or any other entity at the same NPL site for which your group is seeking a technical advisor."

In our view, someone hired by a municipality, namely St. Louis, was not doing work for the State or Federal government. However, the letter went on to say that EPA Region 5 interpreted the regulation to mean that a technical advisor would be ineligible if he or she were also providing services to a federal, state or local government agency…" They had added the word "local" into their interpretation. Again, it felt like harassment. Even though we were prepared to challenge the decision, Scott, however, made it easy for us by resigning his position with the city.

The first thing Scott proposed to do was write comments on the Community Involvement Plan addendum. We had written comments a year before, but Diane Russell had never responded. Also, she had presented half a program to the CAG membership about the addendum in 2016, but had never followed through with the second half. Scott felt certain that commenting on the plan would provide an opportunity for the CAG to lay out its arguments for improved relationships with EPA personnel, thereby achieving a seat at the table for the decision-making process. I expressed an opposite opinion. I wrote, "In my experience, community involvement plans are put on a shelf and not used, and that's the best thing that could happen to them. They don't change or improve upon the established goals of EPA Administrators to involve the community members in discussions and decision-making." Plus, it didn't seem like the best expenditure of our grant money, at $175 an hour, to have Scott essentially rewrite the addendum for Diane. Once again my view of leaving well enough alone didn't carry the day, and Scott took on the project with the approval of our treasurer.

It wasn't only lack of follow-through on the CIP addendum where Diane fell short. I had saved several emails from people in the wider community telling me they had sent questions to her about things, and had never received a reply. In one communication, a former St. Louis resident who now lived out of state said she had emailed Diane twice about a non-working link to the Velsicol website that Diane had published in the EPA newsletter, and had gotten no response. Other emails came to me from CAG members wondering if Diane's disparaging comments about us out in the community were an attempt to get our CAG to give up and go away so she could run her public meetings and availability sessions for EPA without the inconvenient presence of people who knew the hard-won facts.

Another example of lack of follow through, or maybe harassment, was the issue of conference calls. A suggestion by EPA to do more conference calls extended back to the days when Jim Heinzman had been our Technical Advisor. EPA wanted to have exclusive conference calls with Jim as a substitute for the Technical Committee meetings. Now, Diane again began to push the issue of conference calls for only the "technical people." We felt that conference calls could be a good addition to the meetings, as long as two or more members of the Executive were on the call. We told Diane that the calls would need to take place after 5 p.m. Eastern time since our chair, Jim Hall, worked until 5.

The first invitation to a conference call was sent from Diane only to Scott for 2:00-3:00 on a weekday, so Scott declined it. The next one came, and then was cancelled by EPA. Scott inquired as to the reason, and it turned out Diane had a family matter come up. Scott said he thought the call should have continued without Diane because there was such a backlog of issues to discuss, including the groundwater report and the Potential Source Areas 1 & 2 excavation plans. Tom said EPA would prefer to have Diane as part of the discussion, adding, "As the Community Involvement Coordinator, she has a major role in play in discussions with the CAG."

Scott replied to the EPA staff in a long email that called into question their motives, saying "As a direct result of EPA's behavior, the suspicions of the community [our CAG] seem confirmed, and they are very concerned that the EPA appears to be trying to oversee, control and manipulate them and their activities." Tom called me, blowing his top about having his "motives and integrity" questioned, taking the exchange personally, which was how he usually reacted.

The next invitation for a conference call arrived for a Tuesday at 4:00. I told Diane again that the best day of the week for our members was Wednesday, and the best time was 5:00 Eastern. I added, "…let's try to coordinate times that work for the volunteers, and let the paid [EPA] employees fit their work around those conference call dates and time…" Another month went by, another invitation, and another cancellation by Diane "due to lack of availability." I complained in an email to the other Executive Committee members that nothing technical was getting talked about! EPA was avoiding our technical committee meetings, and also cancelling conference calls. Next, Diane proposed, yet again, Tuesdays from 4:00 to 5:00. This time Gary wrote a patient reply explaining why that time would not work for the CAG Chair. Diane replied that 5 p.m. would not work for the project team, and the calls needed to be during the workday. Gary asked her to define workday. Tom said he worked 7 am to 3:30 pm Central Time, 5 days a week. Diane tried again, sending out various invitations, one for October

30th and one for Nov. 1. There may have also been one for the 31st. I said I could attend the Nov. 1 call, but not the 30. Gary said later he had never rec'd the invitation for the 30th! Tom said he could not attend the Nov. 1st call because he would be at another site and too busy. Diane said she thought she should cancel the call since only one of the executive board accepted the meeting request. Scott wrote back to keep the October 30th call to get things started. Diane replied that in the meantime, Tom had said he was no longer available for the call on that day. Things got even more confusing, with Tom saying he had cancelled one of the calls because I couldn't be on it, and he thought that was a rule. Good grief. Jim Hall said he no longer knew what the rules were and figured Diane and Tom were making them up as we went along. Scott tried again, asking for a call to be set for Nov. 6th, and listed items he would like to discuss, and miracle of miracles, we completed a conference call. We talked about technical issues until Diane brought up the Community Involvement Plan addendum and her desire for us to use a meeting facilitator. I mention this, because later we were accused of being the ones to bring up non-technical topics in technical meetings.

Another part of Scott's strategy was to invite the directors of MDEQ and EPA Region 5 Superfund to visit us in St. Louis. He thought if we could talk to the bosses and get them on board, it would help us achieve "meaningful community involvement" and "participation in the decision-making process" (phrases from EPA guideline documents).

We never received a response from MDEQ Director Heidi Grether. Margaret Guerriero, however, agreed to come. She was serving as Acting Director of EPA's Region 5 Superfund section. We asked to have our Executive Committee meet with her prior to the evening meeting, and in a phone conversation, and a follow-up email, Tom said he would drop her off at 4:30 at city hall for our meeting, and then we could all go to supper prior to the evening meeting. Our group arrived before 4:00 to brush up on what we wanted to say. 4:30 came and went, and the clock hands kept moving with no sign of the Acting Director. At 5:00, Jim Hall said he was going to go look for her. He did, and found her in the Blue Shamrock restaurant with other EPA staff. Another harassing slight? Or just a mix-up?

Our very abbreviated meeting with Margaret from EPA and Susan Leeming of MDEQ went poorly. No, it was a disaster. Scott took the lead and emphasized again and again how Tom and Diane were failing us, and even said management should remove them from their jobs if they didn't measure up. Margaret bristled at that, and said they were both excellent employees, the top of their professions, the best Region 5 had. I wished I could have led the discussion, or Jim, or Ed, because we would have talked more about having a seat at the table rather than getting EPA staff removed from their positions.

Later, Scott acknowledged that his suggestion about Tom and Diane being removed was not well received by the agency directors, but overall, he felt the meeting went well and then said we should push our strategy further by inviting Margaret Guerriero back to St. Louis right away. In an earlier letter, we had offered to travel to Chicago to meet with her, and that's what several of us thought should be suggested again. Scott differed with us, saying it would give her "home court advantage" and there would be distractions she would have to address while at work. He still believed we could convince Margaret that Tom and Diane were not measuring up. Doubtful. What I had seen on her face and heard in her voice was a full stop on making any changes regarding her employees.

Nevertheless, a follow-up letter was sent to her, and she wrote back that another visit could take place at a later date. She also argued against several points contained in our follow-up letter, pointing out all the ways her employees were meeting or exceeding expectations for involvement with our CAG. When Scott wanted to respond to this letter with more arguments and examples from our view of things, Ed said he felt a response was unnecessary, since we had already listed ways in which we disagreed with her view. He felt it would "achieve nothing other than hardening positions." I agreed with that view. The majority, however, determined that one more, long letter requesting assistance to establish meaningful community involvement was a good idea. Following close on its heels was yet another letter to Margaret Guerriero, a cover letter for the 20 pages of comments on the Community Involvement Plan addendum.

The response we received began by saying it was to address the various letters sent between June and November regarding community involvement. Then it listed everything our CAG was doing wrong in regards to using TAG grant money, in writing the quarterly reports, and in not hiring a meeting facilitator as suggested in the CIP addendum. In fact, consequences for inaction on the issue of the facilitator were put forth. The letter said, if our CAG "chooses not to pursue those services, I will instruct my staff to reduce their participation in monthly meetings and focus on more productive areas of community involvement." That phrase first sickened me, and then angered me. I was angry that Scott's strategy, which had a good intention, had misfired so badly due to two poor tactics, one of which was to ask for Tom and Diane to be removed, and the other which I will describe later. And I was angry that a government employee felt she was in her rights to threaten a volunteer group of citizens who sought to have a say in how their town was cleaned up from pollution that was no fault of their own, and for which EPA had willingly shouldered the responsibility when they allowed Velsicol to leave town without cleaning up their mess.

As for what we were doing wrong, apparently headings for the quarterly report had been changed in 2009, and no one had let us know. I guess it was assumed that we would be checking for changes on the EPA website for updates such as that, which we had not done. And the misuse of TAG funds had to do with allowing Scott, our Technical Advisor, to take the lead in addressing the relationship issues between EPA and the CAG. I guess that's a third bad tactic, because I still haven't spoken about the second.

As mentioned, the facilitator was first suggested in the draft CIP addendum. Our Executive Committee was unwilling to make a decision about using a meeting facilitator until we had a few questions answered, including how to cease having a facilitator if it wasn't a good fit for us. Diane had told us six months ago that she would find out that information for us and even after subsequent reminders still had not provided us with the answer. This was par for the course.

The threatening letter made an assumption that we had *refused* a facilitator, and other letters and conversations assumed the same. Untrue. We were willing to consider the idea, and needed further information, which was not provided. As we often had to do, we searched the web to find our own answers. I went to the website for EPA's Conflict Prevention and Resolution Center and read everything. Nothing answered our main question of how to end the relationship with a facilitator.

I also went to EPA's Community Involvement University website and found many wonderful classes and webinars for EPA employees. In the reply I wrote to Guerriero's threatening letter, I suggested that the Region 5 EPA staff who worked in our community could gain some skills from the education provided to them through the "university," which included the teaching of sensitivity skills toward the cultures and past experiences of a community. I wrote: "Your staff could benefit from them. As conscientious people, we have tried to learn from the previous insufficient remediation that the EPA brought to our community in the 1980s, and to guard against that happening again by expressing our concerns in context with our history. Instead, your staff asked us why we don't trust the EPA, and then disparaged our reasons."

And the last sentence pointed out that it was not the CAG who had chosen to talk about relationship issues at our Technical Committee meetings, which they now told us was forbidden, but instead it was EPA staff that had first begun the discussion when Diane had joined the EPA team several years before.

My only experiences with hired meeting facilitators were of two extremes. The first was that of a dictator, and he had been provided by EPA to the group overseeing Dow's cleanup in Midland. He allowed almost no input from the members of the board or from the public. He was there to make sure the agencies could deliver information without being troubled by questions from those listening.

My second experience was with the hired facilitator for the governor's working group on environmental justice. He was the nicest person, and obviously in love with the process of how people could interact. As soon as good brainstorming started up, he would interject to enthusiastically name the process we were now engaged in, describing it in detail. The result was a halt to the discussion. The interaction of people's minds and their desire to contribute stopped cold as he explained the process.

Over the almost 20 years of our CAG's existence, the three people who had led our meetings each had his or her own style, but interaction among the membership and with the agency representatives took place freely and usually constructively. In all that time, I had seen only one serious outburst of a CAG member toward an EPA staff member. Soon, though, I would have to say I'd seen two outbursts, and it was the result of the second tactic of our Technical Advisor mentioned above.

Even though Scott had laid out a strategy that aimed to improve relations and information sharing from EPA, three of his tactics foiled the plan. Asking that Tom and Diane be fired if they did not measure up was the first; the second I will describe next; and the third tactic was taking the lead on discussing the relationship issues with EPA at the Technical Committee meetings, although we were all to blame for that, since we didn't know it was out of bounds. We had continued the discussion at our Technical Committee meetings because that is where Diane Russell, Community Involvement Coordinator, had initiated the discussions when Jim Heinzman was our Technical Advisor.

The second tactic that harmed more than helped was all Scott's doing, and centered on the air monitoring plan that EPA's contractors had set forth as part of their thermal treatment of about one acre at the plant site. The *in situ* thermal treatment process would destroy volatile and semi-volatile chemicals in groundwater and soil. The system was designed to self-contain all dangerous vapors, and an air monitoring system would keep track of that effort.

In Scott's view the system was not protective enough for the neighborhood, as the summa canister monitors would only give information days later if there had been a leak of toxic vapor. In the comments he made on the plan, he declared that the whole project should be shut down until the proper air monitors were in place. In his view, that meant photoionization detectors (PIDs) placed around the perimeter of the site to provide real time monitoring. The letter in response to his comments assured us that PIDs would be used by the workers near the drilling and heating area. Scott wrote another letter that said the CAG "demands that the EPA protect the health of our community by adding a real-time monitoring component to the Air Monitoring Plan. If it is reasonable that the on-site workers need real-time monitoring, then the community needs real-time monitoring also." He again stated that the whole project should be shut down until the PIDs were operational at the perimeter.

As written, his concerns made sense to me, yet when I toured the site with EPA and their contractors, the explanation they gave sounded protective of the community and workers both. I wrote my new opinion in an email to Scott, and he replied that EPA was relying on the same strategy used by the engineers at Three Mile Island and Chernobyl, trusting that the system would alert them to releases, and it was not protective.

Because of Scott's vehemence and my awareness that Tom Alcamo was reaching the point of verbal explosion, I dreaded the upcoming Technical Committee meeting. I decided to enlist two other people to have extra ears in the room in case there were fireworks. I asked Dan Morden, director of Gratiot County

Emergency Management, who understood the protection of people from a catastrophic perspective, and Liz Braddock, Director of Environmental Health at the Mid-Michigan District Health Department, who understood the protection of people from a public health perspective. Ashton Bortz, aide to our federal Congressman John Moolenaar, was also in attendance.

Apparently Tom had the same idea of having extra ears in the room, because he arrived at the meeting with upper management reinforcements from his agency, plus several upper management people from the main contractor CH2m/Jacobs and from Terra-Therm that was doing the *in situ* thermal treatment (ISTT). When Tom came in followed by all the others, his face showed that he was looking for a fight.

Scott began the meeting by explaining how it had been difficult to get information from EPA, and how Diane would tell us she would get the information for us and didn't follow through. EPA Superfund Branch Chief Tom Short said sarcastically, "Oh, that all sounds very technical for a technical meeting." As their boss spoke, I saw Diane and Tom Alcamo grinning and nodding. (I guess this was part of their strategy, to show upper management that we were violating TAG rules.)

Scott explained in an even tempered manner that we had plenty of items of a technical nature to discuss, but the relationship problems often got in the way and prevented us from gaining the information we needed.

As an example to show how EPA needed to listen to what the CAG had to say, Scott said if the CAG hadn't spoken up, and if MDEQ hadn't spent the money for sampling, EPA would have completed the sediment work in the river in 2006 and left town without addressing the leaking plant site at all. Tom loudly claimed that was untrue, saying it over and over. Then the current MDEQ project manager, Matt Baltusis, joined in, also saying it was untrue. I loudly told them to stop it, and that we were not going to gang up on people. That's when Scott shouted at Matt, saying "Shut up! You weren't there, Matt, and you know nothing about how it was."

Dan Morden shoved his chair back from the table where he was sitting next to Scott, as if he was afraid a fistfight might break out. Theo von Wallmenich, project manager for CH2m/Jacobs, got up and grabbed his things and headed to the door. I said, "Theo, where are you going?" He said, "I'm not going to stay at a meeting where someone tells someone to shut up." I said I agreed with him, and I added I hoped I wasn't seeing a display of male ego. Scott apologized to Matt, and Theo sat back down. Later, however, Matt got up and left, never to return to the meeting. And that was the second outburst in nearly 20 years of CAG/agency interaction that I count as unacceptable. (The first occurred circa 2012 when Gary Smith threw a heavy copy of the ROD document in front of Tom Alcamo, daring him to find in it what he was claiming was there.) And it was Scott who had gone too far, in my opinion.

As Scott switched gears and began going through his points about air monitoring, Tom and Diane, who were sitting next to each other, rolled their eyes, smiled, giggled, and even whispered to each other. I was near them at the table, and spoke to them quietly, as others were discussing something, and asked them to please keep their focus on what was being said. Diane spoke out loudly, saying "I can talk to my colleague any time I want to." I said again to please listen to what others were saying and to not talk among themselves. She gave me a dirty look and started to say something more. I said, "Just behave!" and I know she will hate me forever for saying that, because others were listening to us by then.

Scott explained that when the CAG sends comments to EPA, we would like to discuss them, and not simply receive a letter in response that says thank you, but we are not going to make any changes. Theo spoke quietly to Scott, saying something reassuring, which Scott refuted. Tom Short said loudly, "Don't you trust Theo?" as if it was totally incomprehensible behavior on Scott's part. Tom Alcamo chimed in and said Scott was being

115

"disingenuous." Diane chimed in and quoted something, adding that the law has to be followed, and if citizens suggest something without merit, no action has to be taken. She said our comments had no merit. She said "We have an obligation to the *community* to move forward with the cleanup." She said they were not going to get "wrapped around the axle" and our comments had no merit. Scott thanked her for her opinion and moved the discussion back to the air monitoring comments.

I began to record in my notes places where Tom Alcamo laughed at what Scott was saying. At one point Scott said, "We'd like to know answers to our concerns prior to the start of a process. Here they are, about to throw the switch, and we are getting nervous." Tom laughed. When the discussion was about relying on the system's controls, Scott used the example of Chernobyl, and Tom laughed again. Diane said Chernobyl happened because they were doing an experiment and it blew up. When Scott spoke about the two places where the SUMMA canisters were placed on the far side of the river, creating a dead zone, or unmonitored area, in that part of the river, Tom laughed.

Diane interjected that she wanted a better understanding of where the comments were coming from. She went on about how people have not articulated these comments to EPA or to city officials. Scott and I began to calmly explain how the people sometimes need time to think about things before questions arise, and how they aren't sure what to ask, because they aren't familiar with the mechanisms of the ISTT system. Diane than demandingly said she wanted names of people, names of organizations of where these comments were coming from, which to my ears sounded like another indication that she didn't believe the people in the CAG truly represented the interests of the community. Scott explained how each CAG member interacts with part of the wider community, each bringing those people's concerns to EPA. I echoed him saying we were conduits. She again forcefully demanded names! I offered an example. I said Lisa Krueger, who was not a CAG member at the time, had called me at home with her concerns about toxins in the air once the ISTT system started up. I encouraged her to attend the EPA Public Meeting that Diane had organized to express her concerns, which she did. I also encouraged her to go on the tour of the ISTT equipment, and she did. Diane dismissed my example and referred to Lisa as "that woman." To me, that suggested that Diane didn't really care about names or the people they belonged to, but only to prove to her superiors that the CAG was not representative of the community.

About then, the project manager for Terra-Therm, Devon Phelan, gave a long explanation of everything we already knew about the system, but I could see by her demeanor that she sincerely wanted to address our questions and concerns. She actually said at one point that our concerns were valid, which was something I have never heard EPA staff say to us in almost 20 years. Several times during the discussion about air monitoring, she gave us new information that was not contained in the Air Monitoring Plan given to us by EPA, and which no EPA or CH2m person had ever told us. Maybe they were learning new information at that moment, as well. She also said time and again that she wanted to make sure she understood our questions and concerns, and that we understood her response. She was a Godsend to that meeting.

Theo was also willing to really hear what was underlying our concerns, and between him and Devon, we were able to make plain that, although the air monitoring plan addressed chronic exposure levels, we were also concerned about something bigger, a catastrophic event. Devon gave great detail about the interlocks and alarms on the system that would alert the three operators who would be living in Alma, should there be an "upset." She and Theo were able to help us see that the real-time monitoring done by the workers with their PIDs, and the system's monitoring and alarms would be sufficient, if not better, than our request to have PIDs at the perimeter of the Velsicol site.

Then Dan Morden asked if we could go back through the CAG's seven abbreviated comments point by point, which we did, and it was during that time we were given new information by Devon that helped to clarify the difference between chronic exposures and catastrophic exposures, and the monitors and alarms being used to catch something catastrophic before it happened.

This meeting, that was the occasion of an outburst and a bad tactic on the part of our Technical Advisor, was later deemed by him as a step forward in our strategy to convince EPA to include us in the decision-making process. Maybe in time I will see it that way. In my present view, the outburst in front of EPA upper management was a fine way to convince them of what Tom and Diane had been saying about us as being difficult people to work with, and the tactic of asking for the whole ISTT system to be shut down was over the top and detrimental to our attempts to get along with EPA staff.

Everything ugly and loud from both agency people and CAG people sickened me, and, in my view, did not benefit the community or the cleanup at all.

Then Scott asked me to share my minutes with him before emailing them to the attendees. That wasn't usual practice, but I didn't see what it could hurt. After reading the minutes, he wrote to say he wanted to check with Tom to see if Scott's and Tom's notes agreed, not wanting anything inaccurate placed in the minutes that might upset "the good forward move in resolving community concerns…" Tom (as usual) did not take notes, and I told Scott that Tom's after-the-fact remembrances would not be included as part of the minutes. I was certainly willing to make factual changes if I had misunderstood something of a technical nature. Scott sent me an altered copy of my draft, changing nothing technical or factual, but adding some qualifiers to what he had said in the meeting, such as "EPA would have done the sediment cleanup and *possibly* walked away." He removed the part where Tom had said it was untrue, saying only that Matt had said it was untrue. I had left out the "Shut up" outburst out of the minutes, but when I emailed Scott to encourage him to apologize to Matt again, Scott claimed he had said" shut up" because Tom and Matt were ganging up on me, but that wasn't the case. No one was yelling at me.

Gary and Jim both told Scott the minutes I took at the meeting were the ones that should be received into the record, and if there were other technical details that needed to be added to them after Scott spoke with Tom, an addendum could be written.

Meanwhile I called Matt and apologized on behalf of the CAG for Scott's outburst. I also spoke with Theo and called Tom to express my dismay. Scott did follow through to apologize again to Matt. The fireworks had ended, but the smell of gunpowder was still in the air.

Chapter 8
(2018 – Part 1)
Boiling Point

Our relationship with EPA reached the boiling point early in 2018. It was set off by the letter from Region 5's Acting Director, Margaret Guerriero, as mentioned in the last chapter. The letter arrived in Jim Hall's email box an hour before our December, 2017 Christmas Potluck and meeting. Diane Russell, the Community Involvement Coordinator, had forwarded it to him at that time.

In addition to finding fault with our CAG's recording process, it had said we had refused to get a facilitator. No, we hadn't, but rather we had asked who, what, how and when questions that were never responded to.

After receiving the threatening letter from EPA, we had written two responses, one factual and the other pointing out EPA staff member failures to follow EPA rules and guidelines. In response to that, I received a telephone call from Tom Alcamo, the EPA project manager for the Velsicol sites. He said he was unhappy with our letter, and that if we continued on this path, EPA was willing to escalate the conflict, and no one would like that. I said that EPA had already escalated things by threatening to withdraw from our meetings if we didn't get a facilitator. As was his habit, he didn't respond to what I said, but went on to point out everything we were doing wrong, including not trusting EPA. In addition, he enumerated further complaints: that we had written 16 letters in the last year; the fact that Scott thought he could tell EPA to stop work when he didn't like the air monitoring plant; that Scott had compared the system to Chernobyl; that Scott had asked for Tom and Diane to be replaced; and that Gary asked questions to try to "catch out" EPA and MDEQ staff members.

I asked him what he meant by "escalate." Was EPA going to pull up stakes and leave town without cleaning up Velsicol's mess? He said no, but that EPA would hold its own meetings, such as Availability Sessions, and Public Meetings. I said the EPA guidelines state EPA has to provide information to the community. Would that information be put in the library? He replied, "What good would that do you, if we aren't there to explain it all?"

I finally said, "Tom, I want you to tell me the truth. Is Diane trying to get our CAG members to quit so she can start another one?" This was not an unfounded question. Her attempts to recruit other people, her telling us we didn't really represent the community, and her obsession with having an EPA-chosen facilitator running our CAG meetings were behind my straight-forward question to Tom. Plus there were all the additional time-consuming requirements the TAG-grant people were now saying we must follow.

Tom said, "No, God's honest truth. She just wants to help you improve. She wants you to do things better." I believed he believed that, but it didn't change my opinion of her motives.

He ended the call by saying he thought it was up to the two of us to improve the relationship – that if things were going to cool down, it had to start with Tom and Jane. I agreed.

Honestly, after that phone call, the only thing I did differently was to pay less attention to the warmongers in our CAG. As for Tom, he tamped down his tendency to be defensive, and also began to give us more information and in a timely manner. But all of this happened over the next several years, and not overnight.

As for EPA holding its own Availability Sessions, that had already begun. Diane had organized one for January and had not notified our CAG that it was going to take place. We learned about it from an article in the newspaper. Gary saw this lack of notification as part of EPA's campaign to exclude and demonize our

CAG, pressuring us to bend, break and comply. Ed counseled that we should celebrate that progress had been made in getting the Velsicol site cleanup underway.

Several of our members attended the poster event at St. Louis City Hall at different times during the availability hours, and other than EPA staff and contractors, MDEQ staff and contractors, and city officials, the main attendees were CAG members. Truthfully, most of the rest of the community relied on us to keep their interests in the forefront in dealing with EPA and cleanups, as we had been doing for 19 years.

While all this was going on, Jim Hall called me with the suggestion that we expand the size of our Executive Committee. Besides the officers, we had three board members, which was the minimum number required by Michigan law for a 501(c)3 non-profit organization. At that time the officers were Jim Hall as Chairperson (employed by Consumers Energy as in Environmental Safety facilitator), Ed Lorenz as Vice-Chairperson (soon to retire as professor of History and Political Science at Alma College), Gary Smith as Treasurer, (retired from working at Velsicol, Total Refinery and Dow Chemical), Jane Keon (later, Jelenek) as Secretary (retired from teaching and newspaper writing). The board members were Phil Ramsey, a former oil worker, who was now in his eighties, and wanted to remain a member but didn't want to attend the Executive Committee meetings; Margaret Hoyt, a mother and grandmother who had worked at the chemical factory packaging PBB early in her life; and Marcus Cheatham. Marcus stepped down because he felt his job as Health Officer for the Mid-Michigan District Health Department conflicted with our increasingly difficult problems with the State of Michigan Department of Health and Human Services over the acquisition of the PBB records for the researchers at Emory University. We voted in Wayne Brooks, a retired pharmacist, to fill the empty slot. Then, at Jim's suggestion, we expanded to five board members, and voted in Caroline Ross, a retired UAW employee who was active on many county boards, and Norm Keon, an epidemiologist for both the Mid-Michigan District Health Department and the Central Michigan District Health Department.

For any new person attending meetings of our CAG, it was difficult to get up to speed. Not only did we have several separate sites, but three operating units within the main Velsicol Former Plant Site. Plus there was ample science and technology to understand, the acronyms, and the context of our long history with chemical contamination, both our own nineteen-years-worth as a CAG, and also prior decades encompassing the DDT and PBB disasters, and the failed first Superfund remediation of the plant site. The new board members not only had to learn or be reminded of much of this, but also we needed their thoughts and opinions in how to proceed in these many areas. I kept that in mind as I wrote emails on issues, and fleshed things out more to help all board members better understand the issues.

I had written a letter to Diane from the CAG, enumerating our questions about the use of a facilitator and, amazingly, she responded right away. In her letter she suggested we have a conversation with EPA's Conflict Prevention and Resolution Center. We agreed to talk with the staff of that center, and Diane said she would make the arrangements.

At our first meeting of the expanded Executive Committee in January, we discussed in depth our questions about what it could mean to have a facilitator run our meetings. Did EPA want the facilitator to run both the Technical Committee (TAG) meeting and the CAG meeting? It was unclear to us if receiving TAG grant funding was connected to saying yes or no to a facilitator. It had been implied by Diane, but was it true? Would we be allowed to interview potential candidates for the facilitator position to see if he or she was a good fit? What was the conflict that caused Diane to want us to use a facilitator from the Conflict Resolution place in Virginia? What evaluation had been done to convince EPA that the meetings were not running as they should? Who made the evaluation? If we decided to stop receiving TAG grant funding, would that mean we didn't need to have a facilitator?

By February, our many questions were still not answered. Phil was dead set against the use of a facilitator. He said, "When they start poking something down our throats, I'm against it." I felt the same way, but I was willing to have a phone call with the people at EPA's Conflict Prevention and Resolution Center. Jim worked with Diane Russell to get a date and time arranged. On the first call would be Jim and I with Ellie and Gina from the center.

Gina asked us to tell about ourselves, and I said, "You probably already know more about us than we do about you, so please tell us about yourselves, first."

The bulk of Gina's work was to supply facilitators for Community Advisory Groups. I asked for examples of other CAGs who had used a facilitator, and she named one in Philadelphia and one in Buffalo. She said the USS Lead site in Indiana had decided to not form a CAG.

Ellie was an attorney and had worked in enforcement mediation for EPA Superfund. She mentioned New Bedford Harbor, and how the challenge there was to start a facilitation process with little thought given as to how to end it. She said as facilitation satisfied people, they drifted away, and the ones that were left were less desirable to work with. She said groups of community stakeholders "may serve a useful purpose for a period of time," but then the group reduces down to those participants who are not representative of the community.

I was glad we had kept her talking as long as we did, because now our suspicions were verified that Diane saw us as not representative of the community, and had passed on her view to the conflict people.

Jim said, "Okay, you've laid out the game plan. What's next?" They didn't understand what he meant. He said, "You've showed us that you think our CAG meetings are no longer useful, so what's next? We are being forced to get a facilitator or EPA will not attend our meetings anymore."

Ellie expressed shock, and said she had misunderstood the situation, and she wasn't even going to tell us what she thought. I said, "I want to know what you thought." As we chatted, what became clear is this: Ellie thought we were EPA staff that wanted a facilitator to "help" the CAG group gradually dissipate, including those "less desirable to work with."

After their profuse apologies, Gina said she had talked with Diane Russell several times over the last months, and her perspective was that communication had broken down. I said the phrase "communication breakdown" didn't really describe the situation. It wasn't a back and forth breakdown, but a one-way breakdown. We would ask for information that we needed to make a considered decision, and it wasn't given to us, or was given to us after a decision had been made.

The one-sided communication breakdown was on EPA's side, and had increased when Diane came on board as the Community Involvement Coordinator. I said, "We believe she thinks our CAG has outlived its usefulness and that she would rather do community events on her own." I listed all the ways the CAG kept the community informed, through press releases to papers around the state, radio and TV interviews, presentations at schools, universities, service clubs and retirees' organizations. We also kept EPA informed of new possible sites of contamination, we sent our members to talk to city residents who were unsure of EPA's intentions when their yards had to be excavated, we brought our state legislators to town for events involving our sites, and two of our members had written books about the activities surrounding the Superfund sites in our town.

We had not outlived our usefulness. In fact, our CAG was operating with the very purpose laid out in EPA guidelines. We were, in fact, the focal point of the information exchange between the agency and the community.

Jim ended the conversation by saying we needed to discuss what we had learned with our Executive Committee, and that we would set up another call for a later date.

Along with us on the second call were Margaret, Caroline, Gary, and Wayne. After some explanation from Ellie and Gina of how mediation and conflict resolutions are supposed to work, Gary and the others took us back to the heart of the problem: we ask for information to guide us in the decision-making process, and it is not forthcoming. Even when Tom or Diane said they would get it to us, if it arrived at all, it was after many reminders from us, and often arrived too late. How would a facilitator solve that problem?

Gina said, "If I were facilitating, my conversation with EPA would be, 'why are you resisting sharing documents?'" She went on to say, that the CAG had the right to see the documents, but a facilitator could not force EPA to share them.

Throughout our dialogue, both women said that we were not required to have a facilitator if we didn't want one. When Wayne said we were being forced to get one, Ellie said it sounded very disturbing to her. The conversation ended with both sides indicating, but not saying outright, that a facilitator didn't seem to be the answer for our CAG.

As all this was going on, EPA continued to put into practice their threat of having their own meetings if we failed to get a facilitator. We wrote a letter about this to the new Acting Director of Superfund at Region 5, Robert Kaplan, pointing out that we had conducted two conference calls with EPA's Conflict Prevention and Resolution Center. Despite this, EPA was carrying out their threat by holding Availability Sessions.

Amid the discussions about a facilitator was the worry that if we didn't get one, TAG grant funding would be cut off from us. That led us into a cost/benefit analysis of having a Technical Assistance grant. The paperwork for the treasurer was extensive, and working with the online systems was frustrating to Gary. During the twelve years I had served as chairperson, I had written and filed the quarterly reports for the TAG grant, and had kept the job when I became secretary. EPA had tacked on a new requirement very recently, stating the CAG had to have pre-approval for work done by our hired Technical Advisor, because if it was later disapproved by EPA, they would refuse to pay. That would mean the $175 per hour expense would fall on our group of volunteers.

When we had received the letter from Region 5 Acting Director Guerriero, stating that we were misusing TAG funds, and that the quarterly reports were inaccurate, both Gary Jim, and I had spent many volunteer hours on the EPA website trying to find out what, if anything, we were doing wrong. From the sample report shown online, I learned that the document was no longer called a Performance Report, but a Progress Report. I also learned that the heading "Activities" had been changed to "Materials Produced this Quarter." Those were my inaccuracies in the reports I had been submitting through the years since 2009. They also preferred a box with columns for "Environmental Results Progress Achieved," instead of list, and I was now savvy enough with a desktop to design such a box for the report.

One of Gary's shortcomings was failing to tally the in-kind contributions of volunteer time as a match for the grant. In our early years as a CAG, when Ed was chairperson, the TAG people at Region 5 had read the reports of our activities and could see that our time contribution greatly exceeded the needed match amount. They even told Ed he didn't need to submit the quarterly performance reports any longer because everyone at Region 5 knew we were going far beyond expectations in time contributed. When I became the new chairperson on 2002, an employee in the TAG program asked for all our back performance reports that the other EPA employee had said we didn't need to write! We did our best to reconstruct them, and from then on we kept submitting the reports even if not asked to. We had always kept track of meeting attendance with time sheets, which helped fulfill the in-kind match requirement.

Now that EPA doubted that our volunteer hours met the match requirement, Gary decided each of the officers and board members should give him a monthly statement of their activities for the CAG/TAG and the hours spent. One more burden on our volunteers, but he felt it was necessary to have the proof of our overabundance of hours spent working on CAG/TAG projects. Phil objected at a CAG meeting, saying he was not going to keep track of his hours for EPA. He said, "The work I do is for the CAG and for myself, and not for EPA!"

I didn't like having to do the extra bookwork, either. It seemed like the last straw. Did we really need a TAG grant, I wondered? The grant was very restrictive and the money mostly went to a paid Technical Advisor. With all the hot water our current Technical Advisor had gotten us into, was it worth it to administer the grant just to pay him to perhaps intensify the tension between the CAG and EPA?

I also thought that by telling EPA we no longer wanted a TAG grant, it would perhaps end their bullying about using a meeting facilitator.

I brought my thoughts to the next Executive meeting, along with information about the EPA's TASC program. We had used the Technical Assistance Services for Communities program many years before, at the time of the 5-year-review of the Gratiot County Landfill Superfund site. We had asked the TASC person to review the written reports about the site, including the recent assessment. We were pleased with the results, because even though she was hired by EPA, she gave objective feedback based on her own science and engineering expertise.

With the TASC program, a CAG tells EPA what they need in the way of technical advice, and EPA does the hiring and all the paperwork. That is in contrast to the TAG grant program in which the group hires the expert and does all the advertising, contracting, in-kind hours of contribution, quarterly reports and other paperwork.

At our meeting, we came up with a few ideas for ways to use a TASC expert. I contacted the TASC person at Region 5 and said we had documents, charts and photos regarding a railroad spur that formerly had run in and out of the chemical plant through what is now a low-income housing area. Tank and freight cars would sit there for days with their contents sometimes leaking, and we thought the soil should be sampled and analyzed for DDT and other contaminants. A TASC expert could look at our documentation and write a report of the findings.

The very day I sent my email, I received a response that the request had been forwarded to Washington, D.C. That pleased me, since one of our concerns was the time it might take to line up a TASC person.

The response from Washington, however, said the site lay outside the Velsicol boundaries (meaning the fence around the actual plant site), and wondered if the recent excavation activities of EPA (in the residential neighborhood) were being done under Superfund and were related to the site in any way.

Oh, my. Of course the yards dug up for DDT and PBB contamination were related to the Superfund site, as was the railroad spur that had transported chemicals in and out of the fenced boundaries of the Superfund site. A chain link fence around a property didn't limit the spread of contaminants!

I responded with a detailed explanation, but heard nothing back. A month later I wrote to the Region 5 person to express my disappointment in the process. She replied that the turnaround time was usually faster, but since it was between fiscal years, it had slowed down. After that, I dropped the effort. It had seemed like a good idea, but if it took weeks or even months to get an expert lined up, it wouldn't serve our purposes which didn't usually allow us that much time to evaluate a problem. I should add that we had been asking EPA to sample the railroad spur property for five years. They had said MDEQ should do it, and a recent letter from MDEQ said

EPA should do it. Once again the community was caught in the middle between agency squabbles.

In one of my phone conversations with Tom Alcamo, he said he wanted to give Gary and me a training session in how to do TAG grants. Gary was the usual one to communicate with the TAG person at Region 5, so he worked with her to set a time and place for the training session. He preferred that EPA come to us rather than we go to Chicago, and I agreed.

We met near the end of March at St. Louis City Hall. The attendees were Gary and me, with Jim on the phone. Six EPA people attended, including Diane Russell. We had a square of tables to sit around, but Diane and another EPA person chose to sit directly behind Gary and me, and they took notes. The plan was for an hour and a half session, but because of all the questions Gary and I asked, and the explaining we had to do, it lasted about three hours.

They showed us a PowerPoint about the TAG program, and from some of our questions during the slide presentation, they told us later they would alter one or two slides to incorporate our suggestions. Gary had previously asked them to provide forms that we could fill out for the TAG paperwork instead of having to manufacture our own, which might not contain all the information they were seeking. They hadn't brought anything and didn't know of anything. The TAG person from Region 1 said he had come up with his own forms and he would be glad to share them with us. True to EPA's reputation, this never happened.

At the training session, we learned their main emphasis, which was that anything we paid out money for, or recorded as an in-kind contribution of time, had to be CERCLA-specific, referring to the law governing Superfund. In their interpretation, that meant any of our activities that related to Velsicol. We mentioned that we had a meeting coming up with the state health department regarding PBB, and they said no, that was not Velsicol-related. We explained that PBB was one of the chemicals produced by the local Velsicol factory, and one which EPA workers were trying to clean up at the plant site, in the river, in the neighborhood, and from the high school athletic field. The instructors didn't know this, and they responded that perhaps the PBB work we did fell into a "gray area". Gary decided later that we should not count the hours we spent on our work as a partner with the Rollins School of Public Health on the Michigan PBB Registry outreach and studies, in order to strictly comply with TAG grant assumptions, even though many of our officers spent as much or more time on the health consequences of PBB exposure than they did on Superfund cleanup. And, as Ed pointed out repeatedly, the Environmental Protection Agency's mission was "to protect human health and the environment, not only the environment."

At the end of the session, the man from Region 1 said we were one of the best TAG recipients he had ever spoken with – that we knew what we were doing and we were doing it well. The main Region 5 person agreed and others around the table nodded.

My hope was that Diane had heard the compliment, and also that she had heard from Gina and Ellie that they were concerned about how Diane was trying to force a facilitator on us. My hope was that the opinions of these seasoned EPA employees might change her opinion of us so that she would cease her attempts to impede our efforts to clean up our toxic town.

As mentioned earlier, in my own mind I had computed a cost/benefit analysis of having a Technical Advisor paid out of TAG funds with the burdensome TAG grant process we had to perform. My conclusion was that the grant wasn't worth it. I was willing to get out of the TAG grant altogether. Gary hated to turn back money that had been awarded to us. The rest of the group was not in agreement about making a change, so we continued on as we were.

Our contract with Scott Cornelius as our paid Technical Advisor was due to expire in April. Prior to that, Scott met with the Executive Committee in a strategy session, during which Jim Hall pointed out that EPA was "pissed off," and that was why they were requiring us to do all the extra TAG work. Jim added, "I'm pissed off, too."

Scott said we were in a situation much like guerilla warfare. "We need to be as nice as can be, but continue to copy people, to get things on paper, to embarrass EPA. EPA wants everything to go smoothly. Their worst nightmare is having a community upset with them."

I said I believed that Scott's strategy from last year was basically a good one, but that two tactics he had used made it fail: First, asking for the removal of Tom and Diane from their positions, and, second, demanding that EPA shut down the ISTT work because of lack of air monitors.

Scott said he believed his demand (to not turn on the treatment system with the air monitors then in place) worked by bringing the technicians to the table who pointed out to EPA that they had failed to address catastrophic vapor releases in their air monitoring plan.

Caroline Ross said instead of clearing things up, everything seemed more hostile. And she knew from her previous work with government entities that when threatened, the government closes ranks.

Wayne agreed and said things seemed chaotic, and that might mean we would not get government funding to get things done.

Later, Jim voiced the strongest opinion against Scott Cornelius, saying he had led us down a rat hole in our relationship with EPA. During a subsequent Executive Committee meeting, he made a motion to fire Scott. I seconded it to see that it got voted upon. Of the seven people in attendance, 2 voted yes and 5 abstained.

Because we now had to receive pre-approval for every project we asked the Technical Advisor to do, we were limited in how quickly we could respond to reports put out by EPA. Sometimes weeks went by with Gary having to remind EPA repeatedly that we had asked for pre-approval for Scott to read and comment on a document. Once we had approval, EPA was very slow in allocating the money into our government account, and then into our local bank account so that we could write a check to pay Scott. Scott felt he should be paid on time, and Gary wanted to pay him out of our Oxford account (money from a court settlement we had gained in the Oxford Automotive bankruptcy), but I protested, arguing that if EPA didn't re-pay us, then we would be out the Oxford money. I wrote in an email, "I think Scott is going to have to wait, just as we are waiting. It may be that he will not choose to do so many things for us if the money is in question, and we will understand if that the case."

Scott sent Gary a list of 10 items for which he was requesting time. At this point I was in favor of taking back letter writing and phone calls that we board members used to do ourselves, before Scott had become our Technical Advisor. It would help save the exorbitant amount of money that Scott charged for those activities.

In reading Scott's list, I chose several of the items to do myself, including a phone call to MDEQ about the railroad spur. I knew David Kline, Superfund Section Chief with MDEQ, and felt we had good rapport. When I sent an email to the Executive Committee and Scott about what I'd learned in my phone conversation with David, Scott responded with an admonishing email to me to say that I should have assigned this technical issue to him as our Technical Advisor; that Scott would have asked follow-up questions; and that David wouldn't have given Scott the excuse regarding the delay that he gave me. He went on to say how it was more appropriate to have the Technical Advisor conduct phone calls with EPA and MDEQ, and if the board members wanted to find out the real reason for the railroad spur delay, they should approve the time he had previously requested to complete this task.

I wrote back telling Scott that his admonishing tone was out of place in speaking to a member of the Executive Committee. I said, "Having a Technical Advisor does not mean that the people of the CAG sit back and let the TA run things. We have hired you to advise us where you can, and the Executive Committee determines which direction to follow, because it is the governing board of the CAG." I pointed out that it was prudent for the Executive Committee to take on tasks that would save us from paying him $175 an hour.

We continued on in this manner, giving Scott less work than he would have liked. Even when it was time to renew his contract, we didn't do it. Apparently, Gary called Scott to tell him the decision to not renew his contract, and in response, Scott decided to resign. He added, however, that if we chose to reverse the decision, he would continue as our Technical Advisor. Jim Hall wrote a nice note accepting his resignation.

Later in the year, when we needed expert advice on an EPA document regarding Area 2 of the Velsicol Former Plant Site, we decided to ask our previous Technical Advisor, Jim Heinzman, if he could read and comment on the report. Gary sought approval at Region 5, and they agreed.

From that experience, it seemed it might be possible to use the TAG grant money in a piecemeal way. Instead of hiring a Technical Advisor for the life of the grant, rather to hire an expert on an as-needed basis, following the format of the TASC program. It was worth a try.

Chapter 9
(2018 Part 2)
Heating and Cooling

For the first time since 1978 when the chemical factory had shut down, some actual cleanup was due to take place on the former plant site. Even though it was only one acre of the 52-acre site, it was a beginning. And that acre, known as Area One, contained many dangerous volatile chemicals, including DBCP, and NAPL composed of mostly benzene and DDT.

Preparations had been underway for several years. A new wide entrance with a gate had been built on M-46. This access from the plant site directly onto the highway would eliminate truck traffic in the neighborhood. We had asked for this many years earlier, and it pleased us to see it put in place.

Service roads were constructed through the plant site, as was a concrete pad to hold all the thermal treatment equipment when it arrived by truck. A high-voltage electrical circuit was laid to carry the power for the heating units and to run all the extraction and heating equipment. It was three inches in diameter, lay just under the soil, and was marked by orange snow fence.

By January of 2018, all 276 heating units, 59 multi-phase extraction wells, 17 temperature monitoring points, and 14 pressure monitoring points were in the ground. The extraction wells would remove both liquid and vapor. Both the temperature and pressure gauges would take measurements in increments from the surface to 30 feet below ground.

Much of the treatment equipment had been hauled in. Tanks, huge canisters of carbon, pipes going in several directions both vertically and horizontally, a smoke stack, and a heavy black plastic vapor barrier over the wellfield were visible from the end of North Street. As one of our CAG members commented, the equipment for chemical destruction looked much like the equipment for manufacturing chemicals. A little irony to contemplate.

The process was a form of thermal destruction referred to as thermal conductivity heating (TCH). Heating elements, similar to the much smaller ones found in a toaster oven, would carry the electricity deep underground into the clay till unit, boiling the groundwater and water in the soil into steam, and vaporizing the volatile contaminants. A vacuum unit would bring the contaminants to the surface, with the gases going into one treatment unit and the liquid into another.

Like most projects, the start-up date moved. A first it was thought that heating would begin in January, but the system wasn't fully set up yet. Then, in February, problems with the thermal oxidizer turning off at 1700 degrees Fahrenheit instead of 1800 likely meant the pre-heat exchanger needed to be replaced. This unit was used to raise the temperature of the vapor prior to entering the thermal oxidizer, which helped to conserve the natural gas used as fuel.

The problem turned out to be an issue with a sensor not sending a signal to the computer, and it was fixed by early March. Extraction began, but the heaters were not yet turned on to full power, so no contaminated vapors were yet being developed. The contaminated groundwater coming up in the wells was moved into storage for eventual treatment, once they were sure the computer was operating correctly.

Our EPA project manager, Tom Alcamo, let us know that he had used a decibel meter to evaluate the noise levels, and even though not all equipment was running yet, he didn't think the noise would be a problem in the neighborhood.

Ever since our fiery phone conversation, Tom and I had been on better terms. He sent email updates without being asked, and I sent him emails wishing him well when he had the flu. With forward progress on the cleanup, all of us had a better outlook.

136

On the afternoon of March 7, when Tom's email arrived saying heating had begun, it gave me a thrill. Finally, the cleanup of the plant site was on its way to becoming a reality!

It was expected that it would take about five months to heat the soil to the boiling point, and then the contract stated that the heating would continue at that temperature for a minimum of 90 days. From calculations, it was estimated that about 25,000 pounds of contamination would be removed from the one-acre area. As time went by, we learned this estimate was low. The major volatiles to be removed were benzene, chlorobenzene, toluene, 1,2 dichloroethane and DBCP (1,2-dibromo-3-chloropropane, a male sterilant). The process wouldn't destroy DDT, but plenty of DDT contained in the NAPL would come up.

Early on, we had requested to have data from the thermal treatment posted on a live website we had hoped to set up. Instead, Tom did it, working with his computer people to set up a website that showed up-to-date readouts of heating at the various levels of soil, air monitoring data, and other information. Photo overlays of how the chemical plant looked while in production could be laid over the maps of current remediation plans.

In addition to the gate onto M-46 being a long-standing request finally satisfied, another request was fulfilled when EPA offered site tours to interested community members and public officials. In all the years we had been working to see this site cleaned up, we had never been allowed onto the property. At different times throughout the years we had asked, and if not the whole group, couldn't the officers go take a look or at least the chairperson? When the river sediment remediation had been underway with the white tent set up over the water treatment equipment, we tried hard to persuade the EPA project manager at that time to give us a tour, and our request was flatly denied.

I signed up for the first site tour, which took place in late April. My first actual tour had taken place late in the fall of 2017 when Tom invited me to take a preliminary look at the equipment being set up. At that time, being inside the fence gave me sensations of history and chemistry. History, because I thought of people I knew, both living and dead, who had worked there, including Michigan Chemical Corporation employees my parents had known, many of whom had left when Velsicol took over. And chemistry, because I knew I was walking on top of all the poisons buried underground that had been killing birds, killing fish, polluting the river, and fouling the water supply for so many years. And then there was the hopefulness that maybe something was really going to happen to help clean up the source of all this trouble. Was our dream going to become a reality? It was quite a mix of thoughts and feelings.

The organized tour in April was interesting because I got to watch the reactions of other CAG members as we walked from the staff trailer out to Area 1 where the equipment was working to heat the ground and bring up the toxins. Margaret Hoyt tried to get her bearings and pointed out the locations of the buildings in which she had worked while employed there early in her married life. Norm Keon also pointed out where the business office had been located where his father had done bookkeeping for the company. Phil Ramsey drove up in his car, since his health didn't allow him to walk much. Theo von Wallmenich, the project manager for EPA's contractor, Jacobs (formerly CH2MHILL) got in the car with him to explain about the machinery we were looking at.

Another tour conducted in May was for the press and elected officials, and I went again.

By that time, 200 pounds of volatile organic compounds had been brought up from underground. Late in May, that number rose to 400 pounds. By then the ground was heated to 65 degrees Centigrade, with 100 being the Centigrade boiling point.

The electrical bill for the first month of heating was $150,000. The City of St. Louis was benefiting somewhat from the high bill, since they produced their own electricity. Not that much, of course, but a deal had been worked out with Consumers Energy, and part of the bill EPA paid went to the city. Our CAG was pleased that the town was benefiting in this way from the cleanup that had caused so much worry and suffering in years past.

Finally, in July, the ground had been heated to boiling. Many more pounds of volatiles and semi-volatiles were coming out of Area 1 than expected. The carbon filters had to be changed out much more often -- an added expense, but worth it.

While I was on another kind of tour, one of an historic home in St. Louis, Ruth Gibbs approached me about someone she knew who had been kayaking and had seen a white, odorous discharge entering the river. I told her to have the man contact me. He did, and described what he had seen and he said it was coming from the newer area EPA was working on. He added, "I love living on this river and hate to see this happening to a river that everyone is working so hard to repair!"

The "newer area" meant the thermal treatment set-up, and it must have been the pipe from the water treatment discharging into the river. I immediately contacted the rest of the Executive Committee, and Jim Hall asked me to contact EPA. Meanwhile, he contacted Dan Morden, the Gratiot County Emergency Manager. Dan and the St. Louis Fire Chief, Rich Apps, and other emergency preparedness personnel had been briefed by EPA and the Terra-Therm company on the equipment and process. Dan and Rich had both spoken to our CAG, assuring us at the time that they didn't expect any catastrophic emergencies in connection with the operation. This emergency was not catastrophic, but it was concerning.

I sent an email to Tom at EPA. Later, Theo responded, since Tom was not in, and said the chalky discharge appeared to be related to biological growth with a biological smell. He also said both Rich Apps and Dan Morden had visited the site, and he had discussed his observations with them.

Jim Hall touched base with Jim Heinzman, our former Technical Advisor, who said we should contact MDEQ's pollution discharge staff about this. He said discharges were not supposed to cause aesthetic problems that could be seen or smelled, and were not to produce undesirable vegetation in the river. He recommended that we look at a copy of the discharge permit the State had issued to EPA. Ironically, our former Technical Advisor, Scott Cornelius, had asked to see that SRD (substantive requirement document) regarding discharge, and we were told by the Region 5 TAG people that they wouldn't pay for our TA to look at a State document, even though it was part of the Velsicol Superfund cleanup.

Jim Hall notified MDEQ and a person was sent out, who observed white/greyish colored material on the cascade prior to going into the river, and some odors. He said he had learned in his conversation with Theo and TerraTherm employees that the general consensus was that the color and odors resulted from aerating the FracTank, and by ceasing that process, the biological growth would lessen. Theo termed the problem an aesthetic concern that didn't pose a threat to the river or human contact.

That evening, Gary Smith and Jim Hall boated over to the discharge pipe and took a video. Gary also pulled out his copy of the SRD and found the section that said EPA had to report any unusual characteristics of the discharge, which included turbidity, color, oil film, floating solids, foams, settleable solids, suspended solids or deposits. What he had seen at the discharge pipe fit the categories of color and deposits. According to the SRD contract, if any of these characteristics were observed, EPA was required to alert MDEQ within 24 hours.

In my phone conversation with Theo, he had said that in June, a month before, they had seen a biomass getting started, and had also detected an odor. He explained that the groundwater in this area contained a lot of iron, and iron-loving bacteria. As the water was treated and became hotter, it encouraged the growth of the bacteria. He said they had been monitoring the situation since June.

He had observed greenish, black and grayish growths, indicating plant growth, reduced iron with iron bacteria, and molds, fungi and other bacteria. The whitish/grayish growth was fungus. The dead or dying cells were creating the turbidity.

He went on to say they had spoken with MDEQ that day about using a couple of additives to address the problem, because any changes to the SRD had to be approved by them. A state biologist would review the additives to make sure they wouldn't harm river life.

The additives were approved. Ultimately citric acid was used to control the growth of iron-reducing bacteria, along with Peroxy X-22, a biocide, also referred to as peracetic acid (PAA). Neither additive was considered harmful to the river, and both would break down in open air and light.

Besides the concern about what was going into the river, the CAG's concern was that EPA had not followed the requirements of the SRD by notifying the state within 24 hours. It appeared that they hadn't planned to notify them at all, and it was only because we had raised the alarm and contacted them that anything was done. Jim spoke to Tom about this, and stressed to him the importance of letting us know when they know instead of having us blindsided about an issue. Jim wrote to us in an email, "All the inspections they got [from the state, county and city officials] could have been avoided had they let us know there was a problem and was being worked out."

Gary wrote in an email, "We have a long history of being misused and abused by the EPA and even the DEQ at times. This is yet another one of those times. The environment is who will suffer from these types of events."

We wrote a letter to Heidi Grether, director of MDEQ, describing what had occurred, quoting the relevant passage of the SRD, and pointing out that EPA had violated its terms by failing to notify MDEQ within 24 hours of their first observation of the unusual characteristics of the discharge. We ended the letter by saying, "We would like to know what consequences EPA faces by failing to report the turbidity, color, odor, film, floating solids, foams and other characteristics of discharge to MDEQ within 24 hours. It is our contention that the discharge would still be polluting the Pine River had not the resident notified our Task Force. That is unacceptable to this community. We need the State of Michigan to advocate for us in situations such as this, and to impress upon the federal EPA the importance of following guidelines laid out by the State."

We never received a reply -- not even a canned response thanking us for the letter. This was typical the whole time Heidi Grether held the position. All of her predecessors had responded to our letters over the years, and that is why it is significant to note that Grether never responded to anything we wrote to her, even invitations to come and visit our Superfund site.

By the middle of August, almost 50,000 pounds of contaminants had been removed from Area 1, almost double the amount anticipated. Over four million gallons of water had been treated and returned to the Pine River through the discharge point on the river's edge. That was a lot of warm water to be adding to the stream. The water entered the river at about 100 degrees Fahrenheit, but MDEQ didn't think the warm water discharge was significant.

By September steam could be seen leaving the tall smokestack at Area 1. Tom wanted me to let the community know that the cooler outside air temperatures contributed to the visible steam, as did the installation of a more efficient cooling tower that had recently been added to the equipment on site. As for electricity usage, they had surpassed the 7.5 million kilowatt hours and had reached 8 million. There was still a month of heating yet to do before cooling would begin. At that point, the city had gained $687,000 from electricity sold to EPA.

Tom confided to me that he was working to sign TerraTherm onto a contract for Area 2 to enable them to move their equipment

142

directly to that site rather than tearing down the equipment, transporting it elsewhere, and then having to remobilize later to come back and set things up in Area 2. Government contracting had restrictions about sole-sourcing a company, but he was hoping to find a way through that bureaucratic maze. His plan would save at least a million dollars of taxpayer money that could be used for actual cleanup. This plan made sense to us, and later, once the idea was made public, and we wrote a letter to the Acting Assistant Administrator of EPA in Washington, D. C. requesting it, with copies going to our members of Congress.

Tom also had a hope that heating could begin at Area 2 while Area 1 began to cool down, but that didn't pan out. Further, he hoped that heating could take place in both Area 2 and the Velsicol Burn Pit Site across the river, but it turned out that there wouldn't be enough electrical capacity to heat both at once.

In Area 1, the 90 days of heating at boiling point was reached in October. EPA had been analyzing the charts that showed diminishing returns of contaminants to help to determine when to turn off the heaters. The day came, and Tom said the treatment systems for water and vapor would continue to collect and treat contaminants for at least 21 days as the cool down began.

During the heating process, 56,000 pounds of contaminants had been removed, far more than the original estimate. Electricity usage reached 9,700,000 kilowatt hours. Over 5,700,000 gallons of water were treated and discharged into the Pine River. Ambient air monitoring showed no *system-related* detections. (The one detection was likely from a diesel-engine truck.) Over a million data points were collected, with 30,000 of them manually collected. Laboratory samples amounted to 560 as the system operated to keep a check on the process.

Now the long months of cooling would begin. Before the ground was fully cool, confirmation samples would be taken to determine how well the process had worked.

As for Area 2, it was estimated that heating units and extraction wells could be in the ground in time for heating to begin in late spring. Instead of one acre, Area 2 would require the heating of three acres, and much debris was buried underground that had to be factored into the use of electricity in that area. Area 2 was the location of the former DDT manufacturing plant, and included a spot where DDT-laced NAPL had been found at a depth of 99 feet.

On the health front, the year started off well with recruitment underway for two new studies on the health impacts of PBB exposure. The first was a clinical trial involving a substance that when ingested would perhaps enable the body to eliminate PBB and DDT faster than the normal half-life of the chemical compounds. The second was a multi-generational study to determine if fathers who had been exposed to PBB could pass health problems via their sperm to their children who had not been directly exposed.

Another bright spot was an assurance that a renewed contract between the state health department (MDHHS) and their contracted public health institute (MPHI) would result in a better flow of past data on original PBB cohort participants to the researchers at the Rollins School of Public Health at Emory University. That assurance dissipated quickly once Dr. Michele Marcus at Emory read the Agent of the State agreement between MDHHS and MPHI. Language in the document prohibited any contact with participants in the original cohort.

Seeing the sentence in the document came as a shock because it contradicted a statement made in a letter MDHHS had sent to Michele Marcus a few months prior in support of a research grant. The statement from the support letter said, "Currently, our Department is assisting Emory and MPHI in recruiting members of the closed PBB Long-Term Study cohort and their unenrolled offspring into a study cohort which you manage." In contrast, the sentence from the Agent of the State document stated, "The Master File database will not be used to initiate contact or recruit participants for the Marcus Cohort," which said, in essence, that MDHHS would not help Emory and MPHI in recruiting members and their unenrolled offspring.

This language blocked necessary activity between MPHI and Emory, and would prohibit the dissemination of research results and educational materials among the people of Michigan who had been exposed to PBB contamination. It would curtail the sending of updates on health outcomes of PBB exposure to those exposed and would even prevent Emory from sending postcard invitations about PBB informational community meetings around the state!

Michele said she believed the Michigan PBB Registry had an ethical imperative to inform people of research results because often the new information led to an early diagnosis and more effective preventive measures for those who had been exposed to PBB. Apparently the state health department had determined that receiving a postcard invitation to a meeting to learn about research results of PBB exposure to human health was too great a threat to public health to be risked. Good grief.

In another change, MDHHS was now asking Michele to return the records of deceased persons they had previously shared with her. The concern was privacy. In the view of the community, now that we knew that deleterious health effects likely passed from the exposed generation to subsequent unexposed children and grandchildren, it was vital that the offspring know about their parents' exposure, but the state health department didn't think it was even legally allowable for family members to request records of the deceased, let alone researchers.

We later learned that MDHHS seemed to be applying a new "broad consent" privacy definition to the current situation. Even though the definition was not retroactive, the state health department was using it in that way in dealing with the records of PBB Long-Term Study participants who had passed away. Michele decided to return the deceased records as a gesture of goodwill, as she was still hopeful that she could work with MDHHS and not butt heads with them. In my opinion, that was a futile gesture on her part, as it turned out to be.

In a phone conversation with Michele, the MPHI director took the position that the new prohibition on contacting or recruiting people was just a matter of wording, and she said she would make sure it was corrected. A month later, nothing had changed.

I sent a memo to our state representative, Jim Lower, alerting him about the ban on contact and recruitment. In it I said, "If the language remains in the new agreement, it effectively severs a lifeline being held out to people whose health may continue to be affected by their involuntary exposure to PBB."

He replied with concern and said his office staff would look into it. At this point, I wasn't asking him to do anything, but was seeking to keep him informed. I hoped that MPHI, MDHHS and Emory could get the wording changed.

Prior to all this, I had spoken with Kory Groetsch at MDHHS about attending a CAG meeting to bring our membership up to date on the PBB records issue. He had suggested that he would like to attend when Michele Marcus could also be there. Since I now knew Michele and her crew would be in Michigan for PBB community informational meetings in April, I invited Kory and others from MDHHS for the third Wednesday of the month, which was the usual meeting date of the CAG, and had been for 19 years. He accepted and hoped to bring others with him.

In our conversation, I mentioned our concerns about the language in the new Agent of the State agreement between MDHHS and MPHI, and told him I'd notified my congressman about it. He said he thought the wording may have slipped into the document in error. Afterwards, I said in an email to the others on the PBB Leadership Team, "my prediction is he will find the wording was not in error!"

During this time we had a conference call with people in Flint who were forming a Lead Registry. They had questions about the PBB Registry, and we had questions about the legislation that allowed them to be termed a "public health registry." They were not sure why they were called that. The formal name of their registry was the Flint Lead Exposure Registry, and it was directly funded by the CDC. It would not only enable the identification and monitoring of exposed residents, but would also connect the people to health services and would allow the registry to conduct research, as well.

After the conference call the PBB Leadership Team discussed the greater scope allowed the Lead Registry, and speculated that if we could become a "public health registry," it would enable us to behave in a public health way by giving participants updates on research results and inviting them to informational meetings.

I contacted our aide to Senator Debbie Stabenow and she found the title and number of the federal statute that had set up the Flint Lead Exposure Registry. Some searching on line led me to the WIIN Act of 2016 that authorized water projects across the country, including $170 million to address the problem of lead in Flint's drinking water. None of the articles I read, however, used the term "public health registry."

What was the difference between a "cohort" and a "registry,' I wondered. It was a distinction that Sarah Lyon-Callo had made several times during my second meeting with MDHHS in 2017. She termed the original study a cohort, and what Emory was doing a registry, and to her that meant that the registry couldn't have all the data the cohort had. At another point, she said Emory's activities constituted a cohort within a registry.

Also, there was apparently a difference between a "public health registry" and a "research registry," because in the phone conversation with the Flint people, they said they were now a public health registry and later would be a research registry. Did they just mean they would conduct those activities at different times?

Michele sent an email to the point person for the Lead Registry at MSU asking for further detail. Not all our questions were answered by her response, but we did find out that within the Notice of Funding Opportunity there were 22 different administrative requirements for them to fulfill. One of those was AR-24 that established the Flint Lead Registry as a "public health authority" related to HIIPA data.

Norm Keon searched the Public Health Code, finding nothing about how to create a "public health registry," and concluding that it was a "loose" term that may refer to any registry created via the Public Health Code. There are dozens of registries within the Public Health Code, including cancer, birth defects, donor, and peace of mind registries, but none use the words "public health registry."

I surmised that the term "public health registry" was a reference to the Lead Registry group having met the AR-24 requirement that established the Flint Lead Registry "as a public health authority related to HIIPA data." Looking at their PowerPoint slides it was evident that their administrative structure allowed all kinds of outreach to the exposed community, and that the kinds of privacy concerns MDHHS was raising about the PBB Registry did not apply to this new long-term study.

Following up on the difference between a "registry" and a "cohort," Ed Lorenz searched historical documents from CDC and USDA and concluded that at the time of the establishment of the Michigan Long-Term Study of the PBB Cohort, there was no difference between a registry and a cohort. The terms were used interchangeably. He also found a 1991 instructor's manual for a CDC course that used the PBB Disaster in Michigan as its training example, entitled "Mixed Bag in Michigan: The PBB Story." Question #14 said, "List and discuss reasons for and against launching a long-term registry follow-up effort in this particular health hazard situation." Ed had gone through the long pro and con answer circling the word registry each time it was used, and in an email to us, concluded that CDC regarded the Michigan Long-Term Study a health registry." He also had found wording on the second page of a 2011 state health department hand-out about PBB that called the cohort study a "registry."

I followed up with an online search for definitions of "cohort" and "registry." A definition from the U.S. Department of Health and Human Services defined a "cohort" as "a group of people who share a particular characteristic, for example age or a medical condition." The National Institutes of Health said a registry "is a collection of information about individuals, usually focused around a specific diagnosis or condition." From those definitions I could see why Sarah Lyon-Callo said the current Michigan PBB Registry was a cohort within a registry. The particular characteristic that made it a cohort was the individual's exposure to PBB. What made it a registry is that information had been gathered on these people about that exposure and the health outcomes from it.

Importantly, from another source I found a list of how a registry fulfills three public health needs: 1) to elucidate the presence or absence of long-term health effects after exposure to hazardous substances 2) to maintain current contact information in order to pass on up-to-date, and possibly urgent, scientific information 3) to be available to answer questions members have concerning their exposure.

It seemed to me that the wording within the current Agent of the State agreement between MDHHS and MPHI was sorely curtailing the public health purposes of the Michigan PBB Registry.

All of our conversations were taking place against the backdrop of State Attorney General Bill Schuette taking many high-ranking MDHHS officials to court over the Flint water crisis, including the agency's director, Nick Lyon and the state medical executive, Eden Wells. Wells was accused of having stopped a research team in Flint who had wanted to notify research subjects about the dangerous Legionnaire's disease bacteria in their water so that they could take measures to avoid sickness. Wells was opposed to notifying people because of the fear of causing alarm. That was a familiar phrase. We had heard it during the PBB Disaster, and even had preserved it in a letter from the governor of Michigan to one of our deceased CAG members, Arnie Bransdorfer, who had been a county commissioner at the time. As for the outbreak of Legionnaire's disease, it killed 12 people in Flint and sickened at least 79 others, and Wells had been charged with manslaughter.

Marcus Cheatham told us he thought these court proceedings were the cause of MDHHS personnel continually putting stumbling blocks in our way. Norm Keon agreed, saying that lawyers had become a major presence within the state health department.

The April visit from the Emory researchers would include a meeting with the director of MPHI, and with Sue Moran and Sarah Lyon-Callo from MDHHS about the Agent of the State language, the records of deceased people, and the benefit in transferring all the data to Emory University, which now had an NIEHS grant and the capability of fashioning a useful data base for registered participants and researchers. Michele wanted the meeting to include some of us on the PBB Leadership Team, but in late March the MPHI director instructed Michele to tell us that she alone was invited to the meeting, and not any of her community partners. Michele decided to go ahead with the meeting, hoping it would help build a collaborative relationship with MDHHS. She felt if the meeting didn't produce results, then we could move toward other options, such as a National Ethics Review of the situation, or legal action.

Michele had received an affirmative reply from NIH to her question on whether it was allowable to use grant money for legal expenses.

Marcus Cheatham had spoken with an attorney for the Mid-Michigan District Health Department about the MDHHS's increasingly hardened position on the release of the PBB records. He told the attorney about our interpretation of the public health code, the opinion of the ethics professor at Emory that the records of the deceased should be part of the research, and other previous attempts to resolve the issues.

Marcus included a 1986 opinion by the former Michigan State Attorney General Frank Kelley who said that personal medical information should be provided to investigators from either the state health department or the local health department. Norm had provided Marcus with this opinion, and Norm had long maintained that it was the legal right of the local Health Officer to ask for the PBB records and that the state health department was obligated to give them to him.

Utilizing the documents we supplied, the Lansing law firm Marcus approached came to the same conclusion we had. He added that the Mid-Michigan District Health Department would not have to follow the same procedure that Emory University was required to follow – namely, to first obtain the consent of the study participants. If MDHHS declined to provide them with the records, then the local health department could pursue legal remedies, including filing a lawsuit.

The time came for our April dinner to be followed by a CAG meeting. Attending the dinner from MDHHS were Kory Groetsch, a toxicologist and director of the Department of Environmental Health, and Sarah Lyon-Callo, an epidemiologist, and director of the Bureau of Epidemiology and Population Health. Other guests attended from the PBB Citizen's Advisory Board, comprised of farm families, from the research team from Emory University, and from the Executive Committee of our CAG. Legislators had been invited but could not attend, although an aide to U.S. Congressman John Moolenaar came to the meeting.

Almost 60 people were there that evening, many of them from farming communities in Michigan, and some were former chemical workers. Michele gave a PowerPoint presentation about the new studies underway, namely, the clinical trial for the elimination of PBB from the body and the three-generation study to determine if men exposed to PBB could pass the epigenetic expression to their offspring.

She discussed the records of deceased study participants. It was known that records of children who were part of the 1978 study were in the folders of the parents, and when the parents died, the records of the children became inaccessible, due to the MDHHS policy. She also contended that if it had been the desire of a study participant to have his or her health records available for research, the desire did not end at death.

She spoke about a new grant applied for that would provide funds to create digital infrastructure for organizing and accessing the PBB records, making them more usable for researchers. The PBB records would be linked to other data bases, such as the National Death Index, the Michigan Cancer Registry and birth certificates. In order to link those databases, identifiable information would be needed, which present MDHHS policy was not providing.

Next Kory Groetsch spoke about the disposition of the 6,866 records of participants in the Michigan Long-Term PBB study which began in 1978. When the study ceased after 20 years, Dr. Michele Marcus began working with the de-identified data in 1997. He praised her cutting edge ideas, especially her exploration of epigenetics. He said the state health department would like to see the work proceed, and would set up a way to get de-identified data to her. That last statement was amazing to hear.

Sarah Lyon-Callo explained that the Long-Term PBB study was given Medical Research Protection status in the Public Health Code, which protects the records from legal subpoenas. That is why individual participants must give their permission to have the records transferred to Emory University. Several audience members spoke strongly about the offspring of deceased participants having access to their family records. Lyon-Callo said MDHHS would figure out a way to do that didn't break state law. Again, we were pleased by that statement and believed the meeting was moving us forward. Sadly, we learned in days to come, that the attempt had been stopped by a lawyer for MDHHS.

Even before the sit-down meeting with MDHHS and MPHI, Sue Moran, a deputy director at the state health department, requested from Marcus Cheatham a new letter requesting the PBB records, including how he, as local health officer, would use the data and how the use of that data would support essential public health services. Marcus requested Norm's help in understanding what should be included in a response. Norm explained that the law under the Public Health Code did not require a health officer to provide any justification for his request for medical records. To ask Marcus to present proof of how the use of the data supported public health was potentially another way to limit his access to the records.

After the April face-to-face meeting, it seemed to Michele that the state would move forward with revising the language in the Agent of the State agreement, and having their lawyers review the law that restricts the sharing of deceased records for continued research. The Emory researchers felt relieved that the problem was on its way to resolution. I wrote a follow-up message to our state representative, Jim Lower, telling him that the representatives of the three entities had met and had verbally agreed to changes in the content of the agreement. Michele had already drafted a document that included the changes that she planned to share with Sarah that week, and she allowed me to include it with my note to Representative Lower.

Not as sanguine about the supposed resolution as was Michele, our Executive Committee continued to discuss the issue and gather information.

Because of the timing of the writing of the 1978 Public Health Code, Ed and Norm suspected that it had been written partly as a result of the PBB Disaster, in hopes of preventing anything like that from happening again. Ed found 8 boxes in the state archives relating to the public health review process, which led to the writing of the Public Health Code. From that research, he learned the name of a retired University of Michigan faculty member, now in his mid-eighties, who had chaired the 1978 Governor's Commission on the Public Health Statute Review.

When contacted, the man responded and said, in part, that "Of course the PBB crisis was certainly well known to our Commission and the legislative committee with which we worked in developing the Code. That's why we decided to deal with the subject when we mapped out our future work plan at our retreat."

Our Executive Committee decided Ed should write back to the U of M professor to establish more of a relationship, and then perhaps Norm and Ed would visit U of M to see both the professor and also Denise Chrysler, an attorney specializing in public health law. Both this attorney and the professor had recently appeared as authors on an article about the Flint water crisis from the public health law standpoint.

Ed had also done research on the HIIPA privacy law and found that after 50 years, privacy laws do not come into play regarding medical records.

We also discussed taking our complaint to State Attorney General Bill Schuette and or to Governor Rick Snyder. I was ready to make an appointment and go now. After all, we had been holding off going for two years, hoping MDHHS would see the public health importance of getting the entire PBB records collection to Emory. Jim Hall and I were both ready to seek help from our highest state officials. Others felt the appointments would be pre-mature, however, and the Executive Committee decided to wait to make appointments until after the November elections.

Chapter 10
(2019)
Learning Lessons

Our chairperson, Jim Hall, learned that he would be accepted into the Emory University clinical trial to test the theory that PBB could be eliminated from the body faster by eating a low calorie diet and taking over-the-counter weight loss pills that contained Orlistat. Jim's blood showed levels of PBB that were seven times higher than people who had worked in the chemical plant while the fire retardant was being manufactured. As we so often observed, the people exposed while still growing up seemed to have accumulated more PBB in their systems and more health problems than those who had been adults during the 1970s PBB Disaster. Mid-way through the clinical trial, Jim told us that a subsequent blood sampling showed that his PBB levels were dropping. Our hope was when the final results of all the participants were analyzed, the Orlistat could be recommended for others to try, under a doctor's supervision.

Both our attempt to procure the complete PBB records from the original cohort established in the 1970s, and the attempts by the Emory University researchers had availed nothing more than the same explanation that as a "medical research project," extra privacy laws governed release of the records. As mentioned in the last chapter, these laws, as MDHHS interpreted them, even meant the data from deceased cohort participants was no longer to be used in ongoing and future studies. In speaking with some of the offspring, they believed that their deceased parents would have wanted the data collected about their own health problems to be included in current studies, even after they had died. As our treasurer, Gary Smith, eloquently said in an email to the rest of us, "Everyone who signed up for that original study didn't give two shits about privacy. They wanted answers. I believe that desire is the same today, whether dead or alive."

Our Executive Committee decided to ask someone who was in this situation to write to the new State Attorney General, Dana Nessel, to ask for help in freeing up the records of the deceased. I spoke with Terri Fountain on the phone, and she agreed to write the letter. I drafted it and she tweaked it to personalize it, and sent it off. Disappointingly, she received a form reply that was no help at all.

Once the new governor, Gretchen Whitmer, was sworn in, our CAG wrote to her requesting help. She sent our letter to MDHHS, and the customary reply letter was written to us from a deputy director of the state health department saying the records were off limits due to the original study being a "medical research project." Somewhat amusingly, the letter began "Thank you for your latest letter regarding…." It was at least our third letter. We were nothing if not persistent.

The bill I had drafted in 2018 that would give "public health authority" to the Michigan PBB Registry had been sent to our state congressional representative, James Lower. He contacted me to let me know he wanted to introduce it in the House. He said he believed the bill, when passed, would enable Emory to gain access to the PBB records, and also to reach out to Michigan communities with new research findings, as public health is meant to do. I was quite thrilled to learn this. My draft had been sent on to be written in language and style acceptable for proposed bills. I asked that I see the new draft before it moved onwards just to make sure it said what we had intended it to say, and I am so thankful I did this.

When the new draft was emailed to me, the whole intent had been altered. Instead of giving the Michigan PBB Registry "public health authority," it gave it to the state health department which, of course, already had it! Its language also required the state health department to continue the actual research into the health effects of PBB exposure, which they had no interest in pursuing, or money with which to do research and analysis. That is why they had turned that aspect of the study over to Emory University years before.

It turns out that it was a lawyer who had misunderstood the plain language of what I had written and had turned the bill upside down and backwards. As time went on, we learned that this was only one example in which lawyers were subverting and undermining the health of the public in our state with their poor understanding of the meaning of public health.

Meanwhile, our PBB Leadership Team was working with people from two universities to plan an event in Lansing with the intention of educating our legislators on the human health effects of exposure to fire retardants, both past and present. It was called "From PBB to PFAS: Policy lessons from widespread chemical contaminations in Michigan." Congressman James Lower was one of the sponsors, as was Senator Rick Outman, who had been our previous state representative and had assisted our CAG in various ways in the past.

In addition to a speaker on PFAS, both Michele Marcus from Emory and our CAG vice-chair, Ed Lorenz, gave presentations, and Brittany Fremion, who was spearheading the PBB Oral History

157

project, displayed posters. Michele's presentation was on the health effects of PBB exposure, and the importance of listening closely to the affected communities. Ed's talk, using St. Louis and the Velsicol chemical factory as his focus, was a short and powerful discourse on lessons that our elected officials should have learned from the PBB disaster that could now be applied to the present day's PFAS crisis.

During the question time, Senator Winnie Brinks from the west side of the state asked Michele if MDHHS had given Emory complete access to the records from the original PBB cohort study. Michele responded diplomatically, but made it clear that the researchers were given less access now than when she had started her PBB research 20-some years ago.

The event was well covered in the press both before and afterwards. Lisa Halbert, daughter of Rick and Sandra Halbert of *Bitter Harvest* fame, referred to a quote from me in one of the before articles as a throwing down of the gauntlet. I had said, "We are hoping that the event will help us with our problem with the State Health Department, which is not fully cooperating to give access to Emory University with the records they need to perform comprehensive health studies of PBB exposure." Most people who had lived through those turbulent times in the 1970s would understand the lack of cooperation as being usual. Everyone knew that the agencies of the state government had covered up the PBB disaster at the time and some people continued to see a continuing cover-up as the cause of present day difficulties.

At the event in Lansing several of us met Francis "Bus" Spaniola for the first time. Bus had introduced legislation in the late 1970s to reduce the allowable level of PBB in human food. Prior to the passage of his bill, the allowable levels for human consumption were higher than what cattle were allowed to consume. Melanie Pearson took my picture as I stood between two of my PBB heroes -- Bus and Dr. Tom Corbett, an early 1970s whistle blower who had researched the potential effects of PBB exposure on mice even before state government had admitted there was a problem in the food chain.

We also met Tony Spaniola, son of Bus, an attorney who was active in bringing attention to the PFAS problem in Oscoda County, a former location of an Air Force base for many decades. Tony told Michele and others that he was in regular contact with one of the key policy advisors to the new governor. He offered to deliver to this person a package of our documents delineating our attempts to resolve the PBB records issue. Marcus Cheatham, CAG member and Health Officer for the Mid-Michigan District Health Department, compiled the package and wrote a timeline showing our efforts from 2012 onward. Seven years! Should it really take this long and be this difficult for the public to resolve an issue with a state agency?

Now that Representative James Lower was busy with a campaign to take over a seat in the US Congress, I decided to contact Senator Rick Outman about passing a bill that would grant "public health authority" to the Michigan PBB Registry. I also encouraged Michele to respond to Senator Winnie Brinks in more detail about the PBB records since the senator had raised the question at the legislative event, and also to ask that we meet with her on the same day we met with Outman.

In thinking about our personnel, it seemed best to me that we have only three people attend the appointments with the senators. I should since I was the one who had drafted the bill, Michele should since she dealt directly with MDHHS and MPHI about the records issue, and I thought Norm Keon of the Mid-Michigan District Health Department would be a good third because of his decades of knowledge about the public health code. The three of us also represented three partners from within the PBB Leadership Team (Mid-Michigan District Health Department; Pine River Superfund Citizen Task Force; and the Emory University researchers).

Before the appointments were set, the researchers learned that they had received a grant to study PBB and cancer, which increased the urgency for MDHHS to give them access to the de-identified data of original study participants.

We decided to make two specific requests of the senators:

First, we requested that they send a letter to MDHHS recommending that the records be released to the Mid-Michigan District Health Department for their determination of the public health needs of PBB-exposed individuals, as current law and regulations allowed. We had a legal opinion on this written by the law firm that represented local health departments.

Second, we requested that a legislative bill be passed that would grant current and retroactive "public health authority" to the Michigan PBB Registry, which would allow the researchers to notify those in the Registry of the evidence linking PBB exposure to health effects, including an increased risk of thyroid dysfunction, breast cancer, and other cancers.

When we met with the senators, they seemed as unhappy and puzzled as we were by the rigid stance of MDHHS in failing to allow research to be done with the PBB records. They both said health policy aides of theirs would look at our documents to help the senators better understand them. We returned for follow-up appointments about two months later. Sadly, Outman's office had done nothing about our issue, while Brinks had reached out to MDHHS only to receive the same response we had been given for years. It was quite disappointing to see no progress with either of our requests. It was beginning to feel like another dead end. The aide sitting in with Senator Brinks said it looked like a lawsuit was necessary.

Another government shutdown occurred at the beginning of the year. Reporters called to get our reaction. I explained that so far we hadn't experienced any hardship at our Superfund sites, even though the contractors were unable to continue their tasks in the field or at their desks. We were grateful that our EPA Project Manager Tom Alcamo had managed to have both money and a contract in place for Area 2 prior to the shutdown. As for Area 1, it was still going through its cool-down phase.

To the best of our knowledge, the *in situ* thermal cleanup in Area 1 had been successful. Once the heating had ended and the ground had partially cooled, soil borings were taken at depth. It was found that any NAPL remaining in the soil had congealed into a tarlike substance that would not be moved by the groundwater, and the substance later hardened like asphalt. Even so, the asphaltic material was being removed when it could be to rid the area of source material to the best extent possible.

We had been presented with a technical memorandum outlining basic steps for addressing contaminants in Area 2. For one thing, the 3-acre site would be split into two phases of cleanup because not enough electricity was available to do the whole thing at once. The lack of electricity also meant that the Burn Pit Superfund Site across the river could not begin until both phases of Area 2 had been completed. The soonest we could expect to have the NAPL removed at the Burn Pit would be in 2021.

Phase 1 of Area 2 would have 52 multiphase extraction wells (extracting both liquids and gases), 242 heater wells, 16 temperature monitoring points at different levels underground, and 13 pressure point monitoring points. Our EPA project manager, Tom Alcamo, talked about lessons learned from the heating in Area 1 that were being applied to Area 2.

First, they would now use two weir tanks instead of one to settle out the liquid NAPL. The collection of contaminants had more than doubled from the estimates in Area 1, and with Area 2 being even worse, they would need more capacity for whatever came up out of the ground. The plan was to separate the extractions from the well field into two streams, which would slow down the flow and allow more NAPL to settle out into the tanks before the filtration treatment phase.

Second, they were adding paracetic acid and bicarbonate up front in the treatment phase to prevent the chalky, smelly substance from forming that had caused such concern in the river the summer before.

Third, the problem of corrosion was being addressed up front. In Area 1 the chlorinated chemicals coming up out of the ground had corroded the blower motor veins, and this time, they had coated the blades with epoxy. Also, thicker pipes were being used for the untreated liquids to again cut down on problems from corrosion.

Fourth, the number of vapor phase extraction wells was increased by twenty.

One thing in the technical memorandum for Area 2 that caused us concern was a proposal to re-use part of the old, 1980s slurry wall. During the first Superfund cleanup from 1978-1982, a clay wall had been built around the chemical site, and a clay cap placed on top. The Remedial Investigation had shown that the wall had failed with gaps as wide as 7 feet that allowed contamination to flow from the plant site into the river.

The Record of Decision for this new cleanup, signed in 2012, stipulated that a new metal wall be placed around the site. To re-use part of the original slurry wall would save money, but seemed shortsighted to us. The clay wall had proved it would fail, both in actuality and in bench tests of the material in a lab. Those tests showed that the mix of chemicals buried at the site ate through the betonitic clay. In addition to those concerns, the idea that the ROD could be changed willy-nilly instead of being an ironclad agreement upset us. We had understood that the ROD was a contract that once signed by all the parties must be adhered to. In fact we had been told that once the remedy laid out in a ROD was underway, the community could not object to anything until the entire remedy had been completed. To ban input from the community along the way and yet to allow the agencies to make changes flouted the American adage of a government of, by and for the people.

We hired hydrogeologist Jim Heinzman to read and respond to the technical memo. He pointed out a number of data gaps for the re-use of the slurry wall, and in many other of the plans for Area 2 treatment. At a meeting of our Technical Committee, Tom Alcamo said they were not going to re-use the part of the slurry wall where Area 2 bordered the river, and that a slurry wall investigation was not part of the design for Area 2. We didn't drop the issue, but rather asked for EPA to give us a presentation on their plans for any re-use of the wall. We made our request in March and Tom put us off until he agreed to do it in July. At the last minute, he changed his mind, saying in an email that it was his responsibility to keep the community informed, and that was what he was doing.

Many years previously, when Richard Karl had been the Region 5 director for EPA, we had requested that "community involvement" be included in one of the documents. He had allowed a paragraph entitled Community Involvement to be inserted, but the text of the paragraph simply said that the community would be informed. Being informed and being involved are two quite different things, and this slurry wall dispute was a good example.

When Tom cancelled the presentation abruptly for July, Jim Hall contacted the aide to our US Congressman, John Moolenaar. Ashton Bortz had asked to be kept in the loop, but she didn't see what she could do at that time.

Finally, we got the presentation in September, so six months after we had asked for it.

The part of the wall for possible re-use would be the stretch from North Street to M-46, behind the houses on the west side of Watson Street. Plans called for drilling out samples from the wall and analyzing them, and also conducting a dye test to see if the wall leaked. That involved piezometers placed at intervals inside and outside of the old wall, introducing dye on the inside and if it reached the outside piezometer, the wall would be considered to be leaking. Prior investigations of groundwater seemed to show that the wall in that area was doing its job of holding groundwater from moving out of the plant site boundary. An assessment of the

163

findings would be made in April, 2020 to determine if more investigation was necessary.

We had planned to keep Jim Heinzman on as a technical consultant for the slurry wall concerns, but he was hospitalized with a serious blood infection, which later led to other physical problems. Jim Hall and I kept in touch with him and his wife, hoping he would improve enough to help us, but he didn't rally for a long time.

We contacted Scott Cornelius about the slurry wall and also the carbon experiment that was to take place on a plot of land downstream. He responded with a Standard Engagement Letter to take the place of the contract we had allowed to expire. Gary sent the letter on to the EPA for their approval, and that began another long, drawn out squabble about use of Technical Assistance Grant dollars.

At first it seemed straightforward. EPA objected to the late fee described in the letter and we contacted Scott and he agreed to remove it. Then we learned that Region 5 EPA had sent the letter to Washington, D.C. lawyers for their input. Tom Alcamo called me to say they wanted to know who our Technical Advisor was, Jim Heinzman or Scott Cornelius. I told him we had two TA's at present because they had different areas of expertise and that Jim was sick and his continuation with us was uncertain.

The other concern from D.C. was the disparity in wages: $80 an hour for Jim and $175 an hour for Scott. Tom said the highest paid EPA TASC person received $158 an hour. We didn't like the high price Scott charged any better than the folks in D.C. and I emailed the Executive Committee and suggested we try to wrangle Scott down to $130 or less.

Gary did some research and learned there were no wage caps for TAG advisors. He also reminded us of how much we had paid an earlier technical advisor, who charged us for lots of staff persons as well as for himself. Gary worried that EPA didn't want us to use Scott and was trying to find reasons for us to decide against using him, but in my phone conversation with Tom I hadn't heard any indication that he was trying to exclude Scott through technicalities. I also pointed out that neither Jim nor Scott had been fired by us. They had both taken breaks to do other things. In a sense they were still hired by us, although not with up-to-date contracts.

Six weeks later we received a written response from Region 5 EPA about Scott's Standard Engagement Letter, which enclosed many of the TAG guidelines and rules. Two days later we sent our response, addressing their concerns point by point, and also included our previous contract with Scott which had been approved by EPA, and which we said we were continuing. Four days later Tom Alcamo called to say that he thought all of the questions and concerns had been answered acceptably with our letter. Twenty-seven days later, however, we still did not have the necessary approval to allow Scott to work on our technical projects. Gary emailed Region 5 again, and we almost immediately received a letter asking for more precise delineation in Scott's letter about the sites and the agencies he would be dealing with as Technical Advisor. Gary drafted another response, and I edited it, but we didn't want to send it until he had clarified a question we had with the Region 5 personnel. It was summer by now, and people were out of the office, so the answer was a long time coming. On August 10th we emailed our letter of response to their July 31st letter, explaining that we were not trying to "duplicate efforts" by having two TA's on the same NPL site, but due to Jim's illness, we desired to have Scott do some things for us until Jim could return. And if Jim was unable to return, we would have someone in place to continue on with us.

We knew Tom Alcamo was planning a presentation at our Technical Committee meeting in August about the slurry wall investigation, and we were feeling a little desperate to have a technical advisor on board to listen to the presentation and educate us from his experience. Gary asked Scott if he was willing to attend the August meeting even though he wasn't yet officially on board with us, due to EPA's concern of whether or not we could have more than one technical advisor. We knew the guidelines for TAG grants allowed more than one advisor, and Gary, who practically had the guidelines memorized after doing the job for 20 years, had given EPA references to help them understand that what we were doing was acceptable.

Scott did attend the meeting, and about a week later, Tom Alcamo wrote to say Scott could start charging the grant, but said further clarification on his contract might be necessary.

During the slurry wall presentation, Tom explained that the information being gathered in this investigation was necessary for the groundwater treatment system whether or not parts of the slurry wall were re-used. Matt Baltusis from MDEQ, now re-named EGLE (Environment, Great Lakes and Energy) explained that most of the information gathered during the Remedial Investigation phase of the cleanup in the early and mid-2000s was for the downgradient section of the slurry wall that bordered the river. It was that investigation that had shown the gaps in the wall, and those gaps were in the downgradient portion of the slurry wall.

Chris Douglas from Weston Solutions, EGLE's contractor, then presented slides on the historical data from two earlier investigations (Memphis Environmental Center and Michigan Department of Environmental Quality) that gave some information for the upgradient section of the wall that bordered the neighborhood. A 1996 Memphis Environmental study concluded that the entire wall was working as intended, (MEC was a contractor for Velsicol), while the 2002 DEQ investigation concluded that most of the wall (the downgradient portion) was leaking into the groundwater and river, with the exception of a section that was now termed the upgradient slurry wall.

Scott Pratt, an employee of EPA's contractor Jacobs presented slides on 2016 data gathered about the upgradient section of the wall, and on the current plans for a more detailed study to find out if the wall was leaking at all. Samples of the wall would be drilled out and analyzed, and a new dye experiment would take place beginning in October and continuing through January. An assessment would take place in April 2020 to see if more investigation would be necessary. The long-term goal was to have the water level inside the plant site area lower than the level of the river. At present it was as much as 6.8 feet higher inside than out. A planned drain around the entire perimeter of the site would eventually channel water inside the plant site to the groundwater treatment facility to be built on site, but that was many years down the road.

At the same meeting we heard about the test plot in an OU-3 floodplain on N. Union Street where previously invertebrate and mammal toxicology had been studied by Dr. Matt Zwiernik of MSU. Granular activated carbon charcoal had been spread on the 45,000-square foot test plot at a rate of 2% by weight relative to the top inch of soil. Baseline sampling of soil and worms had taken place earlier, and the first post-amendment sampling event was scheduled for October 2019 with the second scheduled for May 2020. Three things were being evaluated with this experiment:

1. The method of application, including the amount of charcoal used.
2. The stability of the charcoal.
3. The effectiveness of the charcoal in reducing the availability of contaminants to invertebrates.

The experiment was designed to learn if carbon amendments could be used in floodplains in OU-4 (Madison Road downstream to the confluence with the Chippewa River) to significantly lower the bioavailability of DDT and PBB to earthworms. The floodplains further downstream in OU-4 were less contaminated than those nearer the dam.

Even before Jim Heinzman got sick, we had planned to assign Scott Cornelius to the cleanups planned for downstream of St. Louis. When Scott had been our MDEQ Project Manager for the Velsicol sites, he had the foresight to study soils and sediments downstream to determine the extent of contamination. He had found money to do some preliminary studies, including the sampling of insects and small mammals, and it was the result of those studies that had convinced EPA to take on the downstream portion of the river as operable units of the Velsicol Superfund site. At first the whole stretch of the Pine River from the dam in St. Louis to the confluence of the Pine and Chippewa rivers in Midland County had been termed OU-3. More recently, only the floodplains closer to town became OU-3, and the rest of the river and floodplains downstream had become OU-4.

We were all in favor of having Scott advise us about the carbon amendment study, but some of us were worried about his high fees. Tom Alcamo had told us that the funding for TAG grants was not assured forever, and that we were one of the few places that had a grant. We worried that the money could run out prior to our need for technical advisors coming to an end. In fact, Gary was involved during this time in a request for an extension to our current grant.

Since I had read several of the early scientific papers on carbon amendment experimentation, I suggested to the Executive Committee that Scott should read only the papers that covered the same kind of experiment as ours, and not the ones that took place in oceans and in other settings, as a way to limit the amount of money we would have to pay him. The board agreed that Gary should inform Scott which articles were approved for him to read. We also decided to start Scott off only on the carbon experiment and not have him plunge into slurry wall document reading. It was still our hope that Jim Heinzman would soon feel well enough to take on that responsibility.

At first Scott agreed to read only the designated papers, but later said he felt he needed to review all the documents EPA had read, even if they didn't directly apply to our type of experiment. He was not willing to do "an incomplete review." Gary sent us an email about Scott's reconsideration, and said, "Do we want a complete review and keep our TA or no review and likely lose TA?"

Hoping that Jim would be up to reading documents, I called his wife, Pat, and she told me that from the blood infection Jim had moved into a bad reaction to the antibiotic they had given him, which included liver abscesses and a loss of balance. With his vertigo, he was in no shape to be reading documents, and I didn't even bring that up with Pat.

As Scott began his review of documents for the carbon experiment, he also requested that he be allowed to take part in the October sampling event at the plot. We agreed to that, as did EPA, but the rains that autumn turned the floodplain into a swamp. Scott did take pictures of how the carbon previously applied to the surface pooled in low spots. It wasn't clear to us how worms and voles would take it up into their bodies with it being surface applied, and with the heavy rains, the carbon was no longer evenly distributed.

Another problem we encountered was a privacy issue. EPA would not share the baseline data with Scott because the experimental plot was located on private property. Scott went back into the investigation document that he had generated when he had been our MDEQ project manager and utilized background information from that.

He presented his preliminary findings to us, which raised many questions and concerns from CAG members. With those in mind, Scott wrote two sets of comments for EPA to respond to in writing. The first set had to do with the presently known facts, and the second set addressed what we might know when the data was in from the two sampling events planned by EPA. We sent the written comments to Tom Alcamo, asking to begin discussing them at our November Technical Committee meeting. Tom sent a terse email saying he and his staff didn't have time to respond, and "We are not going back to how things happened previously with Scott. He's not doing oversight." The words "overseeing" and "oversight" had become trigger words for EPA years earlier. The argument at the time made it clear that their understanding of the word was different from mine. My meaning was that our group of citizens monitored the work they did, but their meaning seemed to be that we had the authority to tell them what to do or what not to do.

Even though Tom later said several times that he would respond in writing to our comments, it did not happen in November or December of 2019, or in January and February of 2020. It is the middle of March as I write this, and we are still waiting.

As for TAG approval to pay Scott, that issue continued to drag on. Even though Tom had said Scott could start charging the grant, when his invoice was sent in by Gary, no funds showed up for Gary to draw from to write the check.

Gary raised the issue at our November CAG meeting, and the responses from Tom Alcamo and Diane Russell were heated and confusing.

Gary simply inquired why payment had not yet been deposited in the government account for paying a technical consultant. Diane Russell explained that all invoices now must be sent to TAG grant experts at EPA Headquarters in Washington, D.C. Payment was now made within 30 days of submission of the invoice. This was something new. We had not yet been informed of the 30-day pause. Previously, once the invoice was approved, the money moved electronically into an account where Gary could access it.

Gary also asked why our questions on the carbon amendment experiment had not been addressed. Diane questioned their source. Gary said they were questions and concerns from CAG members and also from our Technical Consultant. Tom said he had barely looked at the questions and has sent them to Headquarters, and if there are any issues, they would get back to us. That was confusing. Why in the world should the questions addressed to Tom need to be sent to Washington, D.C.? I asked that, and was told it was to see if the questions were appropriate or not. I again asked why, as did Gary, and Tom said we were being paranoid. Jim Hall, as chairperson, shut down the discussion and we moved on.

The next day Jim called Ashton Bortz, aide to our US Congressman John Moolenaar. After they had talked, Ashton called me and I tried my best to explain the dialogue exchange, although I had found it confusing. Later, Ashton told me that she had contacted the congressional intergovernmental liaison after the meeting, who then brought Tom into the call.

Ashton related that during the call she had told Tom that the Technical Committee meetings should be held regularly to air these questions in a non-public setting. Tom told her he only attended those meetings if there was something to talk about. Ashton suggested to him that with the heating of Area 2 going on and the carbon study it seemed to her that there was much to talk about. Tom replied that her view was noted. We had last held a Technical Committee meeting in August 2019. It is now March, 2020, and still no meeting.

The day following Ashton's phone conversation with Tom and the liaison, we received a letter from Denise Boone at Region 5 EPA saying they had reviewed our "Comments/Questions" on the carbon experiment which led to their own concerns. The letter said, "The intent of the TAG is for community groups to receive assistance from a technical advisor so community members can understand and more effectively comment on site technical information and decisions…It is PRSCTF's role to submit their comments to EPA."

In our minds, this situation was linked once again to Diane Russell's determination to show that CAG members did not represent the wider community. Despite us explaining that dozens of community members regularly thanked us for being on the firing line, and channeling their questions and concerns through us to the agencies, Diane maintained that since others in the community at large did not take the time to attend CAG meetings, it meant that we didn't represent the community. She was wrong, but failed to accept our explanations.

The letter also failed to distinguish between the two sets of questions we had submitted. Our cover letter had made it clear that we knew the second set of questions could not be answered until all the data was in, and that we wished to begin the discussion with the first set of questions for which there was sufficient data.

In our letter of response, we pointed this out, and commented that Tom Alcamo had said at our meeting that he had "barely looked at the questions" before sending them to Headquarters. As always our response was polite. We said, "We apologize for the confusion it may have caused by sending both sets of questions now. We think this confusion led to your comments regarding an inability for EPA to respond to questions before an outcome of the experiment is obtained, and also to your assessment that we are paying our technical consultant for costs that have not yet occurred. To remedy this confusion, we would advise the project manager to consider at this time only those questions listed in the first section."

Finally, their letter stated that they would not pay for one hour of time billed on Scott's invoice ($175) because it was spent in reviewing internet articles on earthworm behavior. They stated, "TAG technical advisors should possess a demonstrated knowledge of the hazardous or toxic waste issues, academic training in a relevant discipline, and the ability to translate technical information into terms your community can understand at the time they are contracted. TAG funds cannot be used to reimburse an advisor to acquire this technical knowledge or training." Does the phrase "straining at a gnat" fit here?

In our response we defended our technical advisor's academic and experiential background in biology, including earthworms. We went on to say, "If there is a specific Technical Assistance Grant guideline that prohibits a technical consultant from charging for this time to research a reliable source of information on a study's target organism, please point it out to us."

We asked them to reverse their decision about the $175 payment. They refused. Gary found out about a dispute process, and we began that in December 2019. Trust me, we were not doing this because it was fun.

As for a follow-up bird study in the neighborhood, we contacted EGLE over and over, and wrote a letter to the new EGLE director (no reply) requesting a study. Even though David Kline at EGLE sounded willing, our EGLE project manager later said his agency would not do one until the newly planted trees in the neighborhood had matured. That meant in about 30 years! Good grief.

Our EGLE project manager, Matt Baltusis attended only three of our monthly CAG meetings in 2018, and about as many in 2019. The three big issues that we needed him to follow through on (bird study, railroad spur, and Seville Township dump) received very little attention from him. As the PFAS issue became a priority with EGLE, Matt spent most of his time on that. Early in 2020 he sent us an email that we would be receiving a new EGLE project manager for the Velsicol Plant Site and Burn Pit Site. We once again hoped for the best.

Near the end of the year, Jim Hall learned that his job was taking him north into Oscoda County, and he and his wife would be moving there. It was time for our biennial elections, and I was voted in again as chairperson. I had encouraged a newer member, Brittany Fremion, to run for Secretary, and she was elected to that office. Brittany was a history professor at Central Michigan University, and with grant money had initiated an oral history project that collected interviews of people who had lived through the PBB Disaster. We were grateful for her expertise, and her youth!

Chapter 11
(2020)
Extracting DNAPL

Despite the pandemic, the extraction wells in the plant site continued their purpose of bringing to the surface heated DNAPL in both liquid and vapor form, and the on-site treatment facilities continued their purposes of separating out the contaminants and returning steam to the air, and water to the Pine River.

Thankfully, our EPA Project Manager, Tom Alcamo, had both a contract in place with the thermal company, Cascade, and money set aside to continue this work, even as the world shut down most of its activities to prevent the spread of the coronavirus, named COVID 19. There was worry that the contracted workers at the plant site would be sent home and the whole system would not be monitored, or even, perhaps, the heating, extracting, collecting and transporting would have to shut down.

I had called Tom about these worries, and he said because the heating process was automated, monitoring could be done remotely and from a distance. As for the main contractor on site, Jacobs was keeping two people working daily. Both were housed in motels in Mt. Pleasant (about 15 miles north of St. Louis). If those hotels closed due to the pandemic, and the workers were sent home, we were fortunate that another Jacobs employee lived in St. Louis, and could take over the basic jobs of the other two workers.

The suppliers, such as those who brought in new carbon filters, were continuing in business at present, but, Tom said, if the truckers quit delivering, then the whole process of heating and treating would cease.

Our CAG had met monthly for 21 years, with only three times calling off a meeting. In the year of the pandemic, we met in January, and not again until July, and then it was not face-to-face, but via Zoom.

To back up, though, our fourth occurrence of skipping a monthly meeting happened in February, before the coronavirus hit. The meeting was cancelled because some of our Executive Committee were speakers and the rest were registered to attend, a large event at the University of Michigan in Ann Arbor, entitled "From PBB to PFAS: Research and Action to Address Michigan's Large Scale Chemical Contaminants.

I gave a joint PowerPoint presentation along with Dr. Michele Marcus, the PBB researcher from Emory University, about the importance of the community's involvement in scientific studies regarding their wellbeing. I spoke about our CAG's years of difficulty in procuring a comprehensive health study for our residents, followed by Michele who spoke about her research, emphasizing the value of the community's input into the subject and design of her studies.

CAG Vice-Chairperson Ed Lorenz sat on a panel that discussed the lessons learned from how the state agencies had handled the PBB Disaster, with our newest CAG member and Secretary, Brittany Fremion, serving as facilitator of that panel. Tim Neyer, from the PBB Citizens Advisory Board (CAB), spoke about his growing up years on a contaminated and quarantined farm. CAG member Marcus Cheatham, interacted with poster viewers who had questions about the poster from our PBB Leadership Team. CAG member JoAnne Scalf displayed a poster about her volunteer health mapping project of past and present St. Louis residents.

The keynote speaker was Dr. Linda Birnbaum, the former director of the National Institute of Environmental Health Sciences and the National Toxicology Program. I had met her at a previous NIEHS conference in North Carolina, and found her to be a dynamic speaker with a wealth of knowledge to share about the health effects of exposure to fire retardant chemicals. She was a definite draw for this conference in Ann Arbor, and the meetings were full to overflowing. Portions of the program were broadcast live to Central Michigan University and Alma College, with both learning institutions serving as sponsors of the event, along with the University of Michigan. CAG board member, Wayne Brooks, facilitated the showing and discussion at Alma College.

Later that same week, an in-person full group PBB Partnership meeting was held, and it was the last encounter we had with the researchers and each other for the rest of 2020, due to the pandemic. The PBB Leadership Team continued monthly telephone conversations, but all community meetings and appointments for participants in the clinical trial ceased. Emory University suspended all research laboratory work as non-essential. This was another costly blow to the clinical trial studying a substance that animal studies had shown would help the body eliminate PBB, DDT and other like chemical compounds. Great efforts were made by two of the PBB CAB members (Terri Fountain and Bonnie Havlicek) who were nurses, to meet privately with people in the trial to keep their data current for the study. They wore full protective gear, and the Mid-Michigan District Health Department allowed them to use their closed facility in St. Johns.

After much effort by Melanie Pearson and others at Emory, two virtual community meetings were arranged to discuss the recent health findings and give updates on the PBB research. The meetings were very well attended, with 70 % of the people indicating that they were first time attendees, and 95% of the attendees indicating that they were interested in participating in research. Following the meeting, 176 people completed the survey forms, which would later yield possible participants for the current studies, namely, the clinical trial, the three-generation study, and the comprehensive health study.

As for the PBB Records, we continued our pursuit to acquire access to them from the state health department (MDHHS) for family members of people in the original 1970s study. Emory researchers Michele and Melanie reported that they had yet another meeting planned with the state health department personnel in March, but once again COVID 19 intervened and the meeting did not take place.

In March before the shutdown of everything in Michigan, I met with Marcus Cheatham, health officer for our local district health department, and Norm Keon, epidemiologist for several county health departments and who also had worked for the state health department at the time the new public health code was being written. We discussed strategy for utilizing the statement we had acquired earlier from the attorney for Michigan's local health departments that supported what Norm had been saying for years – that the public health code allowed local health departments open access to records, which would include the PBB records from the original study. Again, COVID 19 severely postponed any forward progress in this area, with all public health workers putting in hours and days of overtime due to the pandemic, including Marcus and Norm.

Finally, in October Michele and Melanie were able to meet virtually with Sarah Lyon-Callo, epidemiologist at the state health department. According to Michele, Sarah maintained that the only way vital status updates or the cancer update could go forward was to use temporary IDs that would be destroyed after a short amount of time. Michele was able to help her see that the same IDs were necessary to match mortality data *and* cancer data. She refused to allow Michele to speak directly with the attorney that had drafted the latest Grant of Authority between MDHHS and their semi-private contractor, MPHI.

Michele and her staff crafted a one-page document that made three points: 1) the cancer and mortality data needed to have the same ID numbers and it was only the withdrawn participants that needed new IDs; 2) the PBB Registry was originally set up for the purpose of surveillance, specifically for cancer; 3) the 2018 revised guidelines from the U.S. Department of Health and Human Services made it clear that a portion of a research project could be carved out as surveillance under the state's public health authority.

Norm Keon had been working to acquire documents from the era of the PBB Disaster, contacting various people who had actively participated, from veterinarians to employees of the state health department. One of his recent acquisitions had yielded a document that spelled out the purposes of the 1978 original State of Michigan long-term study of people exposed to PBB, connecting it clearly to possible cancer outcomes.

Both Michele's three-point document and Norm's old document were submitted to the head of Institutional Review Board (IRB) at MDHHS. An IRB is a committee established to review and approve applications for research projects involving human subjects to protect their rights and welfare. After a study of the documents, the head of the IRB sent the Grant of Authority document between MDHHS and MPHI back for a rewrite. This sounded like good news to us.

Meanwhile, with help from Michele, I had crafted a letter to our state senators, Rick Outman and Winnie Brinks, regarding the ID numbers and the necessity for the ability to link data from the PBB participants to both the cancer index and the mortality index. It also pointed out the distinction between "research" and "public health surveillance" as defined in the new federal guidelines. And it emphasized that the original purpose of the 1978 PBB study was to determine the connection between PBB exposure and cancer outcomes.

We don't know for sure, but we think a phone call to MDHHS from the senators may have taken place, aiding MDHHS's decision to seek a rewrite of the Grant of Authority. We base this on an email from an MDHHS employee who mentioned that "upper management" was involved in the decision to send the document back to the lawyers for a rewrite.

Once again, we observed among ourselves the deleterious impacts of having lawyers making decisions about public health. Our local health officer, Marcus Cheatham, wrote: "An overarching part of this story is that otherwise nice people in our government (I'm part of government) permitted and even defended Michigan Chemical's pollution, then permitted the failed clean-up, and now continue to block research into what happened. Time passes but we seem stuck in roles and unable to see a way out." And our CAG vice-chair, Ed Lorenz wrote: "Having worked in government with many wonderful, dedicated people who went out of their way to help meet human needs, it is frustrating when we encounter the use of regulations that are clearly open to varied interpretation used to block assistance that clearly is in the public interest."

There was one more indication that our years of effort to convince MDHHS to be helpful to survivors of the PBB legacy were bearing fruit. At the end of 2020, we learned that the state health department planned to launch a page about PBB on their website. In addition to information, the site offered links to the Michigan PBB Registry at Emory University, and amazingly, offered a bureaucratic way for family members to access the PBB data of their deceased relatives. Finally.

We took some credit for this excellent outcome. Our continuing work to keep the PBB legacy from being forgotten, which had included many letters, face-to-face talks with MDHHS personnel, and with our legislators in Lansing, had brought this about, even if the powers to be never acknowledged that fact.

After no meetings in March, April, May or June due to the shutdown of Michigan society by Governor Gretchen Whitmer, our CAG held its first on-line Zoom meetings in July. Our secretary,

Brittany Fremion, sent us directions of how to download the program, and then she hosted our meetings.

The Executive Committee, comprised of our elected officers and directors, met first about a number of issues, with the most pressing being our concern about what actions to take in regard to the excessive amount of DNAPL being drawn from Area 2, Phase 1 of the plant site thermal treatment process. A prediction by our project manager had been for about 50,000 pounds, and by mid-June over 100,000 pounds had been settled out from the groundwater extracted. Later, when the heat was shut off on September 14, over 182,998 pounds of contaminants had been drawn up and trucked to an EPA-licensed incinerator in El Dorado, Arkansas. The heating and treating had required 12 megawatt hours of electricity.

We decided to ask our paid Technical Advisor, Scott Cornelius to review the 2006 RI (Remedial Investigation report) and more recent EPA documents in regards to DNAPL source areas on the plant site, and then report to us in a Zoom meeting prior to our CAG meeting with EPA in mid-July. Even though we were glad DNAPL was being captured and dealt with, we were concerned that it might indicate a much wider area of contamination underground than what EPA planned to treat with heat. We knew that the RI document had laid out a much larger area to be treated than what EPA had shrunk it down to.

Scott explained to us that MDEQ (now EGLE) had used a geometric method to determine treatment volume, while EPA used modeling software to refine the treatment area. He suspected that not enough information was available to enter into the EPA's model for it to make an accurate estimate. EPA further characterized the site using a point assessment approach, which gave visual detection 10,000 points; DNAPL test kit detection 1,000 points; and the Csat test detection 100 points. Scott questioned the low point assignment given to the Csat test, a method regularly used by industry in similar investigations. The Csat calculation determines the porosity of soil and the viscosity of the DNAPL, indicating the soil's capacity to hold liquid DNAPL.

Later I contacted our still unwell former Technical Advisor, Jim Heinzman, and he agreed that the low points allowed for the Csat test likely changed the ratios and subsequently shrank the remediation areas, causing other sources of liquid DNAPL to be missed. He also pointed out that the borings EPA made prior to remedy selection were spaced 100 to 150 feet apart. If a winding gravel area existed between borings, it could serve as a conduit from one area to another, with DNAPL pulled through it. This could also explain why the DNAPL looked different, as Tom Alcamo had told us, and why it weighed so much, if it was actually from another source of DNAPL located underground and connected to the heating area via a gravelly conduit. The DNAPL they were now collecting weighed 17 pounds a gallon as compared to a gallon of water at 8 pounds.

In our discussion with EPA staff at our July Zoom meeting, we were told that underestimation of DNAPL is usual, and the borings helped them define the right spot, and that the heating was specifically targeted and would not heat to liquefaction DNAPL located in a different area. We were also told they suspected a dip in the till unit below the heating area that led to pooling of DNAPL in that area, which would account for so much more being drawn up. In July, they had expected to fill and send four tanker trucks of DNAPL to the incinerator in Arkansas, and now the number of trucks needed had risen to twelve.

Our Executive Committee decided a letter about this issue should be sent to EPA, with copies sent also to our state and federal legislative representatives, and we did that. The detailed comments with which EPA responded helped ease our concerns, and we agreed with Tom that an approximately seven-foot dip in the underlying clay layer allowed a pooling of DNAPL, with the dip occurring between the original borings.

Even though the contract with Cascade had ended on July 7, EPA was paying them to continue the heating process to bring up as much DNAPL as possible from the area. Tom estimated that the thermal process in Area 2 alone would cost EPA (us taxpayers) close to $50 million.

Also included in our discussion at the meeting was the possible migration of contaminants into the Pine River from the west side of the site, where no collector infrastructure had been built. When asked directly if the site was still contaminating the river, Tom Alcamo said it likely was. The EPA Community Involvement Coordinator, Diane Russell spoke up and said that if monitoring showed a problem, an emergency removal action would take place. When asked what sampling or monitoring EPA was now conducting in the location, we were told none.

Our Executive Committee decided to request an Emergency Removal Action for the west side of the former Velsicol plant site, reminding the acting director of the ERA Superfund Division that we had been voicing our concerns about the recontamination of the riverbed since 2006, when the sediment removal project from the river had ended. Included in the information given to us about the extraction of DNAPL from Area 2, Phase 1 was that the pressure of water built up under the 1980s-installed clay cap was helping to push DNAPL to the heating area. When Gary Smith suggested that the same head of pressure was likely pushing DNAPL to other areas of the site and out into the river, Tom Alcamo did not disagree.

Our letter contained two requests: 1) that monthly sampling of river sediment, river water, and groundwater begin immediately on the west side of the site; 2) that an Emergency Removal Action take place to bring a halt to the ongoing migration of DNAPL from other areas of the plant site to the river.

The response from EPA was a classic example of science-speak mixed with information we already knew well, since we had lived it. Only one bullet point made sense to me: that the completion of the *in situ* thermal treatment in Area 1 effectively eliminated a source of DNAPL on that side of the site that could enter into the groundwater and river. Essentially, the answer to our request was no, an ERA would not take place on the west side of the site, and nothing was said about beginning monthly sampling and monitoring.

During that first Zoom CAG meeting in July, we received some good news about the railroad spur. For years we had been trying to get EPA or EGLE to sample the soil where the train tracks had run, and where carloads of chemical compounds coming to or from Michigan Chemical/Velsicol had been emptied or filled. EPA had refused, saying it wasn't their job to initiate a new investigation. We had argued that it was not new, but part of the ongoing Velsicol Superfund cleanup. EGLE staff had contributed old photographs showing the location of the railroad spur, which matched what we had described, but no further action had been taken.

Just before COVID 19 had led to the first state-wide shutdown, we learned that EGLE was providing us with a different project manager. I "met" him on the phone in early March, and finally saw his face at our Zoom CAG meeting in July.

In our phone conversation I had told Erik Martinson about both the railroad spur and the follow-up dead bird study we wished to have completed. As for the bird study, he reported at our meeting that EGLE was still evaluating both the dead bird and nesting success studies. The railroad spur, however, had seen some progress with access to private properties being sought, including the property owned now by Mid-Michigan Railroad. If access was gained, EGLE planned to do 60 five-foot borings along the former path of the tracks, hoping to begin soon.

We were relieved to hear that progress had been made, yet worried that the railroad company would slow down the plans, as it had in the past. As we suspected, they failed to understand the need for the sampling and were reluctant to give EGLE access. Despite that, Erik had a RR Spur Investigation Scope of Work drawn up, and he acquired access to three of the other four private properties on which the spur used to run. By the end of 2020, Erik and his staff were still trying to work with the railroad on their misunderstandings, and had submitted the required paperwork and paid the fees that Mid-Michigan Railroad charged. Now Erik had hopes of doing the borings in the spring of 2021.

Ever since EPA had refused to pay for one hour of our Technical Advisor's time for an internet article search on worms, our treasurer, Gary Smith, had been persevering through a formal dispute process to gain payment. EPA lawyers essentially said Technical Advisors should already know everything there is to know and if they have to look things up, it is considered to be new training, which Technical Assistance Grants do not pay for.

With the earthworm as the target organism in the Carbon Amendment Experiment EPA was conducting on a downstream floodplain, we in the CAG were glad Scott had reviewed earthworm behavior in preparation for his comments on the experiment.

In an email Gary was told that the Agency Decision to not pay was sent to the Action Official who sent it to the Affected Entity informing of their right to appeal the Agency Decision with the Disputes Decision Official. Their capital letters. Bureaucracy at its best.

As the Affected Entity, we later received word that the Action Official had upheld the Agency Decision to not pay for the one hour of work.

Jim Hall asked in an email: "How much money did they waste to make this decision...And did Scott train or research? Bunch of bull."

It was time for the Affected Entity to appeal to the Disputes Decision Official.

Gary drafted an excellent three-page response with citations from the TAG grant program. We ran it by Ashton Bortz, legislative aide to our U.S. Congressman, John Moolenaar, as she had asked to be kept in the loop. She had no changes to recommend to the letter.

The Disputes Decision Official wrote to say we had not sent relevant documents. Of course we had. Obviously, one of the other bureaucrats/attorneys had not passed them along. Once this problem was cleared up, the decision remained the same: No TAG dollars for the online research of the targeted organism of the study. We had long ago paid Scott out of our own money, and we were glad it was only one hour of his time in dispute.

As for the Carbon Experiment downstream, we remained skeptical of its efficacy. The previous fall our Technical Advisor, Scott Cornelius, had accompanied Tom Alcamo and others to view the flood plain after heavy rains, and the surface-applied carbon had washed and pooled into heavy concentrations in the low spots. Our concerns as community members, with the addition of more scientific and technical concerns expressed by our Technical Advisor, were collected by him into formal comments for submission to EPA at the end of October, 2019. As of March, 2020, we still had received no response, and we wrote a letter expressing our view that four and a half months was an unacceptable length of time for the community to be kept waiting for answers. The letter went on to say: "Many times over, responses from your agency have been delayed until there is no time for input from the community. That appears to be happening again. With the final sampling event scheduled for April 2020, next month, it appears that your delay in addressing our questions and concerns, whether verbally or in writing, is designed to box us out of the decision-making process that is required of your agency in working with a Community Advisory Group." The letter was copied to our state and federal legislators and to staff members at EGLE.

Tom finally responded in March to the comments, and within them was information that was new to us, especially that a second phase of the experiment was likely going to be needed. That addressed one of our biggest concerns – that if the initial experiment had shown positive results, EPA would forge ahead using only the carbon to treat the flood plains --because the carbon did not address all the chemicals in the soil, which included PAHs and bis(2-ethylhexyl)pththalate with elevated hazard quotients, it meant that even though the carbon might successfully sequester DDT (in all its forms) from moving up the food chain in wildlife, the other chemicals would remain and be fully accessible.

In the view of Scott, many of the EPA responses failed to answer the question that was being asked. Because of that, and because of the new information EPA had interwoven in their responses, Scott decided to write a second round of comments.

In earlier years, Tom Alcamo, Diane Russell, and regional TAG staff had strenuously upbraided us for submitting comments to them that they felt were not generated by CAG members, and only by our Technical Advisor. Prior to their criticism, the CAG Executive Committee would discuss our concerns with our Technical Advisor and listen to his more technical concerns, and then would pay the Technical Advisor to write the comments in his style. In recent years EPA had found fault with this, saying the comments were not truly from CAG members. So this time around, I re-wrote in a less scientific style all of the questions, concerns, and comments that Scott had already written. I condensed his seven pages of comments into five, wrote a cover letter, and emailed it all to Tom Alcamo. And I also resolved to never again use my volunteer hours in that manner.

Then Scott wrote a third round of comments. In a phone call, Gary and I agreed that we should wait and submit these comments after the first phase of the experiment was completed. The rest of the Executive Committee concurred. Instead we used some of the information from the comments in our July CAG meeting on Zoom, and we also, at that time, made arrangements for Scott to participate in a conference call with EPA personnel. At that meeting, Scott received the baseline data for the plot of ground where the

186

experiment was underway, data we had been requesting for over a year. One thing the data verified was that the total DDT concentration that exceeded 5 ppm extended to a depth of at least 1.1 feet, far below the surface of the soil where the carbon had been spread. That alone left us skeptical about the efficacy of the proposed remedy.

In addition to his work on the Worm Dispute, Gary put in a lot of hours sorting out the TAG grant for the Velsicol Burn Pit. A few years prior I had learned from the EPA website under the guidelines for Technical Assistance grants that each of our Superfund sites could have its own TAG grant. With that information, we had pursued and acquired a TAG grant for the Burn Pit. At the time, we had expected to be well into the remediation of the site by 2020.

Because vast amounts of electricity are needed for the *in situ* thermal treatment process, calculations showed the Burn Pit would have to wait its turn. There was enough power to heat Area 1 on the plant site all at once, but not for Area 2, which had been split into two phases. At present, Phase 1 of Area 2 was still underway, even though it was supposed to have ended on July 7. It was the excessive amount of DNAPL and other contaminants still being heated and drawn up which caused the schedule to change. Installation of heating elements and extraction wells was well underway in the Phase 2 section of Area 2, readying it for the application of electricity once the first phase was completed. After Area 2, Phase 2 of the plant site, the Burn Pit was next on the list.

Gary had applied for an extension of the TAG grant for the Burn Pit, and was told that he had not sent the proper documents. Of course he had. Once again, a retiring EPA person had not passed on the submitted documents to the new person. They were found, which meant Gary didn't have to reassemble them and re-send.

Gary had compiled a timeline of all the back and forth which had lasted for over four months in seeking the extension of the Burn

Pit grant, and as usual, he had jumped through every hoop, some more than once. How do other small groups of volunteers cope with such ineptitude at the federal level? I am so grateful that we have smart and dedicated CAG members who are willing to persevere with the bureaucratic shenanigans presented to us.

One aspect of existing so long (22 years so far) was acclimating to new people hired at the agencies, with some of the former personnel moving on to other jobs and some retiring.

At Alma College, both the archivist librarian and the head librarian retired in early 2020. Their retirements, along with the intentions of the college to make significant alterations in the college library, raised some doubts for us about our decades-worth of documents stored there. Added to these concerns was the shutdown of the campus during the pandemic and the subsequent cuts in services. Already the Alma Symphony Orchestra, which the college had supported, had been permanently disbanded. Would the college even want our documents stored in the library basement anymore, or would they be tossed?

Years ago the Clarke Historical Library in Mt. Pleasant had written to our CAG, requesting the privilege of archiving our materials. At the time we had three professors from Alma College on the Executive Committee, and they preferred that we ask Alma College to archive the materials, and so that's what we did. We had been told (although it was not in writing) that the college would acquire software which would enable the organization and accessibility of the documents. That never took place.

The person who had done the most work on the project in the library basement was Ed Lorenz, both on his own, and in encouraging librarian Viki Everhart to get involved. Brittany Fremion also encouraged Viki, and connected her with an archivist from Clarke Historical Library who taught her archival theory and methods. That resulted in better organization of the documents.

Brittany, a historian, and the driving force behind the PBB Oral History Project, said it was important to her to see our materials preserved in the best way possible. She had worked with Norm Keon to get Alpha "Doc" Clark's PBB veterinary files preserved at the Clarke library, and was also helping Norm sort through other acquired documents from that era. She now set up a dialogue about the CAG papers between me and Marian Matyn, an archivist employed by the historical library, which is housed on the campus of Central Michigan University.

Marian asked if we had already consigned the rights to the documents to Alma College, or had anyone of us signed a donor form? I searched my files, asked Ed and Murray Borrello to search theirs, and finally, spoke with the president of Alma College to have his staff search to see if we had signed anything. Nothing was discovered. The only document was a brief 2003 letter from a former president of Alma College that said her letter was an "indication of our interest in serving as the formal repository of the archives of your work."

Complicating the issue was Ed's strong desire to keep the documents close by, without having them in his house. I understood his view, yet, as I expressed to him and the rest of the Executive Committee, it seemed to be time to find a permanent home for the papers, now that most of us were in the final stretches of our lives. Even the two younger members of our board wanted to see the CAG documents go to the Clarke.

In the midst of this, both Ed and I remembered that in 2011 the MDEQ project manager had borrowed the boxes of papers from both of us and also Murray Borrello and had them scanned and loaded onto a disc. Well, at least that is what we thought. Both Murray and I remembered having been given copies of the disc. I found mine, and realized that the only documents on it were the ones I had loaned. I assumed Murray's disc contained only the ones he had loaned, and the same for Ed. Neither of them could find their discs.

Brittany began to check websites, such as the Archives of Michigan and MDEQ (now EGLE) to see if the scanned documents were available on line. Her search took her to our new EGLE project manager, Erik Martinson. Ultimately, he was able to send us a link to the documents that had been scanned years before. I had already donated my documents from that era to the Clarke.

Also, our Executive Committee unanimously (even Ed!) voted in favor of a motion to deposit any future documents and records in the Clarke Historical Library. "Future" started at the date of the vote. That left a gap. The documents that had been scanned by the state covered from the time of our founding through 2011. For the documents from 2012 to 2020 there was no decision as yet. Even though I was not the chairperson from 2014-2019, Jim Hall, as chair, had shared every document with me, and, because I had been secretary in those years, I generated most of the letters. It seemed that I alone could fill in the gap pretty thoroughly, if Ed wasn't willing to share the documents he had collected.

As another of his projects, Ed began a reworking of our website. Being confined during the pandemic gave him the time and impetus to tackle the huge project. Helping him were Brittany and our indispensable IT guy, Matt Ogle. Matt had spruced the website up after it had been hacked and virtually destroyed years before, and he uploaded whatever was sent to him, to keep it current. Ed, however, was needed to sort the hundreds of documents into categories and reload many of the photos that had been lost.

Ed was able to recover many long lost webpages using the online Wayback Machine. He began re-writing content and adding links to enable online research among the documents. At the same time, Brittany had lined up a person who could build from code an entirely new website for us, but when Matt reviewed the plan, he saw issues with its long-term access and functionality, as well as security if plug-ins were used. He said it would be very hard to add content, which was crucial to our ongoing projects. We decided to continue on with Ed's renovation of the current site, as he expanded categories and organized information. He sent copies of various sections as he worked on them, and they were, of course, top notch.

When it came time to elect a new person to the CAG Hall of Fame, Ed's name was nominated, along with several others. As the votes came in, there was a three-way tie among Ed, and two other long-time members of the CAG: Bernie Bessert and Norm Keon. We, however, ran into a complication. First Ed, and then Norm, said they preferred to wait for the award after they were deceased.

The award is given to individuals who have given time and talent to the restoration of the Pine River and adjacent land to help ensure a safe and healthy environment for current and future generations. All of the nominees, both living and dead, certainly deserved the award.

Ed's email about declining had gone out to the list of dues-paying members, and CAG member JoAnne Scalf wrote a heartfelt email to Ed and Norm asking them to please "accept your fate as icons in the role of CAG volunteers," adding that she would like to see all the founding members of the CAG "in the Hall of Fame before we close up shop!"

Norm emailed later that he and Ed had "conducted a 'high level' discussion and have decided to not withdraw. We are pleased to be in each other's company on this – and don't want to act like we don't appreciate the group!"

Due to the pandemic, we could not hold our annual Christmas Potluck, to which family members of the Hall of Fame winners are invited and the awards given. Instead I traveled to each of the recipients with his plaque and took his photo for the newspapers.

Back to the clean-up: EPA had conducted a dye test of the slurry wall built during the first cleanup in the 1980s. The test was to show if the wall was leaking, and their plan was to re-use it if it was sound. The dye test had occurred in October, and we were still awaiting the results in April. Finally, on August 31st, in response to our requests for an update, Diane Russell sent an email that mentioned "a small section where the bottom of the wall doesn't completely connect to the clay layer and groundwater can flow through."

We scheduled a presentation to the membership on this issue for our October CAG meeting, and concern was expressed about the breach in the retaining wall, which had allowed contaminated groundwater to leak into the neighborhood of residential homes. The hole in the wall was not new, but had been there since the wall was (inadequately) built in the early 1980s. And it wasn't small, but instead 20 to 30 feet wide.

The ROD (Record of Decision) for the Velsicol Site had called for a new interlocking sheet pile wall around the entire 52-acres, which included frontage on the Pine River and also the adjacent neighborhood. In the discussion at the Zoom meeting, we emphasized to EPA that it was the community's preference for the entire perimeter to be encircled with the new wall, rather than using any portion of the slurry wall, which had been shown many times to have large breaches.

Our Executive Committee followed up with a letter to Tom Alcamo at Region 5 in Chicago, reminding him that the CAG had voiced its concern for more than a year about possible re-use of the old slurry wall. The letter again said the community acceptance in 2012 of the ROD was partly based on the construction of a new containment wall around the entire former plant site.

We sent the letter, along with the comments on the slurry wall investigation written by our paid technical advisor, Cornelius Environmental Consulting. The response from EPA, received in January, 2021, said: "EPA is aware of the Pine River Superfund Citizens [sic] Task Force opposition to the slurry wall investigation…" and went on to say that the ROD was not a binding contract with the community.

Really. We had thought it was, but seeing that EPA didn't hold themselves to it was not a surprise. Thinking back to their contract with EGLE, in which they agreed to alert them in 24 hours if any of the discharged water into the Pine River had visible or odorous changes, we remembered they had violated that contract as well. EGLE would not have known about the violation if citizens hadn't alerted them weeks after the milky, odorous discharge had been flowing into the river. Over the course of our history with EPA, there had been numerous examples of the agency's cutting corners to spend less money, rather than doing the best job possible with currently available technology. I found it disheartening.

I think it factored into my decision during 2020 to spend only three more years working with the CAG. That would give me three more years to chronicle our history, and then I could let someone else take my place.

Chapter 12
(2021)
Working the Railroad

When EGLE's new project manager was assigned to us in 2020, we had again asked to have the railroad beds sampled for contaminants where tracks had led into and out of the Velsicol plant site. Many of us remembered how freight cars and tankers would remain parked on the sidings for days or weeks, and suspected leakage into the soil.

The tracks had run through residential areas and also an area where a low-income housing facility now stood. In our view, the transportation of chemicals via rail created the same need for sampling as transportation via truck, which EPA had performed in the 12-block neighborhood previously, followed by excavation of yards to rid them of DDT and PBB contaminated soil.

As mentioned previously, once Erik Martinson came on board as the EGLE project manager, he agreed right away to tackle the project, and his contractor, Weston Solutions, drew up a work plan.

A hold-up on moving forward came when the railroad company would not sign the access agreement form sent to them by the State of Michigan. I asked Erik if a few of us from the Executive Committee could give input on what to do next, and Erik agreed. A Zoom meeting included the two of us, Chris Douglas from Weston, and three of our CAG members who had grown up in St. Louis: Jim Hall, Norm Keon and Gary Smith. Our Technical Advisor, Scott Cornelius, was also invited to be on the call.

Previously, Scott had requested the CAG to hire him to review the rail sampling work plan, when it became available, even though EPA had told us the railroad areas were not part of the Velsicol site, meaning we could not use the Technical Assistance Grant as a source of payment for the Technical Advisor. For his time spent on the one-hour phone call, we had agreed to pay Scott out of our Oxford settlement funds.

During the phone call, Erik reviewed with us his efforts to get an access agreement signed by the Mid-Michigan Railroad, whose corporate offices were in Jacksonville, Florida. The responses from the railroad's legal department showed ignorance of the area and the project by asking for such things as a lineman on the railroad tracks to flag down trains, even though the EGLE legal department had explained to them that no trains traveled through there because the tracks had been torn up decades ago. Jim Hall encouraged Erik to utilize help from our U.S. Congressman John Moolenaar in contacting the Federal Railroad Administration to act as a go-between. Both Norm and Gary suggested to Erik that the sampling begin on the property not owned by the railroad, but by residents and the Custodial Trust of the Velsicol site, so that the project could start. Scott suggested Erik get the state attorney general's office involved.

Erik did contact Ashton Bortz, aide to Congressman John Moolenaar, and Erik reported to us that it appeared that access to the railroad property would be forthcoming. On the strength of that information, I wrote a press release for our local media outlets about the success after all these years of getting a cleanup of the railroad bed The area would be sampled for TRIS, PBB, HBB and pesticides, including all six isomers of DDT. Both local newspapers and a local radio station reported the good news, and Mayor Jim Kelly of St. Louis wrote to congratulate us, and to reminisce about his younger years of growing up near the tracks in the 1940s and early 1950s.

Our celebration was too soon, however. Erik called to say that once again the access agreement sent to him by the railroad was unacceptable. Of the 27 clauses listed, half were impossible for the State of Michigan to meet, including payment of another $6,500 on top of the $7,000 that EGLE had already paid them, and with no guarantee of access.

Once again, our Technical Advisor proposed that we pay him to get involved, saying "If you want this railroad investigation to be conducted, task CEC (Cornelius Environmental Consulting) to make it happen and provide 7 hours of funding." Scott said he had contacts inside EGLE and the Michigan Department of the Attorney General that could cut through the difficulties and force the railroad to give access through a court order.

Meanwhile, Erik had met with the state property specialist who told him that a court order would require EGLE to show that the property was an imminent and substantial risk to public health. Affidavits would be needed of first-hand accounts of leaking tank cars. The property specialist recommended that a revised draft of the access agreement be given one more time to the railroad company with the changes the State of Michigan would need to see to be able to sign the document.

Ed Lorenz, who understood corporate companies, explained to us in an email that Mid-Michigan Railroad consisted of 33 miles of track to a few grain elevators, and their corporate parent was Genesee and Wyoming, Inc., a railroad holding company with 13,000 miles of track. G & W owned over 100 railroad companies. Ed said, "The people who can make something happen, don't want anything to happen and the result is they drag their feet so nothing does happen."

I asked the Executive Committee for a vote on hiring Scott to make use of his state contacts to try to get a state attorney on board. Most, but not all, approved the idea for a set number of hours, to be paid out of our Oxford settlement money.

Later Scott sent us a report on his efforts, which delineated much that we already knew from Erik, including the meeting with the state property specialist. When we voted to have Scott tackle the railroad issue, it was to learn, yes or no, if he could get the state AG to intercede for us. Indirectly, the report from Scott showed that his conversations had resulted in a "no." That was the question we wanted answered and that is what we had paid for, so it was money well spent.

Subsequently, Scott suggested that we pay him for another three hours to contact other state employees in a further attempt to move things along. Gary Smith and I discussed this and decided that we would first have a telephone conversation with Erik Martinson to learn if any forward progress had resulted from Scott's intervention. It became clear to us that again, it was a "no." As a result, I advised the rest of the Executive Committee that Gary and I thought it would be wise to *not* take Scott up on his offer. Scott had made a good-faith attempt and had learned, as we had already learned from Erik, that the AG needed evidence to show an imminent danger to people and wildlife to be able to get a court order to force the railroad to provide access.

As mentioned, the railroad had actually sold some of its property to a local resident, including a portion of land on which the loaded freight cars and tankers were often parked. That meant that a significant stretch of land where the railroad sidings ran was privately owned between the resident and the Custodial Trust, both of which property owners were willing to have the sampling take place.

Erik said that Weston Solutions was writing an addendum to their original work plan, adding the properties just mentioned. Furthermore, if the samples showed contaminant levels above direct contact limits, those results could serve as evidence of imminent and substantial danger, which would perhaps convince the AG's office to get involved in seeking a court order to sample the property still owned by the railroad.

In the 12-block neighborhood that had been excavated a few years prior, hundreds of samples had shown contaminants above direct contact levels, and we expected the same might be true along the old railway bed.

As for EPA, we disagreed with their view that the railroad areas were not part of the Velsicol site. To that end, we sent a letter to the EPA Administrator at headquarters in Washington, DC, arguing that the railway transportation beds had been used for the same purposes as the truck transportation routes, they were contiguous to the main plant site, and they traversed residential areas as did the truck routes, and should be handled in the same manner during the cleanup of the Velsicol sites. We asked that the administrator, Michael Regan, instruct those who worked under him to reconsider their stance and to include the railroad sidings and the residential yards in the remediation plans for Velsicol.

A response came from the new EPA Region 5 Administrator, Debra Shore, who said a previous investigation by EPA had shown the area to be free of contamination, and therefore not part of the Velsicol site.

Certainly, the railroad bed had never been sampled. Was she referring to the samples taken at the old creamery building located on the south side of M-46? If so, the sampling had not ranged far from that building, and certainly not along where the railroad tracks had run. Shore also said that any contamination along the tracks would be from leakage from rail cars, and therefore the responsibility of the railroad company to clean up. Since we knew that private residents now owned much of that area, would they be liable to pay for cleanup instead of the railroad company? On a Zoom call, however, EPA Project Manager Tom Alcamo assured us that the private property owners would not have to pay for cleanup.

In December, the sampling took place. Our EGLE Project Manager Erik Martinson said that results would be slow in coming due to the short staffing at labs.

Working with our Technical Advisor was a challenge. We all had great respect for Scott's expertise, acknowledging that his past experience as a state remedial project manager for our site gave him technical insights, as well as an understanding of negotiation tactics EPA staff were likely to utilize. The difficulty for Scott was to recognize the limited scope of his present job, in contrast with the one he used to hold.

Our contract with him assigned the CAG Treasurer, Gary Smith, as the liaison between the CAG and the technical advisor. Gary was the middleman, although he and I talked often of how best to handle things. The one area in which Gary and I disagreed was the assignment of tasks. I wanted Scott to be limited to the two areas for which we had hired him -- namely, the slurry wall investigation and the carbon amendment study -- while Gary said we should utilize his expertise in other areas, as well. Also, I felt strongly that we needed to conserve the funds provided by the TAG grant by telling Scott ahead of time how many hours he could devote to a task, while Gary, who was also frugal, felt less comfortable with curtailing Scott in terms of time and money spent on his reviews.

A letter from the Chief of the Remedial Response Branch of EPA Region 5, Timothy Fischer, laid out EPA's concerns about the rate of TAG spending on interim reports Scott wrote and "associated investigations." The letter pointed out that at the rate we were paying TAG funds to our technical consultant we wouldn't have money left for him to review important documents that were still forthcoming.

I sent an email to our EPA project manager, Tom Alcamo, thanking him for the letter from his Chief, saying that "both the high invoice amounts and the critical comments from Scott have been something I have brought up repeatedly to him, to Gary and to our board. The letter will help us make some necessary changes, I think/hope."

The letter did help convince Gary to rein in Scott's spending, saying in an email to the Executive Committee, "We have to have him keep to the script and only bill for that." In a longer email he reported that he and Scott had spoken and that Scott understood that we could not pay him from TAG funds for non-technical commentary.

As I mentioned previously, I had spent hours re-working a set of comments Scott had written to make them less combative. And I wasn't willing to spend my volunteer hours doing that again. I truly hoped that Scott by now understood the boundaries of the TAG funding and would stay within them on his own.

He began, however, to contact Tom Alcamo about technical matters on our behalf without including us in the emails. Tom alerted me to this practice, and Gary then addressed Scott on that issue. From the start of the contract, Scott had known he was supposed to include Gary, Ed and me in his emails, yet now he had slipped away from that understanding, as well. I began to wonder if it was because we were all growing older and more forgetful.

At Gary's request, Tom provided us with estimated dates of document releases on the many projects underway at the Velsicol plant site and downstream in Operable Units 3 and 4. The Executive Committee then met with Scott via Zoom to have him prioritize the documents that we would have him review, keeping in mind the hours he estimated the review would take, which were dollars to us, and becoming scarcer, because so much had been paid out to Scott already.

Meanwhile, Gary was doing the difficult and thankless work of securing a new Technical Assistance Grant for us from EPA for the former plant site. Contributing to the complications were getting used to a new TAG grant manager at Region 5, a notice from EPA's finance section that the grant we were now using was being shut down, the confusion at Region 5 over the fact that we had two TAG grants (one for plant site's four operable units and one for the Burn Pit site), and the ever-tricky Grants.gov web portal.

After the new Region 5 TAG person sent an email to Gary, telling him to "calm down," I stepped in and let the man know that his insulting tone was unnecessary. Thankfully, Tom Alcamo then began to send emails to Gary offering help to get him through the grant processing, and suggesting that Gary and I speak with a TAG expert, and setting up a phone call for us. That conversation answered many of our questions and smoothed the path somewhat. Smoothing it even more was a subsequent email from Tom that he had received permission from the EPA contracting office to allow us to skip going through Grants.gov and simply submit the completed application by email to the contracting office.

A long, detailed narrative was needed for the work plan. Ed and I contributed some of the writing, and Brittany Fremion tackled it with gusto, essentially writing the document for Gary. Gary pulled together numbers and facts needed for the other documents in the package, and, finally, the 20 pages of our combined efforts were submitted. Toward the end of the year, we got the good news that the new TAG grant for the former plant site had been awarded to our CAG.

Even though we had been awarded a TAG grant for the Burn Pit Site several years prior, almost no money had been spent, because nothing was happening at the site. Because so much electricity was required for thermal treatment, the Burn Pit had to wait until the underground heating process at plant site Area 2 Phase 2 reached completion. By 2021, the heating of Phase 2 was still underway, at a cost to taxpayers of about $800,000 per month. Over 135,000 pounds of contaminants had been extracted in this phase of treatment, with no diminishing returns. The contract called for the heating to maintain 100 C (212 F) for at least 90 days, and that milestone was reached on November 5, but EPA made the decision to keep heating until January because of the quantity of NAPL being recovered. This NAPL, which looked significantly different from the NAPL extracted from Area 1, had been analyzed and was found to consist of 80% DDT, which wasn't surprising since the DDT factory had been located in this part of the plant site. By January of 2022, diminishing returns ended the heating process, with 140,000 pounds recovered from this phase of the project, and a total of 382,000 pounds collected over all the phases.

The electricity was one reason nothing had happened at the Burn Pit, and the other reason was a lack of funding from EPA. Ashton Bortz, aide to our U.S. Representative John Moolenaar, suggested that our CAG send a letter outlining the need for money for the Burn Pit cleanup, noting that her boss was now chair of the Appropriations Committee. We did just that.

A proposed bi-partisan infrastructure bill at the federal level was giving us hope, as long as the Superfund program remained part of the proposal. Tom Alcamo informed us that if Superfund remained in the bill, as a whole it could receive billions of dollars. If that happened, it was highly possible that the Burn Pit would be selected to receive some of that money.

Another long-standing item in the backs of our minds was a reinstatement of the federal Superfund Tax. Off and on over the years we had written letters to Congress about resuming the tax on chemical businesses, specifically for cleanups of orphaned Superfund sites, such as ours. "Orphaned" meant that no "responsible party" was available to foot the bill. In our case, the state and federal governments had allowed the responsible party, Velsicol, to leave St. Louis in 1982 for a nominal payment towards the first remediation of the factory site, with no threat of legal follow-up for more money. And, of course, that first remedy subsequently failed.

The original Superfund Tax had been set up during the Nixon administration, and ceased to collect taxes in 1999. For several years, enough money remained in the Fund to continue cleanups at many Superfund sites across the country, and when the money ran out in the early 2000s, Congress had to directly appropriate taxpayer money to pay for cleanups.

Suddenly, in 2021, we heard that Congress was actually considering reinstating the Superfund Tax. It seemed too good to be true. Certainly, it was time for another letter in support of the tax.

Ed Lorenz drafted a letter to the members of the U.S. House Committee on Energy and Commerce, requesting both a restoration of the tax and an increase in Superfund allotments to the Agency for Toxic Substance and Disease Registry (ATSDR) for the funding of human health research related to contamination at Superfund sites, including the direct funding of needed clinical responses for exposed persons.

In addition to our letter, we received urgent emails from other organizations asking us to sign on to their letters. I reminded our Executive Committee that long ago we had made a verbal agreement among ourselves to avoid aligning ourselves with other environmental groups, no matter how well-meaning their efforts. We had a number of reasons for coming to this decision, with a major one being the immensity of our own project to which we, as volunteers, could dedicate only so much time and energy.

For the previously excavated neighborhood, a follow-up bird study was a task we had hoped our new EGLE project manager would conduct. In my initial phone conversation with him, I had told him that both the railroad project and the bird study were important to the community to ensure that the cleanup of Velsicol was thorough. And I reminded him that it was the responsibility of EGLE to monitor properties where EPA had completed cleanups, with the 12-block neighborhood south and east of the Velsicol plant site certainly being one of those. The excavation of residential yards, re-sodding, and the planting of new trees had long ago ended, and it was high time to find out if birds were still dying from DDT poisoning.

Before the world shut down due to COVID 19, our group had been seeking information about grant help from U.S. Fish and Wildlife, and private wildlife funds for a follow-up bird study, because our past EGLE project manager and his boss had allowed our requests that the state do such a study go unanswered.

Erik answered, saying EGLE would not undertake a bird study until the plant site was cleaned up and the new trees planted in the neighborhood had matured. Since the timetable for plant site cleanup was 10 to 20 years away, as was maturity for the trees, we began to discuss, once again, how to accomplish a study on our own. Scott, our Technical Advisor, asked for any past information we had on the study conducted prior to excavation by MSU Wildlife Toxicology professor Matthew Zwiernik.

Matt Z had actually completed two studies for us, one of dead birds and one of nesting success. The birds analyzed in the lab had died of acute DDT poisoning, meaning they had come back to Michigan from down south as healthy birds, and in the course of mating, nest-building, and sometimes feeding young, had eaten worms from the yards contaminated with DDT, accumulating enough in their systems to die. As for the nesting success, it was low due to the untimely deaths of the parents, with two streets of the neighborhood having zero nesting success. As for St. Louis, it now had the dubious reputation of being the place where a collected specimen had the highest level of DDT in brain tissue ever found in a wild bird.

From the beginning of the CAG, the reputation of St. Louis was a high priority for us. The town had gone from its reputation of a place of healing waters to a town that people joked about due to its poisoned waters. Instead of a swimming, fishing and boating delight, the Pine River had become a place to avoid as dangerous. All of the CAG's immediate efforts to uncover the chemical messes and have them cleaned up, including yards where birds would no longer die, meshed with our long-term effort to restore the reputation of St. Louis.

After Erik told us that EGLE would not be conducting a bird study until years later, our secretary, Brittany Fremion, reached out to three faculty members at Central Michigan University, hoping one of them would be interested in undertaking a study. She did find a person who was willing to consult with us if we did our own worm collection/study, but did not have the time to do a study herself.

Meanwhile, I continued to bring up the need for a bird study during our CAG meetings, and finally Erik asked to see the documents produced from the studies Matt Z had completed for us, and also for EPA when they hired him later to conduct a wildlife toxicology study of the downstream floodplains. I had most of them, but not all, and Gary Smith and Tom Alcamo provided the others. We were encouraged that Erik was taking another look at the project.

I asked the Executive Committee for their thoughts on organizing a bird collection program ourselves, following the standard operating procedures as laid out in the Zwiernik SOP. I asked them specifically about how much volunteer time they would be able to expend on the necessary steps.

From the responses, it was evident that we all thought undertaking the collection ourselves was possible, but that we first needed to find out how much lab analysis of the birds' organs would cost. We also needed to find out if the Zwiernik SOP (Standard Operating Procedure) was acceptable to EGLE so that data comparisons would be accurate.

Scott also asked for the Zwiernik documents, and offered to review them for us and present his findings in a PowerPoint program. I made a motion to the Executive Committee that we approve Scott's request, and Gary seconded it. A letter from Tom Alcamo, however, brought us to a halt.

He reminded us that Scott's review would merely "rehash" the information that had already been presented to us by Matt Zwiernik in 2015 and 2017. Did we really want to spend our TAG grant money in that way?

Another concern arose from EPA's desire to take part in this bird study. Tom felt that the study would take time and money away from his attempts to complete the contracting for cleanup of

Potential Source Areas 1 and 2 of the plant site. He said that the bird study was a low priority to EPA. No kidding!

For how many years did CAG member Teri Kniffen report finding dead birds in her yard? At least five. Did EPA or MDEQ/EGLE do anything back then to find out why the birds were dying? No. Finally Teri took three birds to the lab in Lansing, spent her own money, and learned that the birds had died of DDT poisoning. Even with that knowledge, did EPA or EGLE step up to conduct a formal bird study when we repeatedly asked them to? No. The CAG stepped up and spent its own money, and Matt Z stepped up and spent his grant money, to undertake the studies that were done. So it was no surprise that in 2021 neither EPA nor EGLE was willing to conduct a follow-up study to see if the excavation of contaminated yards had solved the problem of birds dying from DDT poisoning.

Late in the year Jim Hall made a phone call to our state senator, Rick Outman, asking how to find money for the bird study. Rick directed him to the chairman of the state appropriations committee, Jim Stamas. When the two Jims talked on the phone, Stamas said he was sure money could be found to allow the study to proceed in Spring, 2022. When our Jim re-contacted Stamas by email in December, there was still no firm reply, and our Executive Committee was still undecided about moving forward on its own.

At least EGLE was accountable to the state legislature. In dealing with MPHI on the PBB records issue, we had we learned more about their lack of accountability to the state. A Detroit News article shared with us by Dr. Lisa Halbert of the PBB Citizens Advisory Board described how the state health department used MPHI to avoid oversight by the legislature of the expenditure of millions of dollars. The article said that through a "master agreement," MPHI was able to execute contracts for MDHHS with no legislative oversight. The article confirmed our low-estimation of the process and of the institute itself.

Recently, an issue had arisen with MPHI that once again involved the PBB records of original participants in the state health department's 1978 long-term PBB study. This time we learned that MPHI had found a folder containing 20 completed transfer consent forms that had never been processed. These forms were from people who had attended the PBB Community Meetings organized by the researchers from Emory University, and had signed the consent forms that authorized the state health department to transfer their original records to Emory University, and nothing had been done to accomplish the wishes of the people.

In our monthly conference calls with the researchers, I said that we should voice our dissatisfaction in a letter to the director of MPHI. Dr. Michele Marcus felt differently, explaining that she was in negotiations over the contracts among MPHI, MDHHS and Emory, and that speaking up about the error might negatively affect the outcome of her discussions. I understood her reluctance, and said that the Pine River Superfund Citizen Task Force, as a representative of the St. Louis community, would write and send its own letter, which we did.

The letter pointed out that over the years we had notified MPHI and our legislators of the deficiencies in record keeping at MPHI, and errors such as this latest one damaged the trust our group had labored to build in the wider community. The letter said, "The PBB disaster itself sorely undermined public trust in governmental institutions, an attitude that has lasted to this day. Our patient efforts to re-engage those participants from the original study, and their family members, suffer a tremendous injustice when an institute relied upon by one of our governmental agencies (MDHHS) operates with such laxity." The letter was copied to several of our state legislators.

The reply from the MPHI director said the incidents recounted in the letter were the result of miscommunication – that instead of laxity, MPHI was showing extraordinary care and doing a "deep dive" into the records. The letter said, "Finding the 20 records in question is a result of that deeper investigation and thoroughness for which Dr. Marcus expressed her pleasure that our team was thorough in their reviews."

No matter the spin the director put on it, the records had been lost by MPHI before they were found, and the people who had submitted the consent forms were unable to take part in the current PBB research being conducted by Emory University.

Late in the year, Dr. Michele Marcus told us that in her other dealings with MPHI and MDHHS, she had made sure they knew she was reporting their discussions to the PBB Leadership Team. Michele believed that the letter we had written had become a helpful reminder to the state health department that the community was paying close attention to decisions made. Also, we learned that MDHHS staff had decided to take back the responsibility of transferring consent forms because, in Michele's estimation, they also saw the mistakes MPHI had made.

As for the PBB studies underway, the COVID 19 pandemic had slowed and complicated all of them. The clinical trial to determine if the weight-loss substance ingested by people would cause a faster elimination of PBB from the body had nearly halted, as in-person contact was necessary at the three month and six month stages, and also because the grant money was coming to an end. We wrote a letter supporting an extension of the funding, citing the interruption of the study due to the pandemic, and were greatly pleased when NIEHS came through with additional funding. Near the end of 2021, we had 93 people still enrolled in the clinical trial down from 100, and according to the experts who know about such things, having 93 out of 100 is topnotch.

Funding for the three-generation study had run out, but the researchers continued to collect names of families willing to take part someday. It was slow going to find families that had one grandparent exposed to PBB and one not, and then their children and grandchildren all willing to take part.

We had plenty of people for the comprehensive health study. In fact, our waiting list for people wanting to have their blood drawn to see if they were eligible for participating in a study was well over 1,000 names long. From the pool of those who had already had their blood drawn, and had filled out the long survey forms, the researchers continued to enroll some of them in the health study when money became available.

Prior to the pandemic, a community meeting and blood draw had been held in Cadillac but due to the lab shutdown during COVID 19, results were delayed. They were finally mailed to participants in the middle of 2021. Of the 197 people from whom blood samples were taken, 52 had highly elevated levels of PBB, which made them eligible for the clinical trial.

In the midst of the pandemic, our local health officer, Marcus Cheatham, reached his goal of retirement. He had worked hard with us to try to free up the PBB Records from MDHHS for use by researchers and family members of the participants, and in other areas of our quest to learn the health effects of exposure to PBB, DDT and other chemicals. Marcus had also served the community as a member of our board of directors and in his work with the Healthy Pine River group on the *E. coli* problem upstream in the river.

Because we were concerned that the next person appointed by the District Board of Health might not become involved in the wider community, such as Marcus had done, Bonnie Havlicek (a retired RN and member of the PBB Citizens Advisory Board) and I decided to speak to both the Gratiot County Board of Commissioners and the District Board of Health. The impetus was to campaign for a community-minded health officer, and also to inform the boards about the PBB Leadership Team and the studies underway. It turns out that the District Board of Health had already appointed a person who we knew. Liz Braddock stepped into Marcus' place enthusiastically, which pleased us.

One afternoon I received a startling phone call from Erik Martinson, our EGLE project manager. He told me that the Custodial Trust had run out of money and the State of Michigan had decided to allow the Trust to dissolve. This was the Trust that had been set up in 2004 by the US Department of Justice with monies earmarked for cleanups of Velsicol sites in St. Louis, Michigan and also in Illinois, Tennessee and New Jersey. Money had come from the Trust to partially pay for the new drinking water for St. Louis, and much of the money had been frittered away by a lawsuit mounted by insurance giant AIG.

I remembered that when Scott Cornelius had been our MDEQ project manager, he had convinced the State of Michigan to set aside $6 million of the funds in the Custodial Trust specifically for future operation and maintenance costs for the pump-and-treat remedy at the plant site in St. Louis. When Erik told me the Trust was to be dissolved, my first concern was about the $6 million. He assured me that the Michigan O & M money was still separated out, and that a Memorandum of Understanding (MOU) was being written that would determine if the money would go into a long-term interest account or into a special response fund. I said that the wording needed to be very specific to prevent the money being used by the State of Michigan for some other purpose, thinking back to the state Landfill Trust Fund with wording that only matched the Gratiot County Landfill.

The Custodial Trust had included not only money, but also property deeds – for example, the deed for property on both sides of where the railroad line ran into the plant site. Erik said that the State of Michigan was working with USDOJ, a state attorney general, and other state lawyers in writing the MOU of how to move forward. He said many of the properties would be moved to the State Land Bank.

I asked if LePetomane (Jay Steinberg's company) that held the deeds to the plant site property had initiated the dissolution, or if the State had. I didn't get a direct answer, but he finally told me he was dealing indirectly (through the lawyers) with Chris Steinberg, Jay's son, who had taken over LePetomane following Jay's retirement.

In setting up a conference call with other CAG members and people from the State, I asked that a person from the Trust be included in the call, and someone from the DOJ. The State vetoed that request. Then I asked specifically for David Heidlauf to be on the call, a former LePetomane employee, and with whom we had worked on a number of issues, including the Breckenridge Radioactive Site. I received a curt email response from Erik that that my request was not appropriate. I replied with expanded information about our work in the past directly with DOJ and the Trust, thinking perhaps Erik and others he was working with were not aware of our history in that regard. I also asked again who had initiated the dissolution. This time the email response said that "EPA/DOJ initiated the discussion pertaining to the lack of funds in the custodial trust."

I decided to call Jay Steinberg and David Heidlauf myself, in case they were unaware of what was going on.

Jay told me the Custodial Trust could not be dissolved until someone else took titles to the Velsicol properties. When I mentioned that the State Land Bank might do that for the Michigan properties, he liked that idea. He said, "Tell me who to deed it to and I will sign the papers tomorrow!"

He told me that David had also received my voice mail message, and after they had spoken with each other, Jay had called his upper management contacts at DOJ, reminding them that an active group of citizens existed in St. Louis. "They said they were aware of that!" Jay told me. He assured me that now that we had the DOJ's attention, nothing would be done without them first talking to us. He said neither he nor David had been invited to take part in the upcoming conference call, and that we needed to be cautious that the state attorneys didn't "put anything over on us."

211

He ended by saying, "I won't desert you. We care about your group and we like how you are with the agencies."

Participants in the call from the CAG were Gary Smith, Brittany Fremion, and me (Ed was on a trip); our Technical Advisor, Scott Cornelius; present and past EGLE project managers Erik Martinson and Dan Rockafellow; and from EPA Tom Alcamo and Brad Emlisch.

We learned that, essentially, the Trust Fund was depleted and EGLE and EPA had decided to draft an MOU that outlined the allocation of the remaining responsibilities and funding for 2020 (about $10,000) and 2021 (about $7,500). As for the $6.6 million set aside for O & M, the dissolution would protect that money from the other states with Velsicol sites, who thought those millions should be thrown into the pot and divided up.

Again, I emphasized that the wording to protect the $6.6 million from being used by the State for other purposes must be very tight and focused, and cited the language used years ago in the Landfill Trust set up by the State of Michigan for the Gratiot County Landfill.

The MOU would change ownership of the properties, but would not change the EGLE or EPA responsibilities for remediation, further investigations and so forth. We asked to see the draft copy of the MOU, and were told that wasn't possible at this time. Later they sent us a copy of the finalized MOU with its pages of signatures. We were glad to see Jay Steinberg's signature among them.

Our elderly, outspoken CAG member, Phil Ramsey, passed away toward year's end. A tall man, Phil had dwindled down to 123 pounds. In his car he made frequent visits to the plant site, and had become a favorite of the people working on the cleanup, especially Scott Pratt, the project manager for the contracting company. Several of us attended a gathering that Lois, Phil's wife, had organized to celebrate Phil's life, and Scott spoke movingly about his friend. Several of us from the CAG also spoke, remembering

Phil's insistence on getting the best clean possible for the plant site, which would include removing the huge underground pile of debris that we had nicknamed "Phil's Hill." For his many contributions, including his years of serving on the Executive Committee, Phil had been voted into the CAG Hall of Fame in 2017. Lois said the honor had meant a great deal to him.

At year's end, I collected new nominations from the membership for the CAG Hall of Fame Award, and two people were nominated again and again: Gary Smith and Jim Hall. Even though we had decided to only choose one person per year, I convinced the membership that both men should be inducted, and they were. It was well-deserved recognition for two founding members who, like Phil, had persisted in seeking the best cleanup possible for our community.

Chapter 13
(2022)
Flowing Money

The headline on one of the newspaper articles said "Velsicol Burn Pit to Receive Millions from EPA for Cleanup." We could hardly believe our eyes and ears, and some of us still kept a degree of skepticism that the money would truly flow into our projects. After 24 long years of worry about having enough money to complete one project at a time, suddenly we would receive enough money for several projects at a time. Not only for the Burn Pit Superfund site across the Pine River, but also for excavating PSA 1 & 2 areas within the plant site, for designing the chemical oxidation plan for PSA 3, for excavating OU-3 floodplains and riverbanks immediately downriver from the dam, and for installing a metal wall to keep the plant site pollutants from flowing into the river. I was on the phone a lot giving interviews to various news outlets.

It was the Bipartisan Infrastructure Law that was flowing the money into our cleanup projects, as it was at three other Michigan Superfund sites, and many others across the country. Despite attempts by various lawmakers to exclude Superfund from the money flow, Superfund stayed in, the bill passed, and was signed into law.

This was one of those times when I wished we were still meeting in person, because we could have handed out Dixie cups of sparkling cider for a toast to the hard work of Tom Alcamo in getting all the preliminary work done at the Burn Pit to make it eligible for consideration, and for our own hard work in persisting two decades ago that the Burn Pit, despite being delisted by EPA, was still a contaminated mess.

Along with new funding, we were assigned a new EPA Remedial Project Manager for the Burn Pit, Jennifer Knoepfle, who Tom Alcamo said was seasoned and hardworking. Tom was

214

overworked with our mega site, plus the lead site in Indiana that he also headed up. He was only a year or two from retirement age, and I was sure that new adventure was also on his mind.

Because of the pandemic travel restrictions for EPA employees, it was several months before we met Jennifer in person. In the meantime, we asked her to give us a refresher presentation on the Burn Pit since many years had passed since the site had achieved readiness for cleanup. Jennifer presented the refresher, and said that most of her time spent so far had been to get extensive documentation written and signed by the administration in Washington, DC to begin the remediation of the Burn Pit site.

One thing slowing the process was the economical choice made by EPA Region 5 to "sole source," the *in situ* thermal treatment (ISTT) contractor that had performed the work at Areas 1 and 2 on the plant site, rather than bidding it out again. We supported their conservation of money. It made sense to us to use the same contractor whose equipment was already set up for treating both contaminated groundwater and gases extracted during the boiling process, and whose workers had gained experience on the plant site. To pay for demobilization and remobilization seemed a waste of taxpayer money.

The idea for bringing the wastes across the river from the Burn Pit to the treatment facility on the plant site would involve pipes and a barge as a sort of bridge. It was during our Zoom conversation with EPA that we first heard about the plan, when our CAG member, Jim Hall, who had encountered a similar process in his work, began to ask specific questions. Also during that Zoom meeting, our Technical Advisor, Scott Cornelius pointed out that the Army Corps of Engineers had a lot of experience with pontoon bridges, and as they were already here to provide oversight services for PSA 1 & 2, it made sense to tap into their expertise, which could also better utilize funding dollars. Jennifer liked the idea, and said she would look into it.

Having to Zoom instead of meet in person had sorely cut into our membership participation. Very few non-board members took part in the video meetings. Our Executive Committee began to explore options for cameras in hopes of having what our young Secretary, Brittany Fremion, termed a "bi-modal" meeting. One of our members, Doug Brecht, also served as a trustee on the Seville Township Board, and he told us about their experiment with an Owl camera that would turn toward whoever was speaking at the time.

Gary Smith attended the next township board meeting, and I Zoomed in, to evaluate the method. It was the first time for the Seville board to use the Owl camera in an actual meeting, and I know they worked out the kinks later, but because of the difficulties they had that evening, both Gary and I had reservations about investing in a camera for ourselves.

As the discussion among the Executive Committee members continued (how to arrange the tables and chairs in our meeting space at city hall in St. Louis to accommodate a camera, how long the cord should be to connect the camera to computer, how those Zooming might or might not be able to participate in the meeting, how to deal acoustically with the echoes in our meeting room, and so forth), I remembered that just before COVID 19 shut down life as we knew it, our CAG had purchased a high quality projector to use for showing PowerPoints at our in-person meetings. Previously, we had borrowed the city's projector, but there were complications both with how it worked and the quality of the picture. The projector we had bought worked through a laptop computer, just as the Owl set-up did. I asked those more technically skilled if we could maybe use the projector at the in-person meeting to show those speaking to those who Zoomed into the meeting on their computer screens at home.

Brittany thought it might work, and we decided to experiment with it, and also with a Bluetooth microphone for those speaking at a distance from the computer microphone. The experiment showed it was possible. So 31 months after our last in-person meeting, finally, in October 2022, we had another. Things were not perfect for those Zooming in, but fixable. The best part was being in the same room with EPA and EGLE people who we hadn't seen in far too long, and meeting new agency people, including Jennifer, and two Army Corps of Engineers men who would be working on the PSA 1 & 2 projects. Not many CAG members attended that evening, and very few in subsequent months. Times had changed.

Participation of a different sort was increasing, however. Ed Lorenz had been spending much time and talent, with some help from one of his sons, in making a new website for the CAG. I, personally, was so grateful that Ed, once again, had taken on that monumental responsibility. Ed had introduced us into the website world back in the early 2000s, and after several invasive acts by outsiders, our website was not only outdated, but a mess. For a while, Gary Smith and I tried to serve as administrators of it, but that didn't work well. Now that the new website was operational, Ed reported that website traffic was up 23%, and unique visitors up 33%, and a few months later, the unique individual number had climbed to 84%. Many of the visitors were from other states. At the same time, book sales on Amazon for my memoir of our CAG, *Tombstone Town*, had climbed. Somewhere there were a few people who were interested in what we were doing!

One reason the U.S. Army Corps of Engineers was overseeing the PSA 1 & 2 work had to do with the intricacies of the project, which included the deep excavation of an estimated 100,000 tons of contaminated soil. Potential Source Area 1 (no longer potential, but actual) was bordered by state highway M-46 on the south and residential backyards on Watson Street to the east. To prevent cave-ins on the residential property, a sheet pile wall was inserted 30 feet into the ground between the excavation site and the yards. The plan had been to vibrate the wall sections into the ground to limit the noise in the downtown area, and that method worked until about the halfway point. Then, a mechanical hammer pounded the steel deeper until only two feet or so of the wall was left aboveground. Also, placed near the houses, were motion monitors. If the levels of vibration reached a point that basements might be damaged, then the work would be stopped. According to Tom, the upper levels signaling danger were never quite reached.

The excavation, which hadn't yet begun, would dig at surface and far below the water table, and would involve difficulties that could benefit from the Army Corps of Engineers advice. Both contaminated soil and contaminated groundwater would be removed. NAPL (non-aqueous phase liquid) was the principal threat waste, and was highly toxic, highly mobile and a risk to human health and the environment. Contaminants of concern included chlorobenzene, xylene, the fire retardant TRIS, and phosphates.

Prior to work starting, the excavation of PSA 1 & 2 had been used by Tom to squelch a follow-up bird study the CAG had hoped would take place that spring. He had told us last year that with open soil at the plant site, we couldn't be sure if the robins and other birds would be pulling worms from the neighborhood or from the excavation site, thereby spoiling the results used to determine if the neighborhood excavation, which had ended in 2016, had been successful. When he announced this, I was sure PSA 1 & 2 would not be at the excavation stage by spring of 2022, and I was right. Now, spring of 2023 is the target date for the digging to begin.

Our EGLE project manager, Erik Martinson, had moved forward on the long-requested railroad sampling. As previously mentioned, the land where the tracks used to run was partially owned by LePetomane Trust and a private resident. Both the Trust and Dale Hamilton were willing to allow sampling, even though the railroad company had refused.

Three phases of sampling by EGLE's contractor, Weston Solutions, showed that DDT was present, and in high enough concentrations in a few places to warrant excavation. To jump ahead, about 50 cubic yards of contaminated soil were removed in 2022, and we are glad for that, but, because access was never gained to all of the property, we are quite sure that more DDT-laden soil is present on the portion still owned by the railroad.

Erik also kept us informed of the progress of transferring the Velsicol properties to the State Land Bank. After we understood that the transfer was a good idea for the State of Michigan and for our St. Louis Superfund sites, our only lingering worry was about a future expense for the City of St. Louis. From what we had learned on-line, it seemed that once the Land Bank held deeds to property in Michigan, they could charge high prices to sell the land to others. We were concerned that if and when St. Louis wanted to own the 52-acre former plant site, with river frontage on two sides, that the Land Bank could price the land at a prohibitively high amount.

Gary and I sat down with Kurt Giles, the city manager, and Tom Reed, the new mayor of St. Louis, to express our concern, and to explain our efforts to learn more. Soon after that, I received an email from Erik that stated in writing that when the time came to transfer the title to the City of St. Louis, the city would not be required to pay *anything* for the parcels of property. That response pleased us and the city officials

The St. Louis officials were also pleased that installation of the last well for their new water supply, shared with Alma, was underway and expected to be operational by early 2023. Back in the mid-2000s, when it was learned that the St. Louis drinking water supply was contaminated with pCBSA, a by-product from the manufacturing of DDT, the city sued Velsicol, LePetomane Trust and others to pay for a replacement of their drinking water source. The suit was settled with St. Louis winning $26.5 million, which was about half the money needed for the project. The remainder of the money would eventually come through EPA.

Also in the mid-2000s, the cities of St. Louis and Alma, situated about three miles apart, joined forces to form the Gratiot Area Water Authority. As the new water wells came on line, wells in St. Louis were shut down, as were a few wells in Alma that were contaminated with compounds from the former Total Refinery. At that time, Alma also quit using the Pine River as part of its drinking water source. Over the years, four new wells had been drilled in Arcada Township, tapping into water from the glacial era, and extensive piping was laid to transport the new water first to the water treatment plant in Alma, and then to homes and businesses in both cities.

As for the health of residents in St. Louis, the researchers from Emory University continued their studies, and CAG member JoAnne Scalf continued her health mapping survey of present and past residents of the town. Even though she now lived in Texas, she and her brothers and sister had grown up in St. Louis. Several of them contended with thyroid issues, and one brother had died at a young age from non-Hodgkins lymphoma. JoAnne had set up a private group on Facebook at which people could contact her to volunteer health information about themselves and their extended families, and hundreds responded with their stories. Prior to the pandemic shut down, JoAnne had displayed posters depicting the work she had done at a conference that many of us participated in at the University of Michigan. By now, she had collected enough data on cancer that she was ready to write a report entitled "The Multigenerational Pine River Superfund Voluntary Health Map Report." To launch it, she came to Michigan and met with a news reporter, and asked me and a few others to sit in on the interview.

Near the end of their conversation, Linda Gittleman, the reporter, asked a great question: what volunteered health information was most surprising? JoAnne said her survey had not asked about infertility, but the information from respondents showed she should have included that topic. Both men and women wanted to know if exposure to the chemicals in the air, water, and food had caused their infertility. She also was surprised by the number of neurological disorders reported, such as multiple sclerosis and amyotrophic lateral sclerosis. The third surprise was the number of family member suicides reported.

We are hoping that the voluntary anecdotal information (much of it supported by medical records), will entice researchers to perform a comprehensive health study of the community.

Of course, we continued to work with the PBB researchers from Emory University. Brittany Fremion, Ed Lorenz, Norm Keon and I all served on the smaller PBB Leadership Team which met monthly by Zoom. We continued to write letters of support as the researchers sought grants to fund their studies.

After the COVID 19 hiatus of both community meetings and our PBB Partnership meetings, the big group of partners finally met face-to-face in 2022. The PBB Partnership included our CAG, the PBB Citizens Advisory Board (CAB), the Mid-Michigan District Health Department, representatives from Alma College and Central Michigan University, and, of course, Dr. Michele Marcus and Dr. Melanie Pearson of the Emory research group. At the meeting, the members of the CAB finalized a decision they had discussed with us previously -- to join our CAG as a committee focused on PBB.

It was at the Partnership meeting that we began to talk about the fact that 2023 would be the 50th anniversary of the PBB Disaster, which had begun in 1973. Should we celebrate? Celebration didn't really set the right tone. The word "commemoration" seemed more appropriate. Jane Ann Crowley suggested that we honor PBB Heroes at the event, with hopes of having 50 of them to honor. Several members of the Partnership formed a committee to begin planning the 50th anniversary and to seek grants to pay for it. As the plans coalesced, it was decided to hold the event at Alma College on May 18-20, 2023.

I chose not to be on the committee. I did write letters of support for grants, tracked down several PBB Heroes, and edited all the hero biographies for the event program.

As for the smaller PBB Leadership Team, a continuing aggravation was the PBB records roadblocks set up by the state health department (MDHHS) and their contractor MPHI (Michigan Public Health Institute), which, we had learned, was really a business that helped MDHHS avoid legislative oversight of their activities. In addition, MPHI was a subcontractor with the research team, so it was "our" NIEHS grant money that was paying them to review the records.

The review of the PBB records began when MDHHS decided it needed to audit more than 2000 consent forms submitted by participants in the original 1978 State-run PBB long-term study – consent forms from people who had *formally requested* to have their records transferred from MDHHS to the researchers at Emory University. Why reviewing those legitimate consent forms was necessary in the eyes of the state, we didn't know. To us, it appeared to be an unnecessary task. Because there was a time factor in the NIEHS grant awarded to Emory to match the PBB health records with the death index and cancer indices in the states of Michigan, Ohio and Florida (the most likely places for original participants to reside), the State's audit of the consent forms meant "our" grant money was being spent to pay MPHI employees to review the records, and time was passing with no actual research taking place. In fact, employees of the Emory research team spent much of their time in finding consent forms that MPHI had lost!

Additionally, MDHHS said that 120 consent forms signed by parents for their children were not valid unless birth certificates were produced proving that the children were actually related to the adults. Lawyers were consulted, and the response was that it was unheard of to ask for a birth certificate when a parent consented for a minor child. Moreover, a decade before, MDHHS had *approved* the parental consents that they were now questioning!

I wrote a letter as chair of the CAG expressing the view of the community as we shook our heads at the ineptness of MPHI employees. For instance, MPHI had even sent their *only copies* of forms to Emory, and then didn't count them as consents because they couldn't find them. The letter emphasized the time and taxpayer money being frittered away instead of having the money go towards the research for which it was intended. The CAB also wrote and sent a letter.

Michele came to Michigan to meet with MDHHS staff about the problems. In addition to the mistakes mentioned above, she learned that a box of 71 records of deceased people had been discovered that were never entered into the State data base. The mismanagement continued to astound us.

Like most bureaucratic responses, the response from MDHHS to the CAG letter talked about the process, the importance of privacy of information, and a listing of the federal and state codes regarding privacy. The importance to the community was acknowledged, and it was stated that MDHHS would continue to work with the Emory researchers. Whatever. The fact was, the audit was using up grant money that could be going for research to provide answers to health problems among the public MDHHS was meant to serve. Plus the audit was using up time so that the grant money was running out.

As mentioned earlier, memberships in the CAG had plummeted with the COVID 19 quarantine of both members and agency personnel. We didn't rely on the dues (still only $5 per year) for operational expenses, but we did rely on the numbers of people attending meetings. Those numbers became part of our in-kind contributions that allowed us to receive Technical Assistance Grants from EPA for both the Velsicol Superfund site and the Burn Pit site. We were down to 15 dues-paying members from the 50 or more who had participated in years past. And some of our aging members left us permanently.

We grieved CAG member, Caroline Ross, who had served on our Executive Committee for several years, and who had enthusiastically supported the Superfund cleanup out in the community. I sent the news of her passing to our email list, and laudatory responses came not only from other members, but from the former mayor, EPA personnel, and the editor of a newspaper. She was respected and liked, and we would miss her.

The famed PBB veterinarian Alpha Clark also passed away. During the 1970s PBB Disaster, Dr. Clark had valiantly stood up to officials from the Michigan Department of Agriculture and others who blamed farmers for their sick and dying cattle, remaining convinced that the cows had ingested a poison. His efforts resulted in threats to his wellbeing, but he persevered and was proven right when PBB was discovered as the poison in the cattle feed. A few years prior to Doc Clark's death, CAG member Norm Keon had befriended him, and convinced him that his boxes of data from the PBB era be donated to the Clarke Historical Library at Central Michigan University. This was done, and the papers are now accessible for researchers.

We were surprised that another five years had passed since the last 5-year Review of the Velsicol plant site proper. A letter came from EPA Community Involvement Coordinator, Diane Russell, asking for input from community members for the review, and also for an update to the Community Involvement Plan. EPA had hired a facilitator from Consensus Building Institute to conduct interviews on our individual perspectives of the plant site cleanup, and to hear our ideas about how EPA could expand or modify communication with the community. I sent an email to 36 of our local CAG members, encouraging them to take part in the interviews.

When the first draft of the report was mailed to us, some in the CAG were upset that the author had not used direct quotes from individuals. The situation was reminiscent of a time many years ago when public comments were left out of an EPA ROD document. Gary Smith conducted an email exchange with the facilitator, and she was conciliatory, but made it clear that a summary of comments was her intention from the start. A second draft was shared late in the year, asking for help in proof-reading the document. I spotted small errors, which were included in an email to the facilitator, and also pointed out two larger changes. One was about the length of time our CAG had remained intact, and I asked that her vague term about "all this time" be changed to "25 years," and told her about the Michigan State University sociologist who had interviewed us at about the 10-year mark in our existence. The sociologist commented that an axiom among those in her profession is that groups of people organized around a cause last no longer than seven years. An inaccuracy I asked the facilitator to correct said that the CAG had given talks in St. Louis about the cleanup. I told her that in addition to St. Louis, we had spoken in many nearby towns, at several universities in Michigan, and at conferences in three states and Washington, DC

I know the CAG history is more important to us than it is to EPA or the wider world in general, but accuracy matters, and that is the reason I am recording the events of the CAG as factually as I can from my point of view.

Back in 2006 the river sediment remediation near the plant site had been officially finalized. Since then, activity on the plant site and in the groundwater had taken place, and EPA wanted to take a look at the river bottom to see if it remained clean. Also, they wanted to see what infrastructure, such as utility cables, might be buried, and to locate debris, if any, from the early 1980s destruction of the chemical plant. When it came time to install the new perimeter wall of steel around the plant site, they needed to know what they might hit as the sheets of metal were pounded deep into the river bottom.

225

A bathymetric survey was conducted using sound-echoing equipment and other detection devices, and only two unknown metal structures were found buried. Otherwise, the state of the river bottom was good, and EPA, after spending a hundred million dollars to clean up that portion of the river, was glad to see that at least visible recontamination had not occurred.

As for invisible contamination, EPA continued to have their workers on the plant site monitoring the projects and themselves for possible DBCP exposure. Our CAG had always wondered why DBCP was contained in the mix of chemicals at the plant site, since we had found no documentation showing Velsicol manufactured that compound. Speculating yet again about the chemical, Ed said his recent rechecking of agricultural chemicals produced at the plant included soil fumigants for nematodes. He wondered if DBCP was contained in a fumigant.

Tom Alcamo had his chemist, Jason Cole, weigh in, and Jason explained that it is likely that both bromine gas and hydrobromic acid were used at the chemical factory to produce trimethylene chlorobromide (TMCB), and that poor control of the process could have resulted in a form of DBCP, which would have been disposed of as an unwanted byproduct. He also thought Ed's idea of it being used in a fumigant seemed possible.

This discussion highlighted the extensive unknowns about the chemical plant. In the end, though, we just wanted it cleaned up!

For strategic reasons, the downstream stretch of river below the dam in St. Louis had been divided into two operable units. There were a total of four operable units included in the Velsicol Superfund Site: OU-1 was the plant site itself; OU-2 was the 32-acres of millpond and river impoundment area behind the dam; OU-3 began just below the dam and extended about 1.5 miles downstream; OU-4 began where OU-3 stopped and extended another 30 miles to where the Pine River joined the Chippewa River at the

Chippewa Nature Center in Midland County. The nature center had been started by a World War II DDT expert, Eugene Kenaga, a former Dow employee, and a most helpful early CAG member, who had died in 2007.

Tom Alcamo's strategy for dividing the downstream river/floodplain area into OU-3 and OU-4, allowed him to finalize the paperwork for OU-3, while investigations were still taking place on OU-4. We now had the Feasibility Study (FS) for OU-3, available funding, and hopes of seeing excavation begin the following year.

Yes, excavation. The EPA investigation had shown that the best plan was to dig up the contaminated soils and haul them away, instead of trying to keep them in place. Of course this would disrupt natural habitat and would impinge on private property, but in the end would further our mission of restoring river and land to being safe for people and wildlife.

We were also pleased to see that the standard for the downstream cleanup of DDT in the soil was now set at 1 ppm rather than 5 ppm, which had been used in the neighborhood. The report said this lower number could be justified because of the much more extensive and diverse wildlife in the floodplains, in contrast with the neighborhood yards.

The obligatory EPA Public Meeting for the OU-3 Proposed Plan was held on line. Our Technical Advisor, Scott Cornelius, wanted the CAG to request a 30-day extension of the comment period, which was already 30 days long. I drafted a letter to that effect, but did not send it. Several on the Executive Committee felt 60 days to make comments was not needed since we approved of the method (excavation) and the DDT cleanup level. Also, why slow down EPA if not necessary?

Tom Alcamo announced that he would retire at the end of 2023, and he was optimistic that the Velsicol Plant Site would be entirely walled, capped, with an operational groundwater treatment system by 2027. For once in the 24, almost 25 years of the CAG's existence, I felt very hopeful that I might see the project finished in my lifetime.

Chapter 14
Pending Projects
(2023 – Part 1)

The Upgradient Slurry Wall, the Downgradient Vertical Barrier Wall, the PSA-1 metal wall, the Burn Pit fencing wall…whether we agreed or disagreed with all the proposed walls going up, the main thing was that the chemical clean-up was moving forward. The federal law allowing Superfund to tap into the infrastructure money to accomplish the physical aspect of remedies had set our projects on a pace far different from the snail-paced normal.

CAG member and former secretary, Carol Layman, would have been enthusiastic about the pace. Year after year she would exhort EPA and MDEQ to work faster, saying "the construction season is going to be gone before you even start!"

We lost Carol in the spring of 2023. Her remains were buried on a beautiful day in May in the walled garden behind the Presbyterian Church. She is missed.

As mentioned, our EPA project manager, Tom Alcamo, had announced that he was retiring at the end of the year, and he voiced the hope that the remediation of the plant site itself might be completed by 2027. Other projects, such as the separate Velsicol Burn Pit Superfund Site and the Former Plant Site Operating Units numbered 3 and 4, located downstream from the plant site, might take longer.

Because so many projects were underway, we were swamped with reports to read, questions to formulate and letters to write. It also meant a greater outlay of our TAG grant money to pay the Technical Advisor to keep up with the reports.

Previously, reports from EPA's contractor CH2MHill had combined many aspects of a project into one document. AECOM, EPA's contractor for the PSA 1 & 2 excavations, prepared separate reports for each task, repeating much of the same wording for the descriptive parts about our site. At first we were paying our hired Technical Advisor to read reports that, upon later reflection, were unnecessary for our needs. After some trial and error, Gary Smith and I decided that he and I and, we hoped, a few others on the Executive Committee would read the documents prior to giving approval to the Technical Advisor to read them, to help weed out the ones we didn't need to spend money on.

Because of a 2017 requirement tacked onto the TAG grant process by EPA, first Scott had to let us know what reports he would study and how many hours he estimated it would take. Then, if our group approved his plan, we sought approval from EPA. If they said yes, finally actual work could begin.

In the past, when projects were barely moving, this process was cumbersome, but didn't put us at much of a disadvantage in terms of expressing our opinions, concerns, and questions. With the present speed of reports, decisions and start-ups of projects, we *were* put at a disadvantage.

After discussing the dilemma with Gary, I wrote an email to Scott, asking him to review a document and share informally with us right away what we should be concerned about, rather than writing formal comments to share with us. The formal comments could come later. Also, Tom Alcamo was willing to have online meetings as soon as Scott was ready to discuss a document, which could help us a move forward a little faster. Scott agreed to both ideas.

We asked Scott to prepare a PowerPoint presentation for an online Technical meeting with EPA. In my opinion, the presentation was less than helpful, simply regurgitating things we already knew, most of which we had already discussed in meetings with the EPA. I decided I would keep my opinion to myself. Gary wrote to me the next morning, however, saying he hadn't learned one thing from Scott's PowerPoint that he didn't already know from reading the document, and questioned if we were getting our money's worth. I replied that maybe it was worth the money for the rest of the board members to have the presentation, since most of them were not reading the documents. I added, however, that I felt sitting through the PowerPoints was a waste of my time, as well as wasting TAG money. Gary and I decided there would be no more PowerPoints that we would ask Scott to prepare.

Another stipulation that EPA had laid down some years before was that written questions come from CAG members, and not from the Technical Advisor. We had complied with this. Individual members would send me their concerns and questions, and Scott would send me his more technical questions, and I would combine them into a letter to EPA, without noting who was asking what. Prior to this practice, Scott's questions/comments sent to EPA would often find fault with *how* EPA was doing their job. By seeing Scott's comments first, I could prune his remarks, and sometimes reword his questions in a way that sounded less like a Technical Advisor and more like a CAG member, to abide by the stipulation that comments come from members and not the Technical Advisor. Copying and pasting aided this tedious task.

Suddenly a set of comments arrived from Scott that could not be utilized in this manner, and could not even be printed out. I asked Scott to re-send in a format I could use to write the letter to EPA with the CAG questions. Scott replied to me and to Gary, saying (incorrectly) that the accepted protocol was to attach what he had written, unchanged, to the CAG letter. He also listed concerns about the method we had been using for several years, and said that his way maintained "clear and transparent communication with the regulatory bodies."

Despite being reminded of the EPA stipulation that required us to glean insight from our Technical Advisor and then write our own comments, Scott continued to insist that his complete comments be submitted along with our letter. As I thought about this latest difficulty, I wondered if Scott's concern was that a negative reaction from EPA to one of the comments might reflect on him, even though we never used his name in our comments, and we had never attributed our ignorance on an issue to Scott. His reputation as

231

consultant had never been besmirched in our comments to EPA, and never would be. His new worry about the method we used to comply with the EPA stipulation was both a surprise and a worry to us.

Nothing was resolved in 2023.

The topic on which we were to write comments was the MW-19 (monitoring well number 19) located on the west side of the former plant site. For years the CAG had urged EPA to address the leaking of NAPL into the river from that side of the plant site, where the 1980s slurry wall was a crumbled mess. After many years of denying it was happening, their tune had changed in recent years to agreeing with us. A 2022 investigation of the area found chemical leakage, with a monitoring well having collected 5 inches of DNAPL. In 2023, however, their agreeing stance changed. Even though visible DNAPL was observed in a 2023 investigation of the soil, the report concluded that it was not widespread in the area. The monitoring well still had 5 inches of DNAPl, and because the level had not changed, EPA concluded that no large accumulations of DNAPL existed in that area. It was their contention that the *in situ* thermal treatment in the northwestern part of the plant site had taken care of most of the problem.

Because of their conclusion, EPA no longer planned to install a second collection trench near MW-19. They also stated they would propose an amendment to the 2012 Record of Decision, to delete the plan stated in the ROD to install the second collection trench.

Another possible explanation for the unchanged level of DNAPL in the well that Gary and I speculated on was that liquids were flowing both in and out of the site. Everyone agreed that the slurry wall on the western side of the former plant site was a leaking sieve, and if DNAPL was continually flowing out of the site through that crumbling wall, and also continually flowing into the monitoring well from sources within the plant site, that would account for the unchanged level.

One thing EPA could do was to pump the 5 inches of DNAPL out of the well and watch to see if it filled up again. Maybe in 2024 we will persuade them to at least do that experiment.

It seemed like every time we expressed concern about this or that remedy at the plant site, EPA brought up the perimeter drain, as if it was a perfect fail-safe measure. In their reports, they stated that even if walls and heating and collection trenches didn't do the job, the future perimeter drain would catch the flow. In reading one of the documents, I wrote at the top of it, "there is too much reliance on the perimeter drain!" and I expressed this opinion in a meeting or two. Doesn't it make sense to stop the leaking first? Twenty years ago when EPA finally acknowledged that the plant site was leaking into the river, wouldn't that have been the time to install a drain around the entire site? Why wait? It wasn't like a perimeter drain would interfere with their installation of a new wall around the site, or any of their other projects, except maybe the final capping of the site. Certainly I'm not an engineer, but doesn't it make sense to *stop the leaking* after paying almost $100 million to clean up the river sediment, as they had done from 1998-2006?

As mentioned, the old slurry wall on the west side of the former plant site had deteriorated drastically and was allowing leakage into the Pine River, and the riverbanks outside the slurry wall were highly contaminated. Even though the slurry wall surrounded all 52 acres of the site, EPA nomenclature had separated the one wall into two portions -- the stretch along the river was referred to as the Downgradient Slurry Wall, and the portion butting into residential properties was referred to as the Upgradient Slurry Wall. They did this because they planned to treat the sections of wall differently, even though the 2012 Record of Decision called for an interlocking heavy gauge metal wall to be installed outside the old 1980s slurry wall around the entire site.

233

The CAG wanted the metal wall, but not at the expense of an extreme narrowing of the river. EPA's initial plan was to install the metal wall as far as 75 feet out into the riverbed, filling in the gap between land and wall with soil. We questioned the necessity of that, and the wisdom of narrowing the river stream that much, which, of course, makes for a more powerful flow.

We had spotted this plan in a report on another topic, and I raised the issue during a Zoom meeting, asking our EGLE project manager, Erik Martinson, if the State Department of Natural Resources would allow such an alteration of the riverbed. By his reaction, we knew he had not heard of the plan until that moment. Subsequently, Tom and others met with the Water Resources Division of EGLE, and argued that because EPA had removed 670,000 cubic yards of sediment from the river 17 years ago, they could certainly add in about 25,000 cubic yards of soil. The argument seemed dubious to us, but apparently EGLE accepted it. In a recent PowerPoint presentation given by EPA, the extent of the wall into the river had been reduced to 50 feet. Still a lot.

Other than that concern, we recognized the necessity of the wall and were in favor of it. Construction is due to start in 2024.

As for the Upgradient slurry wall repair and re-use, that was a different kettle of fish. As early as 2019, EPA had begun talking about possible re-use of the slurry wall that blocked the flow of groundwater from the site into the adjacent neighborhood, and vice versa. Even after they found a 20 foot breach in the wall that was allowing groundwater to leach into the neighborhood, they maintained that a re-use of the wall was warranted. In 2020, the CAG sent Tom Alcamo a letter describing the issues that concerned us about that plan, and citing the 2012 ROD that determined that an interlocking sheet pile wall should be erected outside the existing 1980s slurry wall around the entire site to contain the site's contaminants.

EPA responded that CERCLA law allowed a remedy to be modified if new information was obtained. They pointed out that the ROD document was based on information from the Remedial Investigation, and since then the former city drinking wells had been abandoned, meaning there was less pull on the waters inside the slurry wall. Several of their responses leaned on the fact that a future perimeter drain was planned for the site that would capture water within the walls and funnel it to a proposed water treatment facility to be located on site, inside the walls. Again, I felt it was unwise to rely so heavily on something not yet proven to be perfect in its performance. And we knew Velsicol had used a perimeter drain for the 1980s remedy, and it had not functioned as designed.

EPA concluded from their groundwater modeling that if the Upgradient Slurry Wall had more leaks in it than the 20-foot-wide hole they had found, the groundwater inside the wall would not "mound," meaning hesitate in its flow and even become stationery. Our Technical Advisor offered an alternate theory. He said that the walls could be slowly leaking, allowing outside water to enter, but that inside water would slow and mound for a time even if it was slowly leaking out the other side of the site. Since we knew the Downgradient Slurry Wall was leaking in many places, the theory seemed plausible to us.

EPA's contractors continued to investigate, performing dye tests on the Upgradient wall, installing piezometers, taking some soil borings, performing hydraulic conductivity testing, and installing temporary wells outside the breach in the wall to determine if a plume of contaminated water was moving into the neighborhood. They concluded no plume was leaving the site, that the groundwater MCLs (maximum contaminant levels) were below the concerning stage, and that the Upgradient slurry wall was performing as designed in most locations.

The CAG wrote another letter to EPA about the Upgradient Slurry Wall in 2023, stating that community members did not want any portion of the slurry wall reused, but instead desired the

235

interlocking sheet pile wall to surround the entire 52-acre site. We pointed out that groundwater tests EPA had conducted showed that the non-leaking portions of the slurry wall installed in the early 1980s were performing *almost as good* as a sheet pile wall would. Almost as good is not the best. We said we did not want 1980s technology, but the best 2023 could offer.

We were told then, and in a subsequent discussion about the wall in early 2024, that slurry walls are still being built and, in the words of one of EPA's experts, a slurry wall becomes "a permanent geologic structure" that never disappears unless someone digs it up.

Many years ago, when we were learning that EPA's definitions of words were very different from accepted meanings, I had asked how many years would something need to last for EPA to call it permanent, and the response was 30 years. Well, we are holding out for the "impermanent" interlocking sheet pile wall that will last 50-70 years.

As mentioned previously, downstream of the city dam, the many miles of degraded floodplains had been divided in two (Operating Units 3 and 4). OU-3 included the high school and middle school athletic fields built on a flood plain. The fields had received an emergency surface remedy in 2015, but since then, DDT contamination had been found deep inside the riverbanks surrounding the athletic fields. Plans were in place to excavate those areas, plus two more floodplains downstream.

In OU-4, however, the carbon amendment experiment was continuing, and we were beginning to get positive feedback from EPA about its effectiveness. Worms were more abundant, and shrews, which eat worms, were being found where they hadn't been found before.

The CAG remained neutral. It was our viewpoint that even if adding carbon to the soil made DDT less bioavailable to wildlife, all the other contaminants in the soil, including heavy metals, would remain to contaminate them.

In addition to the field studies, laboratory studies were being conducted by a toxicology professor at Alma College. The studies were inconclusive in both arenas, and we continued our wait-and-see stance.

Regarding health, our partnership with the PBB researchers at Emory University continued, as did our frustrations with the State health department (MDHHS).

Back when the researchers had applied for an NIH grant to match PBB registry participants with cancer deaths in three states, MDHHS wrote a letter of support, with the understanding that the mortality analyses would be completed by 2021. The necessary data was not provided to the researchers by MDHHS until 2023. The delay was partially caused by mistakes made on the part of MDHHS, and in straightening out the issues, time passed, and money from the NIH grant was paid to the MDHHS contractor, MPHI, to untie the difficulties.

I wrote a letter from the CAG to a few of our legislators, which expressed our disappointment that the people from Michigan were left still wondering if their exposure to PBB was connected to cancer deaths of their loved ones. We requested that the legislators require MDHHS to pay MPHI for the work yet to be done, and, later, in an email to Kory Groetsch at MDHHS, I asked that the State make up the money to the researchers so that the study could move forward, as outlined in the plans that had won the grant money from NIH.

Kory's response floored me at first, because of the legal language he used throughout. I pictured him with a lawyer holding a gun to his head as he wrote the response. Ever since the Flint Water Crisis, lawyers had been ruling the State health department, which seemed less concerned with public health than in staying out of court. Finally I responded to Kory, and again made the point that the way the money had been spent did not advance us to an answer for the PBB-exposed population of Michigan, and again I requested that MDHHS restore the money for the purpose it was intended. We will see what I receive in reply.

As for the plant site itself, with cleanup progressing so quickly with the BIL money, Tom Alcamo recommended that the CAG, the City, and the State Land Bank (holder of the deed), meet to discuss re-use of the site.

Back in the early 2000s, the City had received an EPA Brownfield grant to make a re-use plan for the property, and going back to that early plan seemed a good place for our CAG to start its thinking process. Using the report generated from that time, I made a PowerPoint presentation for the group. The first re-use plan had utilized the entire 52 acres of the former plant site, and a colored illustration showed recreation fields, an amphitheater, a park, and a commemoration area. Now, many years later, we knew that a permanent water treatment facility would take up numerous acres of the property. Another big change was that, at present, the State Land Bank Authority owned the property, and their ideas might not align with ours for re-use of the former plant site acreage.

In his last months as our EPA project manager, Tom Alcamo arranged for the Land Bank development director to attend a CAG meeting, along with the St. Louis City Manager, and a representative from SKEO, a contractor with EPA to help communities plan redevelopment of formerly contaminated properties.

During the SKEO presentation only one thing seemed odd to me. Most of the same plans were laid out for the site as in the 2004 re-use plan, but the new plan showed a road along the river, rather than the boardwalk with fishing platforms. My questions about it didn't elicit a reason for the road, but I surmised it was to be an access road for the water treatment facility. What a poor use of river frontage, in my opinion. A second meeting, at which we are to offer our ideas, is tentatively planned for March, 2024.

More than a decade ago, we had learned from Jay Steinberg (president of the Trust designated by the USDOJ to oversee the Velsicol sites and financial settlements) that many boxes of Velsicol's records were stored in a warehouse in Chicago. Our CAG officers had talked of taking a field trip there to peruse the records, and had discussed how to scan the ones we wanted. We never followed through.

At some point, the City of St. Louis had acquired from the Trust 40 banker's boxes of Velsicol's records. Gary Smith learned about this, and I contacted City Manager Kurt Giles about having a group of us go through the boxes to make lists of their contents. He agreed, and found a room for us in city hall where we could spread out and work.

For three weeks, Margaret Hoyt, Gary Smith and I spent many hours going through the huge boxes of records, with help from Norm Keon, Doug and Brenda Brecht, and Brittany Fremion.

Some of the boxes contained notebooks and files of many years' worth of sampling and monitoring records. Other boxes contained correspondence, maps, photos and news articles, and gave us much more information.

Among many other interesting items in the boxes of records, we found a letter to Mr. Joe Phillips at Velsicol from Grant Colthorp, a North Street resident who lived across from the chemical plant.

To quote from his 1978 letter:

"It was with sadness and gladness that we watched the Chemical leave. We couldn't grow a tree. I started many but they all died. All big trees were bare of leaves by the end of July. There weren't any earthworms. All aluminum windows and siding were pitted. I rarely put over $2 of gas in the tank because I wanted to stop in every couple of days and wash the windshield. The hood, trunk lids and car tops turned brown—paintless-- if stored outside. There were times at noon when you couldn't see my garage 100 ft. away. My house turned colors on a wkly basis. The white paint acted as a signal to the community that the Chemical had released something into the air when it turned pink, orange, or brown. For years about once a month I'd stop over at the Chemical to harass them in a friendly manner. They often said they were expecting me as they'd noticed my house had changed colors.

I knew many of the employees and several were among my closest friends, so it was with sadness that I watched their departures.

It has turned into a much more pleasant area in which to live. I'll probably live out the rest of my life here so I felt that I needed to once again seek a closure to the lot that's only a foot from my house."

For many years, Colthorp had written letters to Velsicol, asking them to sell him the lot next door to his house. Finally, in 2023, EPA had worked out a deal to allow Colthorp to own the lot that he has taken care of for decades. The lot was part of the property belonging to the chemical company, then to the DOJ sanctioned Trust, and would have gone to the State Land Bank along with the rest of the former plant site property except that EPA found a way to allow it to be deeded to Grant Colthorp. I know it pleased Tom Alcamo to accomplish this, and it pleased the CAG members, too.

The year before, plans got underway to acknowledge in 2023 the 50 year mark from the start of the PBB Disaster. In 1973, bags that should have contained magnesium oxide, a livestock feed supplement, and instead contained the fire retardant, PBB, were shipped to a Farm Bureau mixing facility in Climax, Michigan, added into the grain, and thus began the entry of PBB into the food chain. The idea for the 50th commemoration began at a PBB Partnership meeting, and we recommended that the event should include discussion of the ongoing fallout from the food poisoning disaster…namely, the health consequences of human exposure to the contaminant. A team, which included several people from the CAG, began meeting regularly to organize a conference. Sponsors included Alma College, Pine River Superfund Citizen Task Force, Emory University, the Saginaw Chippewa Indian Tribe, the EPA Community Involvement Coordinator, the PBB Citizen Advisory

Board, Mid-Michigan District Health Department, Central Michigan University, the National Institutes of Environmental Health Science and others.

The three-day event held in May showcased speakers, such as Elena Conis, author of *How to Sell a Poison*; artwork by local artists depicting the event in photos, paintings, and dance; a bus trip to various nearby sites, including the plant site; panels with questions and stories taken from the audience; opportunities to tell your personal PBB story on video; and 50 seconds of silence to acknowledge all the PBB heroes, living and dead, those in attendance and those not.

It was Jane Ann Crowley who had suggested that we honor PBB heroes at the 50th event. Nominations for PBB heroes ranged from people who had raised the alarm back in 1973 to groups, such as ours, which were still promoting comprehensive health programs for those people exposed to PBB and their progeny. At least three people prominent for their early work to bring the PBB Disaster to light took part in the May conference held at Alma College. They were Dr. Thomas Corbett, an MD who had performed very early research showing possible outcomes of ingestion of PBB; Edie Clark, an aide to the Michigan Speaker of the House at the time, who relentlessly informed the State legislators about the danger of PBB to the residents of Michigan; and Francis "Bus" Spaniola, a former State House representative who helped get legislation enacted that lowered the allowable levels of PBB in human food, and that earmarked money for a long-term health study.

Another PBB Hero Award went to Jim Buchanan, who had been employed by the chemical company, and served as local president of the Oil, Chemical and Atomic Workers union at the time of the disaster. After having failed to convince management to provide showers and other protection for the chemical workers, he had filed a report with the National Institute for Occupational Safety and Health (NIOSH) which helped to bring the practices of Velsicol into the public eye.

Another award went to Richard "Dick" Allen, a deceased member of the State House, and later the State Senate from 1969-1982. He had pushed through legislation to create the Landfill Trust Fund to help pay for the remediation of the Gratiot County Landfill and its operation and maintenance costs. The landfill had been a depository for Velsicol waste, including tons of leftover PBB, and also the gravesite of myriad chickens and some cows that were slaughtered during the disaster. It was the actual first Superfund site in the country, having been dealt with prior to CERCLA law passing, but using the standards set forth in the law.

Another deceased recipient of the PBB Hero Award was Thomas Ostrander, a former chemical worker who had been heavily exposed to PBB. His blood work showed PBB levels 180 times higher than the mandated tolerance levels for cattle at the time. A magazine used his photo on the cover with the caption saying: "PBB Poisoning: If this man were a cow he would have been shot."

Video clips collected at the conference were later used in a Continuing Medical Education Course on endocrine disrupting chemicals, with the PBB Disaster as a case study. Other videotaped portions of the conference were to be part of a future documentary. In addition to these forms of reaching the public, several CAG members were interviewed for newspaper articles, and for radio and TV airings. WOOD-TV out of Grand Rapids did a thorough four-part series on the PBB Disaster.

In our view, and that of many others, it is crucial to remember the largest food-contamination event in U.S. history to avoid its repetition in future years, and we have willingly shared our knowledge with wider audiences.

Chapter 15
(2023 – Part 2)
Finalizing Projects

One day I received a phone call from a reporter from Reuters News Agency about the Burn Pit. It took a minute of conversation before I understood what he was asking. It had to do with human health and a 2013 evaluation of the Burn Pit by ATSDR (Agency for Toxic Substances and Disease Registry). A presentation had been given to us at the time, and soon I began to remember the details.

ATSDR had provided money for the state health department to do a cursory study of data regarding the Burn Pit Site, and publish a report on their findings. The bottom line recommendation in the ATSDR report was that EPA should simply monitor the Burn Pit, and not clean anything up. This was in spite of the site having no walls, cap or fence, with low-income housing full of children located a stone's throw away, and a golf course butting up to it. I guess they based their recommendation on the fact that during the 1980s remediation of the site 68,000 cubic yards of contaminated waste had been dug from the site, trucked to the plant site, and buried under the plant site cap. Apparently ATSDR had overlooked the sampling of the Burn Pit by MDEQ in the mid-2000s that had revealed extensive contamination below ground level, and still plenty on the surface.

As can be imagined, at the time of the 2013 ATSDR report, our CAG advocated for action. And that is what I told the Reuters reporter. Back then our written comments stated that private drinking wells should be sampled for contaminants, the ash piles at the site should be excavated, and the underground contaminated soil dug up or otherwise eliminated.

Talking this over with the reporter, I realized that with the passage of years our persistence on a thorough cleanup of the Burn Pit had won the day. A new water supply had been furnished to the residents in that area, the ash piles were to be excavated and removed, and the entire site, including underground, would be heat treated and/or excavated.

In terms of the water supply, during the past several years EPA had contacted nearby residents, urging them to abandon their private wells and hook up to city water, which was now piped from Alma and from Arcada Township. The last hold-out property owners lived in the Orchard Hills subdivision, and in recent months even they had agreed to the plan. During the 2023 work season, EPA's contractor had completed the project of connecting all the residences to the city water mains. Getting property owners off private wells was a proactive measure to protect their drinking water from possible contamination from the Burn Pit Superfund Site, once the underground heating began. The concern was that heated DNAPL, located in extensive quantities at that site, would travel and contaminate their wells.

Also, in a recent Zoom call with our Burn Pit EPA Project Manager, Jennifer Knoepfle, she had agreed that the ash piles would be removed, rather than reburied on site, with confirmation sampling to take place in the soil beneath them. If more excavation was needed, EPA would do that, too. This had been one of our adamant suggestions following the ATSDR evaluation.

And, with work underway to begin thermal treatment on the huge pool of DNAPL located beneath the site, it was evident that all of our concerns expressed in our responses to the ATSDR report in 2013 were now being addressed in the planned remediation of the Burn Pit. The Reuters reporter was amazed to hear this, and his phone call left me with a feeling of pleased relief to know that after 10 years of voicing what was best for the community, we were able to get a better cleanup than originally planned.

To give a little history of the Burn Pit site, it was just as the name implies – an area across the river from the plant site where the chemical factory both piped liquid waste and trucked solid waste to be set on fire. The city also used the area as a dump. One of our historical photographs shows a huge, black cloud rising up from the Burn Pit, and we know it moved east across St. Louis over Saginaw Street, where almost every resident woman developed breast cancer in the 1970s, and on to the town of Breckenridge, where an outbreak of non-Hodgkins lymphoma occurred.

As mentioned, during the 1980s Superfund remediation, surface waste from the Burn Pit was hauled to the plant site for burial under the clay cap. A flat area in the middle of the plant site became a hill made by the waste from the Burn Pit and from much of the wreckage from tearing down the factory infrastructure. Our CAG member, Phil Ramsey, detested the mound and demanded that its disappearance be part of the final remedy for the plant site. We nicknamed the mound Phil's Hill, and agreed that it should go, although current plans do not call for its removal.

After the 1980s Superfund remediation ended, the Burn Pit (known then as the Golf Course Site) was delisted as a concern by EPA even before it was listed on the National Priorities List (NPL). Ed Lorenz had spotted this anomaly back in the early 2000s, and the CAG then began advocating for sampling to take place there. As a result, MDEQ (EGLE) had conducted a remedial investigation, and the extent of the contamination in the Burn Pit convinced EPA that the site needed to be part of the overall Velsicol cleanup. For a while, the Burn Pit was attached to the plant site as part of the same site, and later was again separated out as its own Superfund site. The separation allowed us to acquire a Technical Assistance Grant for it, in addition to the one we used for the Former Plant Site. The downside was that the Burn Pit had gone to the bottom of the list for federal funding, since it was considered a "new site" by EPA, despite its long history and despite our protestations.

Now, the recent Bi-partisan Infrastructure Law was providing the funding needed to get the clean-up underway.

We knew the first project planned for the site was *in situ* thermal treatment, and Tom warned us that much more DNAPL would be extracted from this area than from the previous three located on the former plant site. EPA sampling had estimated 150,000 gallons pooled underground. Some of the monitoring wells contained 12 to 19 feet of DNAPL. Luckily, the geology at the site was bowl shaped, and has served as a collection lagoon for the DNAPL all these years, preventing its flow to the river. In 2024, when the thermal treatment begins, the first job is to bring up the accumulated DNAPL from the monitoring wells. The DNAPL will go into weir tanks to settle out from other liquid, and then will be transferred to tanker trucks that will take it to an EPA location for incineration.

Following a long wait for the government contracting to be put in place, work began in 2023 to build the extraction well field for the Burn Pit thermal process. An access road was constructed to get equipment to the site -- not through the golf course, but through private property in the neighborhood east of the Burn Pit. Also, electricity had to be brought in.

The workers drilling holes for the thermal treatment were garbed in Level B protective gear due to the high quantities of toxic DBCP known to be present at the site. They drilled 419 holes for the extraction wells and heating elements. Soil cuttings were collected in barrels to be trucked for disposal in a landfill that could accept chemically contaminated waste.

Over the past several years, when thermal treatment had been used on the plant site, heavy black plastic had covered the well field. This time, concrete was poured, Styrofoam laid on top, and another layer of concrete poured over that. The idea was to better contain the heat in the ground, and also to trap stray vapors.

At the end of the 2023 construction season, a 50-foot high barrier was built around the Burn Pit area, using telephone poles as the uprights. The fence was designed to keep out wildlife and golf balls.

Also, barges were spiked into the bed of the river on which a catwalk was built to carry pipes across the water to the treatment equipment located on the plant site. One pipe would transport vapors to the treatment equipment still located on the plant site. A second pipe would transport partially treated water. Polluted water would receive its initial treatment on the Burn Pit side of the river, and then be piped across for its final treatment and release into the Pine River. The original plan had been to directly transport liquefied contaminants as they came from the ground, but EPA had determined it too dangerous to the river in case of spills. Actually, two sets of pipes ran across the catwalk. In case problems arose with one set, the other set could be used, without slowing down the underground heating. The ground was due to begin heating up in April, 2024.

Finally, one more of the sites we had been overseeing for 25 years would begin its cleanup process.

A completed project was the new well field to supply drinking water to the cities of Alma and St. Louis (joined together as the Gratiot Area Water Authority). Well No. 12, located on Luce Road southwest of Alma, had been slow to complete due to supply shortages during and following the COVID 19 pandemic. But now, the last new well was on line, helping to provide clean water to both small communities.

Back in 2012 when the City of St. Louis had sued Velsicol and won a $26.5 million settlement, the amount left after lawyer fees were paid had not been enough to fully fund the new wells and water transmission lines. At the time, EPA had been reluctant to help provide the remainder of the funds to St. Louis because of their worry that many more cities around the country would follow suit in asking for a replacement of their drinking water wells. Even so, the federal court judge worked out a deal, with all parties agreeing that much of the money would come through EPA to bring on line new wells located far away from the Velsicol Chemical Corporation property. EPA's contribution to the project amounted to about $33 million. Water now travels seven or eight miles to reach the homes in St. Louis. With the first transmission main completed in 2013, the construction project took 10 years to accomplish, and now was done.

Instrumental in gaining the new water supply for St. Louis was former mayor George Kubin, who was also a former board member of the CAG. George had been tireless in his rallying of state and federal legislators and agencies to the city's need for a new water source after St. Louis city wells were found to be contaminated with the DDT byproduct, pCBSA, in 2005. He and Joe Scholtz (also a former mayor, now deceased) had led the charge with a lawsuit against Velsicol and the Trust that owned the Velsicol properties, gaining the monetary settlement for the community. Because of his extensive contributions to the CAG and the community of St. Louis, George was voted into the CAG Hall of Fame, and his name now appears on a large plaque hung in the St. Louis municipal building, along with many other deserving people (including Joe Scholtz).

As mentioned earlier, a sheet pile wall had been pounded into the ground to protect houses near PSA-1 prior to excavation. The wall had been installed to help prevent cave-ins.

Potential Source Area number one had been named over a decade before when an MDEQ investigation had shown that the soil was saturated with substances that could continue to pollute the river (potential source of pollution). More recent sampling by EPA had shown that the contaminants were primarily refinery waste, because McClanahan Refinery had been located in that area along M-46 and Watson Street from the early 1930s until Velsicol acquired the property in the 1950s.

Slightly northwest of PSA-1 was PSA-2. About 115,000 tons of soil was expected to be dug from the two areas, with the excavation to extend 30 feet below the surface; hence the metal wall pounded deep into the ground.

The first giant hole was dug in sections. Because GPS instruments were used to inform the person running the excavator of the depth to dig, no person was needed down in the hole. Also extensive surveying took place prior, during and after the digging. We were impressed with the safety precautions taken and the precise estimates the contractor, AECOM, used in their work with oversight from the U.S. Army Corps of Engineers.

During the digging, huge tank bottoms were uncovered and brought to the surface. We knew from old photographs that the refinery tank storage area had been located in that area. The metal was cut up and removed.

The contractors expected odor to be a problem due to the soils being saturated with old oil and other refinery wastes, and they were right. To help combat the stink, a substance was sprayed on piles of excavated dirt that helped seal in the odor, and also controlled dust from spreading. The substance made the piles look bluish, and the odor was similar to sprayed bathroom fragrances.

Our CAG personnel received a few complaints about the odors ("something rotten," "sewage," "pig poop") and also about dust. The first phone call I got was from a man who had been driving into St. Louis from the west, and he said a truck had exited the plant site in a cloud of dust so thick that he couldn't see the car immediately behind the truck. The man was concerned about contaminated soil leaving the site in an uncovered and unlined truck that had not been washed. I emailed Tom Alcamo about what I'd been told.

A second mister was set up to help control dust on the site, and Army Corps personnel stationed themselves outside the gate to inspect the trucks leaving the site. Also, a street sweeper stayed in constant motion, cleaning any dirt residue from the highway. Later, when I toured the project, I watched as a truck was prepared via a machine that spread giant plastic sheets to line both trailers on the "gravel train" truck. And the loads, of course, were covered.

By August work at PSA-1 was completed, with about 109,000 tons hauled away, which was about 28,000 tons more than expected from that area. At the peak of the project, about 30 double-trailer trucks were coming and going, traveling to a landfill and back about three times a day with each load weighing 1,500 to 2,000 tons.

Work began on PSA-2, with about 35,000 tons of contaminated soil removed (again, more than predicted). By November, the project was completed. The whole area was filled in with clean soil, compacted, hydroseeded, and when the grass came up, geese flew in to enjoy it.

PSA-3 was still pending. In that area, chemical oxidation would likely be used. It seems an odd remedy, because more chemicals would be added to the groundwater in that area, but in theory their addition would neutralize the chemicals of concern. An investigation of the area had been completed in late 2022, and in early 2023 we asked for more information on ISCO (*in situ* chemical oxidation) from our Technical Advisor, Scott Cornelius. After reading his report, we formulated questions and sent them to Tom Alcamo. He replied in writing, and we also had an on-line Technical Committee meeting with EPA to learn more about the process. We learned that much preliminary work would be necessary to determine which oxidants would work best to destroy the target chemicals, namely DDT, HBB and PBB.

Once again, we were approached by a person asking to feature our group in a documentary he was producing. Once again, it was the PBB Disaster which had interested the person first. This time the person, Colin Gray, had spoken with participants at the PBB 50th Commemoration at Alma College about his idea of doing a limited series on the PBB event, with one segment focused on the Pine River Superfund Citizen Task Force.

My enthusiasm level was pretty low because of past experiences. For instance, a person had actually filmed PBB community meetings at various towns throughout the state, and filmed a PBB Partnership meeting, intending to make a documentary, and then had disappeared. Another had begun with the PBB Disaster, learned about our extensive clean-up effort, and, over several years, had filmed and interviewed various CAG members, taken a tour of the plant site, and then disappeared. He, at least, told me that the scope of our cleanup projects was so big that the story got away from him.

Gary and Brittany had high enthusiasm. When my husband and I went west that winter, I asked Gary and Norm to follow through with Colin Gray and the "shopping agreement" he wanted us to sign. Gary took the agreement to a lawyer friend, who altered wording here and there and cautioned us about other aspects of the document. Brittany checked with colleagues of hers at Central Michigan University, and also came back with suggestions. When I got home, I set up a Zoom meeting with Colin to help us all understand the limitations of the contract, and to hear what his long-term goals might be.

The conversation helped considerably. Colin agreed to some word and phrase changes in the agreement, and most of us subsequently voted to go ahead and allow him to interview some of our members, and to "shop" the agreement to streaming outlets. He spoke of possible profits and we, of course, as a non-profit could not accept them, but arranged that they should go to the Michigan PBB

Registry to enable the researchers to resume blood tests of Michiganders who now lived in other states.

Birds and fish had been on our long term agenda for years. Residents continued to contact us when they found a dead bird in their yards. And I continued to let EGLE know that a dead bird follow-up study was necessary. Finally, in August, Erik Martinson, EGLE project manager, said that a bird study would take place in the spring/summer of 2024.

When the study had been done in 2013, prior to the excavation of yards in the 12-block ANP (Adjacent and Nearby Properties), it was found that adult birds had died of acute DDT poisoning, meaning they had come back north healthy in the spring, but their diet of worms and insects in the neighborhood had contained so much DDT, that they went into convulsions and died. Ever since the completion of the ANP clean-up, we had been asking both EPA and EGLE for a follow-up study. It was great news to know that one was finally in the works.

A long-term goal from the start-up days of our CAG was to someday have the state fish advisory lifted that cautioned all people against eating any fish, in any quantity, at any time from the Pine River downstream from Alma. People had long ago developed fear of the contaminated river, and rarely used it for recreational fishing. With a nod to the future, our CAG member, Joe Scholtz, had advocated starting a catch and release fishing derby on Michigan's free fishing weekend so that people wouldn't forget that our Pine River was supposed to be a recreational resource. With a little help from us, Joe started the derby, and since his death in 2011, we have continued to help first his family, and then organizations, continue to run it. A free lunch is offered each year, and we foot the bill for the hotdogs.

This year 315 people registered for what his family had named the Joe Scholtz Memorial Free Fishing Derby. In years past, registrants had numbered from 500-800.

Despite the drop in DDT levels in fish captured and tested by EGLE and EPA, the state health department continued its cautions against eating fish from the Pine.

Two fish sampling events were planned for 2023, one in the impoundment area by EGLE, and one downstream in the OU-4 region by EPA. Neither one would be a comprehensive study, which troubled Gary Smith. He stressed to the agencies at our meetings that the studies should replicate the earlier sampling events so that the data could be viewed over time. He also suggested that the age of the fish mattered. For instance, during EPA's 1998-2006 river sediment remediation, lots of fish had lost their lives. In more recent years, when EPA sampled for DDT in fish, they found that the DDT levels had dropped significantly, and took it as proof that the various sources of contamination leaking from the plant site had been eliminated or were under control. Gary argued that the reason could be that younger fish now living in the river simply hadn't had enough time to accumulate much DDT in their fat. We requested that EGLE determine the ages of the fish.

Erik passed on our request to the state-level people who compile the fish advisory guidelines, and was told that the age of the fish had no impact from a human health standpoint.

We responded that human health was not our focus right now, but instead, the completeness of the clean-up. The age of the fish could let us know how much DDT had accumulated in young fish versus older fish that had lived in the impoundment longer.

We think the people at the State who compile the fishing advisory guidelines are not the ones who should be doing the fish sampling to rate the success of a Superfund cleanup.

As for the OU-4 fish study, there were many holes in the plan, including no reference sampling at a known clean spot far upstream, and no consideration given to the fact that fish do not stay in one small sampling area, but swim up and down the river. The object of the EPA sampling in OU-4 was to determine the extent or lack of contamination in the river along a few floodplain shore lines, but of course the fish could have eaten contaminated food at other locations.

When we see the results of both fish sampling events in 2024, we hope to have reason to think the fish in the river are closer to being clean enough to eat, at least by some people, some of the time.

In a way, a finalized project was our relationship with our long-term EPA Project Manager, Tom Alcamo. November was his last meeting day with us, with his formal retirement to begin at the end of the year. I planned a dinner at a restaurant for his send-off prior to our November meeting, and almost all of the Executive Committee attended. Also, Diane Russell asked for a blurb from me to include in the EPA newsletter about Tom's retirement, which I was happy to supply. Our relationship with Tom had markedly improved since 2022 when he and I had determined to work to achieve better interaction between EPA and the CAG. For me personally, it was a relief to have EPA finally providing us with information in a timely manner and not have to fight battles to get it. The result for Tom was fewer times when we had to pressure him for the information, helping him become more genial. Gary referred often to the "nice Tom" we were experiencing in the last days of our relationship with him.

At our membership meeting that evening, Tom gave his farewell to everyone, and Gary and I encouraged Tom to become a member of the CAG. "Nice Tom" thought it was a great idea, paid his $5-a-year dues, and received his membership card. So, in a way, another project finalized!

As mentioned earlier, a second meeting with the State Land Bank people was due to take place in early 2024. Meanwhile, they had left us with two concerns. The first was that the plant site would again need a monument (*another tombstone?*) as a warning marker,

254

and the second that the marker needed to state that radioactivity was contained under the site's clay cap.

For years we had verbally questioned and written letters to EPA asking about radioactivity in the mix of contaminants under the capped site, with our latest letter about it sent earlier in 2023. In the letter I listed what we knew: that the 1982 Consent Decree required actual words on the tombstone that warned of "low level radioactive waste;" that maps left by the 1980s contractor, Conestoga-Rovers and Associates, showed a number of places labeled radioactive; that old reports stated that metal sheets had been laid over the radioactive areas prior to construction of the cap. And in the letter we asked the EPA project manager point blank, "Have you looked for radioactive spots on the plant site? What methods did you use? What have you found to support the maps and consent decree language?" Also, "If the radioactive material was dug up and removed to the burial site known as the Breckenridge site, have you found any reports indicating that action? Was the Nuclear Regulatory Commission (Atomic Energy Commission) contacted to check their reports regarding radioactive waste left on the plant site?"

The EPA response stated that they had not investigated the site with the specific objective of locating radioactive materials. They had, however, found a metal plate beneath the cap in what I will call a northwest "corner" of the plant site. The plate was about 3 feet wide and 20 feet long. No sampling took place there. Later, the information about the pit covered by the metal plate seemed to be corroborated by what we found when going through old Velsicol records.

Because past reports described radioactive waste being buried in PSA 1 and PSA 2, the soil in those locations had been evaluated for radionucleotides prior to excavation, and showed no evidence of any radioactive soils.

As for checking with the NRC, no, EPA had not done that, instead relying on the Conestoga-Rovers reports and the RI investigation performed by MDEQ.

We had hoped to find in the Velsicol boxes early records from the Michigan Chemical Corporation era, but there were very few, and those were generally inclusions in correspondence from the Velsicol Chemical Corporation era -- essentially from the time the plant shut down in 1978 until the time when EPA came back to do a second cleanup of the site in 1998.

The topics were spread throughout all 40 boxes. Our work in October simply listed what each box contained. Afterwards, I typed a 76-page document of our handwritten lists, detailing what was in each box. Maybe in the next few years, someone will go through that long list and make topic lists that show which boxes contain documents pertinent to that topic.

One topic that showed up in numerable boxes was the scrap metal dilemma. The contractor for the 1980s cleanup, Conestoga-Rovers, wanted to sell the scrap to help fund the cleanup. Some of that scrap metal consisted of the railroad tracks that came into the Velsicol property. The ownership of the rails came under contention when Velsicol's contractor had begun to rip out the tracks to sell, and the railroad claimed they owned the tracks. The dispute was settled when Velsicol bought the tracks from the railroad and, when they couldn't be sold for scrap, buried them within the plant site. Although the steel rails were not found during the excavation of PSA 1 & 2, 45 tons of railroad ties were dug up and transported to a landfill.

At the time of the 1980s remediation of the plant site, many of the offsite shipments of metal were returned when the owners of the scrap yards learned about the contamination at the former chemical factory, or tested for it. This included scrap metal contaminated with PBB and metal that tested for radioactivity. Some scrap was sold to a place in Ohio where it was to be melted down. Some kitchen appliance metal was sold for food-making elsewhere. Much of the metal was returned and buried on site.

Also buried on site was a bulldozer that a sub-contractor had left in place too long. After notifying the owner several times to come and get it, the workers burying debris and readying for the cap finally buried the bulldozer, which, of course, led to a lawsuit.

There were a number of lawsuits detailed in the correspondence, including one about the deep disposal well located at the Robert and Marcelle Crumbaugh farm on Madison Road, east of St. Louis.

Their son, Rex, and his wife, Kathy had been fighting Velsicol for over a year by the time our CAG formed in 1998. The couple attended our early meetings and brought the issue before us. We, of course, sided with them. At the time of the trial, which took place in Circuit Court in Gratiot County, I was able to attend two days. Gary Smith attended most of the proceedings. When the decision came, our local judge ruled in favor of the Crumbaugh family.

As far as we know, this is the only court case that Velsicol actually lost, and we are pleased that it took place in our county. Velsicol also lost their appeal. Further, the letters showed that Velsicol considered going to the Michigan Supreme Court, but determined they would lose there, also.

The court had determined that Velsicol had to cease putting contaminants down the deep well at the Crumbaugh farm, and also had to remove their infrastructure and plug the well.

In addition to the waste stream from the plant site, the records showed that contaminated leachate had also been pumped to the Crumbaugh well from the Golf Course Site (now the Velsicol Burn Pit site) from 1980-1984.

The Velsicol records revealed a contamination problem of which we were ignorant. Both soil and groundwater at the Mill Street electrical substation in downtown St. Louis was discussed, with details of sampling and analysis documented in the mid-1990s. Apparently, digging at the location had resulted in chemical odors and discolored soil being detected. When MDEQ sampled the soil in 1994, they found VOCs, PNAs, DDT and heavy metals. Contaminants in the groundwater included many of those, plus

Endrin. The substation had been built on soil hauled in to fill a flowing mill race that had powered a saw mill in the early days of St. Louis. The mill race had been built by channeling water from a dam (now gone) into a narrow stream, which turned the power wheel at the saw mill. This earlier dam was located upstream from where the present dam now exists.

The filling-in of the mill race occurred in 1955, long after quantities of chemical waste had been released into the Pine River and mill race. Furthermore, it was speculated by MDEQ that "free fill dirt" from Velsicol was used to fill in the mill race, which likely added to the extent of contamination.

At present, the community swimming pool is located where the saw mill used to sit, and the substation is located where the mill stream ran before it turned back and joined the river, behind the former bathhouse of the now-gone Park Hotel.

I made copies of the documents I found about the Mill Street Substation in the Velsicol records and gave them to St. Louis City Manager, Kurt Giles. As our CAG members read through the files, we kept on the lookout for a document that would let us know how the problem of the Mill Street contamination was resolved, but could not spot one. Later, we learned the outcome.

I wrote up a talk to give to the CAG at our Christmas Potluck about interesting things we had found while perusing the Velsicol records, and emailed a written version of my Velsicol Records talk to those on our mailing list. Former mayor George Kubin responded with more of the story about the Mill Street substation. He said that when the city applied for a permit to rebuild the substation, MDEQ had notified the city of the need to examine the site, identify the contaminants, and to prove that the city had not placed them there. At this time, the State was saying it would compel the city to remove all the contaminated soil and pay for the project, even though the city manager and city council knew the city was not responsible for the contamination.

There was a public hearing in the council chambers, during which an environmental chemical scientist from Michigan State University attended on behalf of the city. When MDEQ asked where the contamination had come from the scientist, with hundreds of pages of documents in hand, told them it was obvious where the contaminants originated – from the former chemical factory. As a result, the state issued a permit to the city to enlarge the substation with the stipulation that there would be no digging beyond the point necessary for the foundation.

Obviously, the contaminated soil that smelled bad and looked bad is still present underground along the former mill race.

I drafted a letter requesting that our new EPA Project Manager for the Velsicol sites, Jennifer Knoepfle, sample the soil on the surface and at depth along the path of the former streambed to determine the levels of DDT and other chemical waste still in the soil.

I didn't sign the letter or send it, but left that up to the new chairperson. In December we held our biennial elections, and, happily, Brittany Fremion, young, fully capable, and a Central Michigan University history professor, was elected to chair the CAG into the future!

Glossary of Acronyms

AEC	Atomic Energy Commission
AIG	American International Group
ATSDR	Agency of Toxic Substances and Disease Registry
CAB	PBB Citizen Advisory Board
CAFO	Concentrated Animal Feeding Operation
CAG	Community Advisory Group
CDC	Centers for Disease Control
CERCLA	Comprehensive Environmental Response Compensation and Liability Act
CIC	Community Involvement Coordinator
DBCP	1,2-dibromo 3-chloropropane
DOJ	United States Department of Justice
DDT	dichlorodiphenyltrichloroethane
DNAPL	Dense Non-Aqueous Phase Liquid
DNR	Michigan Department of Natural Resources
EGLE	Environment, Great Lakes and Energy
EPA	United States Environmental Protection Agency
ERA	Emergency Removal Action

FOIA	Freedom of Information Act
FPS	Former Plant Site
FS	Feasibility Study
IRB	Institutional Review Board
ISCO	In Situ Chemical Oxidation
ISTT	In Situ Thermal Treatment
LNAPL	Light Non-Aqueous Phase Liquid
MCL	Maximum Contaminant Level
MDEQ	Michigan Department of Environmental Quality
MDHHS Services	Michigan Department of Health and Human
MMDHD	Mid-Michigan District Health Department
MOU	Memorandum of Understanding
MUCC	Michigan United Conservation Clubs
NAPL	Non-Aqueous Phase Liquid
NIEHS Sciences	National Institute of Environmental Health
NIOSH Health	National Institute for Occupational Safety and
NOAA	National Oceanic and Atmospheric Agency
NRC	Nuclear Regulatory Agency
NRD	Natural Resource Damages
NWI	Northwest Industries or NWI Land Management
O&M	Operation and Maintenance

OSHA	Occupational Safety and Health Administration
OU-1	Operable Unit 1 (the plant site)
OU-2	Operable Unit 2 (impoundment area of the river)
OU-3	Operable Unit 3 (downstream portion of the river)
OU-4	Operable Unit 4 (downstream to Chippewa River)
PCBs	Polychlorinated Biphenyls
PBB	Polybrominated Biphenyl
pCBSA	para-Chlorobenzene Sulfonic Acid
PID	Photoionization Detector
ppm	parts per million
PRP	Potentially Responsible Party
RCRA	Resource Conservation and Recovery Act
RI	Remedial Investigation
ROD	Record of Decision
RPM	Remedial Project Manager
SEP	Supplemental Environmental Project
SOP	Standard Operating Procedure
SRD	Substantive Requirement Document
SVOCs	Semi-Volatile Organic Compounds
TAG	Technical Assistance Grant
USACE	US Army Corps of Engineers
VBP	Velsicol Burn Pit
VOCs	Volatile Organic Compounds

Made in the USA
Monee, IL
01 December 2024

71861668R00149